not just JAVA

A Technology Briefing

Second Edition

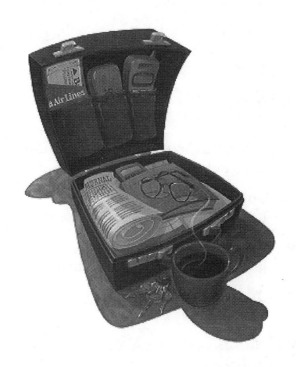

THE SUN MICROSYSTEMS PRESS
JAVA SERIES

▼ **Core Java 1.1** *Volume I: Fundamentals*
Cay S. Horstmann & Gary Cornell

▼ **Core Java 1.1** *Volume II: Advanced Features*
Cay S. Horstmann & Gary Cornell

▼ **Graphic Java 1.2,** *Volume I: AWT*
David M. Geary

▼ **Inside Java WorkShop 2.0,** *Second Edition*
Lynn Weaver

▼ **Instant Java,** *Second Edition*
John A. Pew

▼ **Java by Example,** *Second Edition*
Jerry R. Jackson & Alan L. McClellan

▼ **Java Studio by Example**
Lynn Weaver & Leslie Robertson

▼ **Jumping JavaScript**
Janice Winsor & Brian Freeman

▼ **Just Java 1.1 and Beyond**
Peter van der Linden

▼ **Not Just Java: A Technology Briefing,**
2nd Edition
Peter van der Linden

not just
JAVA

A Technology Briefing

Second Edition

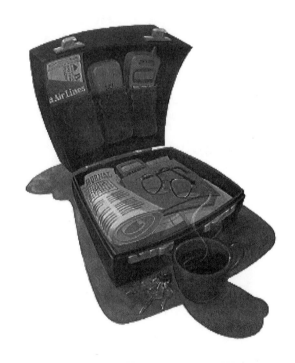

PETER VAN DER LINDEN

Sun Microsystems Press
A Prentice Hall Title

The publisher offers discounts on this book when ordered in bulk quantities.
For more information, contact: Corporate Sales Department, Phone: 800-382-3419;
Fax: 201-236-7141; E-mail: corpsales@prenhall.com; or write: Prentice Hall PTR,
Corp. Sales Dept., One Lake Street, Upper Saddle River, NJ 07458.

Editorial/production supervision: *Joanne Anzalone*
Cover design director: *Jerry Votta*
Cover designer: *Anthony Gemmellaro*
Cover illustration: *Karen Strelecki*
Manufacturing manager: *Alexis R. Heydt*
Marketing manager: *Kaylie Smith*
Acquisitions editor: *Gregory G. Doench*
Sun Microsystems Press publisher: *Rachel Borden*

10 9 8 7 6 5 4 3 2 1

ISBN 0-13-079660-3

Sun Microsystems Press
A Prentice Hall Title

Contents

Chapter 1

Industry Trends for the New Millennium, 3

Computer Industry Players, 5

Sun Microsystems, 5

Compaq Corporation, 8

Hewlett-Packard Corporation, 10

IBM/Lotus, 12

Intel Corporation, 15

Microsoft Corporation, 17

Chapter 2

The Internet and TCP/IP, 25

Internet Origins 26

All About the TCP/IP Protocol, 30

Case Study 1: Using the Internet for Learning 36

Summary 39

Chapter 3

The World Wide Web, 43

Hypertext Leading to the Early Web, 44

HTML—Hypertext Markup Language, 47

Browsers, 49

On-line Web-Based Business, 51

Searching for Web Sites, 51

Difficulties of Regulating the Web, 53

Internet Casinos, 53

Competition between Browsers, 55

Why Browsers Are So Important, 58

Software "Lock-In" through Unique Features, 60

Case Study 2: A Basic Commercial Web Site, 61

Summary, 63

Chapter 4

Programming Techniques in a Browser, 65

How to Say Where to Look: URLs, 66

Somewhat Technical Aside, 67

Browser Plug-Ins, 69

Executable Content in a Browser: Applets, 71

Sending Data to the Server: Forms and CGI, 71

JavaScript, 77

DHTML, CSS, and XML, 82

CSS—Cascading Style Sheets, 83

DHTML—Dynamic HTML, 83

XML—Extensible Markup Language, 84

Example of XML, 85

Summary, 87

Chapter 5

Java Applets, 89

The Java Phenomenon, 89

Distribution of Executable Content: Applets!, 92

Why Is It Useful to Run a Program from a Web Page? 93

Java on the Client: Applets., 95
> Write Once, Run Anywhere (WORA), 98

The Java Plug-In, 101

Platform Independence, 101
> Volume Drives Everything, 104
> Portability through API and ABI Standards, 107
> Why Source Standards Aren't Much Help, 108

Who Has Java?, 116

Summary, 117

Chapter 6

The Internet and E-Commerce, 119

How the Internet Runs, 120

Distributed Administration, 120

Connecting Your Company to the Internet, 122

Web Meets Net, 124

Evolution of On-line Commerce 125
> Stages of E-Commerce, 126

On-Line Commerce Today 128
> Products Best Suited for E-Commerce, 129
> Build It and They Will Come—Not!, 133
> Challenges Ahead for E-Commerce, 133

Case Study 3: Web-Based Retailing 134

Summary 137

Chapter 7

Distributed Processing Security Issues, 139

What Is Security?, 139

Web Site Security Measures, 141

Java Security Measures, 145
> Security for Java Applets, 145
> Security Measures for Applets, 146
> Early History of Security Attacks, 151

Security Comparison: Java, DNA, Plug-Ins, 152

Case Study 4: Lack of Security with DNA, 153

Why DNA's ActiveX Is Unsafe for Internet Use, 155
Finer-Grained Security, 156
Other Security Issues, 157
    Decompiling, 157
    Denial-of-Service Attacks, 158
    Encryption, 158
    Netscape's SSL, 160
    Internet Security versus Openness, 160
Summary, 165

Chapter 8

Java Language Specifics, 167

The Java Philosophy, 167
Object-Oriented Programming, 174
    The First Tenet of OOP: Encapsulation, 175
    The Second Tenet of OOP: Inheritance, 177
    The Third Tenet of OOP: Polymorphism, 179
Language Features: Uniform Data Types, 183
    What Happens on Overflow?, 185
    Language Features: Threads, 187
    How to Prevent Race Conditions, 191
    *Language Features: Automatic Memory Management
    (Garbage Collection), 194*
    Language Features: Exceptions, 197
Case Study 5: USPS Use of Java, 203
Summary, 205

Chapter 9

Java Libraries, 207

The Java Libraries—The Process and the Purpose, 207
    1. The Core Libraries, 209
    2. The Standard Extension Libraries, 210
    3. The APIs for Specific Hardware or Applications, 212
    The Java Media Framework APIs, 214
    JavaBeans API, 216
    The Java Swing API, 217

A Java Program to Draw an Oval at an Angle, 221
Internationalization, 222
Related Initiatives, 224
    Programmer Certification, 224
    100% Pure Java, 224
    The Java Lobby, 225
Java in Operating Systems, 226
Some Final Words on Productivity, 228
Case Study 6: How Java Affects Programmer
Productivity, 230
Summary, 233

Chapter 10

Client/Server and the Intranet, 235
What Is Client/Server?, 235
    How Is Client/Server Different from Timesharing?, 236
    Why Client/Server?, 236
    Advantages and Disadvantages of Client/Server, 239
Scaling Up: Intranets and Extranets, 241
    Intranet Security, 246
    Java Security, 247
One-, Two-, and Three-Tier Systems, 249
Case Study 7: Multitiered System across the Internet, 253
Summary, 257

Chapter 11

Network Computers, 259
The Hidden Costs of PCs, 259
The Iceberg Model, 260
    Other PC Costs: Security, Reliability, 262
How Microsoft Has Addressed Fat Client PC Costs, 264
What Is a Thin Client?, 269
Network Computers, 273
Where Are the Network Computers?, 275
    Where Can a Network Computer Be Used?, 277

What Java Brings to NCs, 281
The Changing Role of ISPs, 281
Summary, 283

Chapter 12

Component Software, Enterprise Computing, and Databases, 285

Software Frameworks, 285
In the Beginning, There Was DDE, 286
Compound Documents, 287
Microsoft's COM Model, 290
JavaBeans, 296
Enterprise JavaBeans, 299
The Industry's CORBA Model, 300
Interface Definition Language (IDL), 304
Java and Databases: JBDC, 305
About SQL and Relational Databases, 305
The JDBC-ODC Bridge 308
Java Blend, 308
Summary, 310

Chapter 13

Conclusions, 313

The Changing Computer Industry—
Retooling the COBOL Programmer, 316

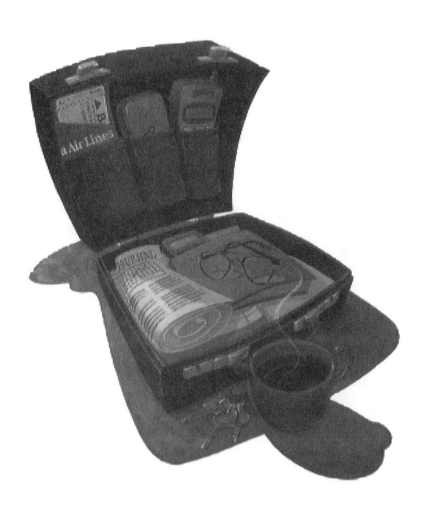

CHAPTER 1

- Computer Industry Issues
- Computer Industry Players

Industry Trends for the New Millennium

The computer industry is still a young industry, and because of its youth, it has always been characterized by change. The Java language has come onto the scene at a time when several other forces are also promoting rapid changes away from older kinds of system design. New network paradigms, new desktop interfaces, and now highly portable object-oriented software are combining to uproot existing expectations of communication, cost, and capabilities. Users are expecting more for less, and they're getting it.

← ? network paradigms (intranet ?) e.g.

Periods of rapid change bring opportunities to create new winners and losers. This chapter summarizes some of the corporate characteristics of the key players in the computer industry. What is their place in the industry overall? What are their plans for Java? Events are unfolding rapidly, so there is an element of timeliness to the scenarios described here. At the time of writing (late 1998), the main issues in the computer industry as a whole can be summarized as:

- Deploying secure electronic commerce
- The need to reduce the PC total cost of ownership
- Introducing specialized low-administration appliances *← ? like what?*
- Uncertainties of regional downturns, acquisitions, Federal legal action
- Converting the Web into value-adding middleware *← ? "middleware" ↗ Dummies Client/Server p. 351: "Software that sits between clients & servers"*
- Shipping products that leverage the "computer/telephony" convergence
- Reducing the cost and time to market of software, and increasing robustness

(deploy: unfold, open out/extend, place strategically)

3

Overlaid on this is the normal jockeying for position of the various players and competitors, each of which has unique strengths and challenges. Throughout 1997 and 1998 the computer industry has been in a state of great flux, making it harder than ever to read the industry and make accurate predictions. It is a rapidly changing world, and some of the factors today are going to be supplanted by new issues tomorrow. A few figures are presented below so readers can make comparisons between players. The meanings and definitions of these figures are:

Revenues: the total annual sales of the company. A measure of the size of the company.

Employees: the number of regular employees. An indication of the size of the company, and the staffing needed to accomplish its goals.

Net income: Net Income is the revenue that is left over after paying all the direct and indirect costs of making the product.

$$\text{Net Income} = (\text{Sales Revenue} - \text{Cost of Goods Sold} - \text{Expenses} - \text{Taxes})$$

The Net Income is the amount available for profit, dividends, or reinvestment by a company.

Profit margin: The profit margin is net income expressed as a percentage of sales. It says how many cents in each dollar of sales are pure profit for the company.

$$\text{Profit margin percentage} = (100 \times \text{Net Income})/\text{Sales Revenue}$$

Table 1-1 shows the profit margins of some industry vendors.

Table 1-1 Profit margins

Hardware Vendor	1998 Profit Margin	Software vendor	1998 Profit Margin
Intel Corp	27.7%	Microsoft	31%
Sun Microsystems	7.8%	Symantec	14%
IBM	7.7%	PeopleSoft (1997)	13%
Dell Corp	7.6%	Oracle	11%
Hewlett-Packard	7.1%	Baan (6 month)	4%
Compaq	5.3%	Inprise (6 month)	−12%

Most manufacturing businesses can sustain profit margins around 5 to 10 percent. Software companies have very low manufacturing costs, so they often have higher margins, in the range of 10 to 15 percent. A figure much different than that indicates special factors are at work.

Computer Industry Players

Sun Microsystems

> 1998 revenues: $9.8 billion
> employees: 19,000
> net income: $763 million
> profit margin: 7.8%

Strengths

As the developer of the Java system and a manufacturer of industry-leading servers and desktop systems, Sun is one of the very few companies that can deploy both hardware and software products. The combination along with stewardship of the Java APIs puts Sun in an ideal position to benefit from all aspects of the new paradigms. It may move Sun's SPARC processor architecture up from fourth place in volume after Intel, MIPS, and PowerPC (in that order).

Along with IBM, Sun is the only other company that has a complete vision encompassing all aspects of the Internet. Sun has sustained and evolved this vision over more than a decade, and during that time it has experimented and invested constantly in the technology. Sun didn't stumble blindly into Java—it funded it as one of several research projects. Sun hit the big time with Java because it was looking in all the right places.

The Solaris operating system is an enterprise-ready operating system with quality, scalability, and robustness that NT can only aspire to, but not yet come close to attaining. Solaris is available for both the SPARC architecture and the Intel x86 architecture, so there is no hardware cost for NT users who wish to try it.

Sun has clearly learned from the pointless fragmentation of the UNIX standard that took place in the 1980s, and readily licenses its Java technology to anyone. The open strategy gives other companies an interest in Java success and helps build volume use.

Sun is a network computing company, pure and simple. This has been its value proposition from its earliest products. The mainstreaming of the Internet has given Sun the chance to take its message and products to a much wider range of customers.

Finally, among Sun's other advantages is its leadership position in UNIX. Much of the innovation in the computer industry over the last two decades (multiprocessing, encryption, networking, widespread graphical user interfaces, dynamically linked libraries, high performance graphics, threads, C++, Virtual Reality, Java, computer security, etc.) has been pioneered or popularized on UNIX, and Sun is the undisputed leader in that sector. Sun can ship improvements to the Java platform faster than Microsoft can ship improvements to the Windows platform.

Weaknesses

Sun has historically been viewed as a hardware company for whom software is a distraction needed to sell the product. That is changing with the maturing of Java, but Sun still lacks experience with mass-market software. Sun failed to "execute outside the box" in the 1980s and push workstation prices down aggressively enough for them to be a contender for high volume desktops. Microsoft was able to use this lack of competition to gain a lock on the PC desktop.

Opportunities/Threats

The challenges for Sun revolve around reaping the return from the fertile Java seeds it has sown. This requires time, follow-through, and sustaining the momentum, but you can take little for granted in an industry this volatile. People ask, "How will Sun make money from Java?" noting that the compiler is given away for free over the Internet. The goal isn't to extract a profit from the Java language itself, but rather to build a business on what Java enables. As Java gets onto every desktop, application software will no longer be an issue for UNIX vendors. As Java becomes the software of choice for e-commerce, Sun server systems become the obvious hardware of choice.

Sun is coming from a position that is behind on desktop volume and ahead on servers, but Windows NT, while still lacking the robustness and scalability to deploy on enterprise systems, is creeping into the low end of the server market. Equally worrying for all UNIX vendors, including Sun, is the encroachment of NT onto technical workstations. Intel's latest Pentium II chips have caught up with Sun's SPARC processor in terms of speed and capacity. If applications software is ported to NT, Sun will inevitably lose some workstation sales, although it is fighting back with very low-cost Solaris desktops.

The opportunity for Sun lies in doing an end run around PCs. Sun must find a way to replace expensive-to-administer PCs with networks of thin clients and Sun servers. For this, the JavaStation needs to become established and successful. Java applications software needs to appear. The lack of standard Java in the leading browsers has been solved (ironically) by Microsoft crushing Netscape. Now it is clear to everyone that the Java Plug-in is the way to deploy applets on an intranet. Interesting rumors circulated in 1998 about an IBM friendly takeover of Sun. The two companies are pooling their resources to hasten and improve thin client Java computing.

As the componentware market takes off, Sun must champion JavaBeans and introduce/justify the concept to the UNIX world (which is frankly unfamiliar with and confused about componentware and ActiveX). Sun now sells more to the commercial market (35 percent) than to the technical market (30 percent), and it needs to continue to beef up its support for ease of use in its software. This seems like an opportunity that is tailor-made for Java because the GUI is so quick and easy to program.

Java Strategy

Sun's Java strategy is

- Position Java as a platform in its own right, as good or better than Windows but which runs on all computers.
- Fight Microsoft's attempts to undermine Java portability with an industry coalition, with a lawsuit, with PR, with whatever it takes
- Cooperate with partners throughout the industry to give them a stake in Java
- Replace fat-client PC's with Java-based thin clients and Sun servers.
- Encourage other companies to produce Java applications software, but do not dilute effort by working on it directly. Encourage programmers to contribute to Java by making the source code freely available.
- Deploy Java as the universal language for all low-end devices: controllers, PDAs, embedded systems, and even smart cards. Java is already decisively beating Windows CE in these segments.

Compaq Corporation

(Figures include Tandem and DEC)
> 1997 revenues: $37.6 billion
> employees: 87,400
> net income: $2.0 billion
> profit margin: 5.3%

Strengths

Compaq surprised the computer industry twice in 1997–8, by buying first Tandem (for its enterprise-ready server software and sales expertise), and then Digital Equipment Corporation (for its service and support network). It had first made a bid for DEC two years earlier. Compaq was already the world's largest PC vendor. With those two acquisitions it squarely declared its ambition to become a full-fledged supplier of enterprise computing equipment.

Compaq has proven that its management has imagination and the ability to seek strategic alliances. In the early 1990s, Compaq considered partnering with Sun, but chose to continue to focus on PCs instead.

Weaknesses

For at least a year or two, Compaq management will be preoccupied with merging three large organizations. Compaq is faced with the challenge of thinning out products from three overlapping and wholly incompatible lines. Customers need to see credible migration paths to protect their existing investment.

Compaq has to assemble some compatible products out of these computer/OS lines.
- DEC UNIX on Alpha chips
- VMS on Alpha chips
- VMS on the VAX architecture
- Ultrix on MIPS chips
- NT on Alpha
- SCO UNIXware on Merced (Intel's 64-bit Pentium successor). Compaq is in a consortium to port this software to Merced.
- Tandem NonStop Kernel (formerly Guardian 90) on MIPS chips
- Tandem NonStop Kernel on Tandem's own chipset.
- NonStop UX on MIPS chips
- Windows and NT on PCs

The company needs to be careful not to let the new purchases derail product plans and schedules. It announced a barrage of new products in 1998 partly to show it could continue to deliver.

Compaq is wholly dependent on Microsoft for its PC operating system. It cannot promote Java too enthusiastically to solve product incompatibilities without incurring Microsoft's wrath. Adopting Microsoft's vision of a "Windows-only" Java doesn't solve Compaq's needs.

Compaq has yet to prove its credibility in the enterprise computing world. Selling individual PCs is a lot different than selling 24-by-7 servers for the corporate glasshouse. Can Compaq grow from being a "box provider" to being a provider of end-to-end computing solutions? It may need to make further acquisitions to bring the necessary competencies in-house, further diluting management focus.

Compaq needs to come up with an enterprise storage management solution that is better than "let EMC have it." Enterprise storage comprises 30 percent of the value of some high-end sales, and it's a bad idea to rely on another company to supply this fraction. Enterprise storage is a shared consolidated data repository for many systems.

Finally, Compaq is currently being out-maneuvered by Dell, which was the first PC vendor to see the possibilities of selling direct via e-commerce. Compaq uses distributors and retail channels, and is at a costly disadvantage. The channels are killing Compaq, but it cannot abandon resellers until it has something better, like Web site sales.

Opportunities/Threats

Overnight Compaq boosted itself from being an assembler of PCs, into membership in the computing industry's Big Three, along with Hewlett-Packard and IBM. Counting only computer-based revenue, Compaq is actually larger than H-P by $3 billion. The opportunity for Compaq lies in acquiring a reputation for selling enterprise software that works. The threat lies in increased pressure from more established competitors.

Compaq is trying to revive DEC's Alpha CPU as a server system running NT (rather than DEC UNIX). This is surprising as it makes Compaq dependent on Microsoft whereas a UNIX/Java approach would let Compaq control its own destiny.

Java Strategies

As a PC vendor, Compaq had essentially no core competency in software. Tandem and DEC both adopted Java, but neither was seen as having any particular depth of expertise.

In August 1998, Compaq announced that they will bundle Java application server software on its servers to help customers build server-side Internet applications. It is licensing the software from Novera Software.

Compaq's overall Java strategy has yet to emerge. It has something to gain from Java in solving its product incompatibility issues.

Hewlett-Packard Corporation

>1996 revenues: $43.9 billion
>employees: 110,000
>net income: $3.1 billion
>
>profit margin: 7.1%

Strengths

Hewlett-Packard is an established computer company, widely respected for both its engineering talent, and the integrity of its business practices. The company is well-diversified having subsidiaries that manufacture medical equipment, scanners, printers, and general instrumentation as well as its Kayak PC and PA9000 UNIX line. H-P was recently added to the portfolio of stocks that make up the Dow Jones Industrial Average.

H-P's biggest strength is perhaps its ability to provide "one-stop shopping" for enterprise computing. The company is renowned for its worldwide service and support organization.

Weaknesses

H-P used to be weak on the low-end PCs, but recently modernized and repriced its line of laptops and portables to be competitive. H-P's decision to throw its lot in with Intel, and merge the HP9000 architecture into the design of Intel's Merced chip is now seen as questionable. At the time it looked like a clever move which would leverage the industry volume platform while retaining compatibility for a very large customer base of HP9000 users. As more time has gone by, H-P is seen as an increasingly junior participant, informed of Intel's decisions but not helping shape them.

H-P started its migration to the Merced chip prematurely, marginalizing its own UNIX product. A major issue for H-P is managing the conversion to NT without losing existing customers. As both NT 5.0 and Merced encounter delays, and slip further into the future, H-P's PA9000 customers feel increasingly like orphans and are open to approaches from alternative vendors. H-P's software destiny is controlled by Microsoft with its NT product. H-P may ultimately be reduced to the role of systems integrator, bundling Intel boards with Microsoft software.

There is a saying within H-P to the effect that the company only starts a project "when it sees its competitors' tail-lights," meaning it is slow off the mark. H-P was very slow to recognize the Internet, very slow to recognize e-commerce, very slow to recognize Java, and very slow to recognize thin-client computing. H-P is viewed by some as the epitome of an old-fashioned technology company.

Opportunities/Threats

The lead that H-P held in the printer market may be passing to more nimble competitors, Canon and Epson. The downturn in Asia, and the 1997–8 PC price war are affecting all PC vendors, but particularly those who are slow to respond to change. In summer 1998, H-P imposed a 3-month pay cut for its middle managers in an effort to control costs. When H-P targeted the home PC buyer, it wisely decided not to try to charge a premium for the H-P name. Instead it set its prices to slightly undercut its main competitors, notably Compaq. Can H-P sustain its unusual foray into consumer computing, as margins become razor thin?

H-P is in an excellent position to deploy thin-client platforms, but its current "thin-client" products are actually just dumb terminals. H-P needs to balance its mellow company culture with the need to anticipate paradigm change, and especially to aggressively design and deploy new products.

If H-P fails to anticipate new ways of doing business (e-commerce, thin clients, Java computing, etc.) it could end up as IBM was in the early 1990s: a complacent money-losing dinosaur. In 1997, H-P bought the Verifone corporation to acquire some e-commerce expertise.

Java Strategies

H-P came out with its own version of Embedded Java for the handheld, and needlessly provoked an argument with Sun over whether this would be compatible with the Java standard or not. Microsoft quickly bought a license to the possibly incompatible H-P JVM. H-P is not a leader in the Java world, and seems to be doing just enough to say "me too."

As a chip integrator and supplier of embedded systems, H-P has much to gain from Java software which can drive all of these products in a unified way.

IBM/Lotus

1997 revenues: $78.5 billion
employees: 270,000
net income: $6.1 billion
profit margin: 7.7%

Strengths

IBM has *the* position of computer industry leadership, built on reliability. IBM products never set any world records in technological advancement, or ease of use. They were, however, dependable. If an MIS department spent the right amount of money, they would eventually get all systems running correctly. This led to the old saying that "Nobody ever got fired for buying IBM," meaning IBM computers were a safe, low-risk choice for procurement officials.

A little-known fact is that $12.8 billion of IBM's 1997 revenues came from software, which makes IBM the second largest software supplier in the world, after Microsoft. With its purchase of Lotus, for which IBM paid the high price of $3.2 billion, IBM also brings leadership in the knowledge-worker groupware realm into the fold.

Weaknesses

IBM is handicapped by its need to support compatibility for a massive existing user base, some of whom still use punch cards in batch systems. IBM's track record of pedestrian products isn't a particular weakness now that it has embraced Java. It can bring technology in-house much more easily. It is interesting to note that a successful outcome from the ill-fated IBM/Apple Taligent joint venture would have been a Java-like system three or four years earlier.

The existence of old technology mainframes isn't IBM's biggest problem. Its biggest problem is that it has essentially six completely separate product lines with only limited interoperability between them: mainframes, minicomputers, UNIX workstations, two kinds of PC, and thin-client systems. IBM spent enormous sums over twenty-five years on SNA to gain cross-platform compatibility, without a result that generalized to the client/server world. Of all companies, IBM has potentially the most to gain from Java, and it was surprisingly quick to realize this, and invest in Java as a strategic technology.

IBM has awesome research capabilities, but has sometimes had difficulty in transferring ideas from the Thomas J. Watson lab into products.

Opportunities/Threats

In 1996, IBM finally dumped the Prodigy joint venture with Sears. Ironically, this is a venture that stands to do very well as on-line commerce takes off. IBM is positioning Lotus's Domino product to rule the electronic commerce space. It is investing in and heavily advertising its e-commerce/intranet/Internet capabilities.

Another move that is strongly in IBM's interest is to throw its weight behind the development of platform-independent Java applications and to convince other software vendors to do the same. It currently has a project code-named "San Francisco," which is developing Java class libraries for high-level business applications—general ledger, accounts payable, inventory control, etc.—in partnership with 50 other software development companies. The San Francisco project was started by IBM's AS/400 division but has now spread to other platforms, including AIX, MVS, and OS/2, as well as non-IBM operating systems like Windows NT and HP-UX. The class libraries use CORBA for cross-platform communication.

IBM's Lotus Division has folded Java into its entire product line. Lotus bundles the Marimba Castanet software into Domino. Lotus also supports Object Management Group's Internet Inter-ORB Protocol (IIOP) as the way Java classes on the client access Domino objects on the server, from release 5 on. Eventually, Lotus Notes will be available in a browser.

Lotus is already shipping a suite of office applications built around the JavaBeans component architecture. The suite is known as "e-suite" and is available for download at http://esuite.lotus.com. E-suite is suitable for use on a personal computer or a network computer.

IBM is possibly the only company that stands a chance by itself of unseating Microsoft's ambition to own most of the Internet-related commercial possibilities. With Lotus, IBM can produce its own electronic commercial applications. IBM is large enough that it can produce and even impose its own electronic-commerce infrastructure as a global standard. Finally, IBM is a soup-to-nuts company that does everything from the silicon foundry to the application software. It can produce network appliances, and it is well placed to dominate the embedded products market over the next few years. Under Lou Gerstner, IBM is once again the 500-pound gorilla of the computer industry.

Java Strategies

IBM is the biggest, oldest, and most traditional company in the computer industry, and it is the biggest proponent of Java.

- IBM has the most to gain from Java and intranet technology, and it has grabbed onto them in a really big way. IBM has dedicated fully 25 percent of its $6 billion R&D budget to Java and Internet technologies, according to Unigram (November 16, 1996) and it has been doing this for the last two years. Various reports claim that IBM has over 2000 Java programmers—more than Sun.

- Java is now supported on all IBM operating systems. IBM is shipping a product that provides Java connectivity to its CICS transaction processing system and DB2 and IMS databases.

- IBM has announced that *all* of its top 150 accounts are already working in Java or have plans to do so. IBM, the world's largest computer company and a cautious adopter of new technology, is into Java in a very big way.

- IBM is partnering with Sun to advance the JavaOS, which is the operating system for Network Computers. NCs will take root because IBM has the resources to nurture the concept until it gets it right. Cooperation among competitors with a common strategic interest is called "co-ompetition" in Silicon Valley.

Intel Corporation

>1997 revenues: $25.1 billion
>employees: 63,700
>net income: $6.9 billion
>
>profit margin: 27.7%

Strengths

As Intel's remarkable profit margin indicates, the company has a monopoly on desktop hardware. It produces the chips and motherboards that go into 90 percent of the world's desktop computers.

Although Intel has a hardware monopoly, corresponding to Microsoft's software monopoly, it is perceived as a less arrogant company than Microsoft. Unlike Microsoft, Intel paid attention to warnings from the Department of Justice about misuse of monopoly power.

Intel's business model relies on continually delivering value by designing faster processors and putting them on the market at premium prices.

Weaknesses

Two things could upset Intel's business model: a delay in its design schedule, or a market decision that, while older chips may not be "the fastest," they are fast enough for most purposes. In 1998 both of these factors occurred.

Unspecified problems are delaying the Merced schedule. Merced is Intel's 600MHz flagship microprocessor for the millennium. It is a 64-bit architecture, and all major server vendors planned to incorporate it in their product lines. Merced was originally announced for volume shipment in 1999. It has been pushed back to mid-2000.

In spring 1998, Intel's earnings fell by one-third, compared with the same quarter a year earlier. It was a dramatic sign of how Intel was wrong footed by the price war in the PC industry. Intel reacted to control expenses by cutting 3000 jobs over the next six months. The problem was that Intel had not at all anticipated the growth of the low end, at the expense of the high end, and this allowed competitors like Cyrix to get a toehold in the market. The sub-$1000 PC segment didn't exist in early 1997, and a year later it was 27 percent of all PCs sold retail in the United States. Belatedly, Intel launched the Celeron chip for low-cost systems.

Intel also failed to anticipate the emerging mass market for "information appliances"— set-top boxes, network computers and the like. Again, competitors got a foothold in the market before Intel could react. General Instrument is supplying the set-top boxes to cable company TCI, and other contenders like MIPS, and Hitachi are waiting in the wings. Nonetheless, Intel is a powerful and resourceful company, with seasoned and capable management.

Opportunities/Threats

In 1998, the United States government announced an anti-trust investigation of some of Intel's business practices. The Department of Justice is concerned about Intel's ability to harm competitors by denying them chip information.

Intel remains vulnerable to the continuing price war in the industry. Vendors are selling the low margin sub-$1000 PCs at the expense of the high-end, high-profit models. That, coupled with a drop in growth rate of PC sales, from 15 percent annually down to 10 percent annually has been a major issue industrywide. When NCs ship in volume, there will be further price pressure on Intel.

Intel appears to have enough doubts about the NT operating system that it is recruiting other OS vendors to provide the 64-bit software to match the Merced hardware. In particular, Intel has provided confidential information to Sun, among others, to port Solaris to Merced. NT 5.0 (itself delayed until some time in 2000) will not support 64-bit hardware. That undermines acceptance of Merced, forcing Intel to recruit additional software partners.

Java Strategies

Intel's Java strategy is "stall, cooperate and celebrate." Ideally, Intel would like Java to go away. Intel lobbied (unsuccessfully) to try to prevent Sun launching Java as an ISO standard. But now Java is successful, Intel would like it to be seen to be most successful of all on Intel hardware.

- Recognize that Java is playing a key role in new application development throughout the enterprise, from the smallest embedded systems to the largest database servers.

- Work to make Intel architectures the fastest to run Java tools and applications. There have been unconfirmed reports that part of the delay in the Merced schedule is caused by the late addition of elements to make it more compatible with Java. Sun in turn has changed elements of Java's floating point model to make it more compatible with Intel's designs.

- Work with Sun to provide key libraries for the Intel architecture. The first implementation of the Java Media Framework library was written by Intel for its x86 systems. Intel wants the best audio and video implementations to run on its products.

Microsoft Corporation

1998 revenues: $14.5 billion
employees: 27,300
net income: 4.5 billion

profit margin: 31%

Strengths

Microsoft's biggest strength is its desktop software monopoly. It owns the Windows APIs that in various forms are on more than 300 million PCs. Because of this huge installed base Microsoft captured the bulk of the independent software vendors. The realization has at last dawned on everyone in the computer industry that *software applications* are what make or break a desktop platform. Microsoft also has a very successful application software business of its own, and this business is helped by the fact that it owns and can extend the underlying APIs as needed.

Bill Gates was unwilling to concede in the 1998 U.S. Senate hearing that Microsoft has a monopoly on desktop operating systems. He also claimed not to be aware that Microsoft's profit margin was 400 percent that of other computer companies, and 200 percent to 400 percent that of other software companies. The fact remains that in Microsoft's chosen areas, desktop operating systems (90 percent market share), and desktop office suites (85 percent market share), the company dominates utterly and completely. Superprofits from these segments bankroll Microsoft for all the other areas it wishes to get into.

Microsoft is a well-run company with excellent industry vision, and the resources to execute on that vision. It has carefully planned its path, and grown as the PC industry has grown. It has displayed great tenacity in targeting other software vendors until it either breaks them, or enriches them by buying them out. This power and practice are so well known that software venture capitalists actually have a term for cashing out of a start-up venture by interesting Microsoft in buying it: they call it "waking the giant."

Microsoft has also shown that it is not a ponderous company. Bill Gates reshaped it around Internet principles at the start of 1996, and had some quite acceptable products within 18 months. The company has pioneered the use of restrictive contract terms and exclusive license agreements as significant elements in growing a business. When Bill Gates talks about "freedom to innovate" he is not referring to software technology as people naturally assume. He means Microsoft's right to impose whatever contract terms are necessary to force people to keep using its products or deny them the ability to ship or use competing products. Microsoft's innovation is in licensing terms and restraint of trade, not software.

Finally, Microsoft's annual report reveals that it has tremendous financial resources: about $14 billion in cash and short-term investments as of June 30, 1998. Microsoft is willing to pay handsomely when it is in its strategic interest to do so. It pays ISPs to give their members Internet Explorer and exclude Netscape's browser. It pays content providers including CBS, and the Sportline Network $300,000 per site to use its NetShow Streaming Media server software. It pays college professors $200 "expenses" for mentioning certain Microsoft products in talks they give. In a 1997 lawsuit Borland (now called Inprise) alleged that Microsoft paid Borland's chief of R&D Paul Gross a $1M sign-on bonus, and increased it by a further $0.5M if he would leave Borland immediately, even though wedding plans would prevent him reporting for work at Microsoft for a further three months. Borland alleged that Anders Hejlsberg (principle architect of Borland's Delphi product) was hired away with a $3M sign-on bonus. No matter how much we may favor million-dollar bonuses for software staff, these look more like attempts to remove key employees from a competitor. The lawsuit was settled out of court on undisclosed terms.

Weaknesses

Corresponding to many of Microsoft's great strengths lie some hidden weaknesses. Although it owns the desktop APIs, these APIs are spread out across five different platforms (Win3.1, Win95, Win98, WinCE, NT) with varying degrees of compatibility. Microsoft is limited in its ability to stay compatible with existing software because it must drive users to new products in order to keep the cash for OS and application upgrades coming in. Microsoft products are often late to market because they have been prematurely announced to stall sales of competing products. Users are frustrated when their old word processor cannot read files created by their new word processors. If users can get the applications they want on any OS platform, Microsoft is highly vulnerable to customers switching vendors.

Microsoft is just not very good at software development. The company buys or copies most of the innovation it introduces. Some examples include MS-DOS (bought from Seattle Computer Products), Excel (copied from Lotus), Windows (copied from Apple), SQL Server (copied from Sybase), NT (copied from UNIX and VMS), Internet Explorer (bought from Spyglass), JScript (copied from Netscape), DCOM (copied from OMG CORBA). Its products have invariably been late and buggy. Software development is arduous, and if Microsoft has to start competing on the quality of its software, rather than the fact that it has a huge installed base, it will have a problem.

A further weakness of Microsoft is the lack of security in its system software. When the user base was comprised of stand-alone PCs, the issue could be ignored and pushed off onto customers. In the age of Internet working and downloading code from inside and outside the enterprise, that just isn't good enough. Microsoft operating systems and browser products have suffered some highly visible security breaches which jeopardize customers' data. The company has tried to plug the gaps with code patches, press releases, and public relations spin control; but just as a house needs a sturdy foundation, a secure software product cannot be built on top of system software that lacks a secure architecture.

Microsoft appears to have a partnering strategy modeled on the "Black Widow" spider which first seduces its mate and then kills it. There is a very long list of companies that have partnered with Microsoft and ended up damaged or destroyed. The only thing that is more dangerous than being a partner of Microsoft, is being a competitor. There's a joke in Silicon Valley that goes like this:

Q. How many lawyers does it take to negotiate a technology agreement with Microsoft?

A. Two. One to negotiate the agreement, and one to file chapter 11 (the US bankruptcy proceedings).

IBM was damaged by its cooperation with Microsoft over OS/2. Sybase shared its database access knowledge, believing it was embarking on a partnership, only to see Microsoft launch the competing SQL server product a few months later. Citrix worked with Microsoft to develop a successful networking product. Microsoft then told Citrix that it planned to either buy the sole rights to the product or develop its own version. Citrix stock plummeted, and the company eventually had to agree to sell its interest out to Microsoft in order to stay in business at all. Microsoft collaborated with Auto-By-Tel, an on-line car purchase service for 18 months. After learning the business, Microsoft started a competing agency. There are many, many other examples of Microsoft partners who unexpectedly found themselves competitors: Stac Electronics, Go Corporation, Argonaut Software, Worldspan (travel agency), Real Networks, to name a few. The latest Microsoft partnership also ended in acrimony. Sun licensed Java to Microsoft, then felt compelled to launch a (still ongoing) lawsuit alleging Microsoft attempted to subvert the language. A judge ruled that Microsoft could not label its product "java-compatible."

Microsoft has forfeited the goodwill of many in the computer industry, The Software Publishers Association adopted a set of "Principles of Competition" to guide legislators on how antitrust issues applied to software. The principles are common sense fair things like "A dominant operating system should not be used to favor Internet content that is owned by the operating system vendor." They may be read at http://www.spa.org/gvmnt/tos/compprinciples.htm. Microsoft complained bitterly that its competitors pushed these principles through the SPA, but it never did specify which of the principles it objected to.

People sometimes perceive Microsoft as an arrogant company. Microsoft has a reputation for crushing partners and competitors with equal relish because it can. Microsoft often crafts its messages using excellent PR staff. Early in 1998 this rebounded on the company, though. Microsoft was facing the Federal antitrust case, and felt it would benefit from a better public image. Apparently it thought it could buy one. The Los Angeles Times broke the story of Microsoft's "Strategic Deception Initiative"—a plan for a campaign to influence legislators by faking the evidence of grass-roots support. Agencies would be paid to write apparently spontaneous letters of support for Microsoft to politicians and newspaper editors. Columnists would be paid to write columns in favor of Microsoft. Deception in a court of law is known as "prejury" and is a felony offense. Is deception intended to influence legislators any less serious? After the story broke, Microsoft dropped the plan, but not without a lingering tarnish on its reputation.

Finally, the high "total cost of ownership" of PCs is a weakness for Microsoft. In the new world of network computers, being tied to desktop PCs may be like being tied to a boat anchor. No matter how much money your company has stashed away, it's hard to compete on price when your competitors' costs are lower than yours. Thin clients cost less than fat clients in every area: hardware purchase price, system administration, ease of use, and training. A PC price war erupted early in 1997 partly as a response to network computers. This war will not be successful in stopping the adoption of NCs because hardware capital cost is only one small component of the total cost of computer ownership. Even if PCs were given away free, you cannot avoid the current costs of system administration.

Opportunities/Threats

The two big opportunities for Microsoft are

- to extend its desktop monopoly up to the server. This is the purpose of the NT operating system product.
- to dominate electronic commerce. This is the purpose of its browser strategy, its WebTV investment and many other strategic investments and partnerships.

The biggest threat currently facing Microsoft is the popularity of the Java platform. Historically Microsoft has always lagged behind the state of the art, but that didn't matter because it had a cheap operating system with large volume. So application developers flocked to Microsoft. But now for the first time a competing platform—

Java—is threatening that advantage. Previous competing platforms, such as OS/2 and NeXT, always had low volume and so were unattractive to ISVs. But Java runs on top of Windows as well as all other platforms. It presents an opportunity that is larger than the installed base of Windows. There are 340 million existing computers that can run Java, and fewer than 100 million that can run Windows 95. And Java is not expensive either—it is free. So for the first time Microsoft has to compete on the basis of merit. It has never had to do this before. It poses a huge threat to Microsoft because of a key weakness—it is better at marketing software than it is at developing it. And Sun can ship improvements to the Java platform faster than Microsoft can ship improvements to the Windows platform.

Microsoft is also threatened by the existence of thin clients running JavaOS, but so far both this threat, and the Microsoft reaction to it, are potential rather than actual.

The United States government antitrust action against Microsoft is a worrying distraction for Microsoft. There are very few organizations with enough power to overcome Microsoft. The entire computer industry is one, and the federal government is another. The government has filed its charges, including some telling evidence in the brief. The depositions will possibly uncover some more dirty laundry for the press to air. It remains to be seen if the charges can be proven in court. One possible outcome from a successful anti-monopoly prosecution is that Microsoft would be prevented from engaging in anti-competitive behavior like preannouncing products or keeping specifications from competitors. These two sanctions were applied to IBM 30 years ago, and the industry was the better for it.

It is also possible that Microsoft will be broken up into an OS company, an applications company, and an on-line content company. AT&T was subject to this break-up penalty in 1982, and the nation now enjoys cheaper and better phone service than at any time in history.

Finally, the Linux operating system poses a threat to Microsoft, unlikely as it may appear. Linux is a freeware reimplementation of UNIX, originally written by superprogrammer Linus Torvalds, but now a cooperative development by many programmers. It is available, with source, for free, and is noticeably better, faster, and more stable as a file/print server than NT. Commercial support is available for Linux, and it is enjoying a surge in popularity. Mainstream applications vendors have announced ports to Linux, and its progress is regularly mentioned in the trade papers.

Java Strategies

Microsoft's Java strategy is simple.

- Microsoft's Java strategy is "Kill cross-platform Java by grow[ing] the polluted Java market" according to a memo from a Microsoft employee submitted as exhibit 101 (MS7 033448) in the 1998 Federal antitrust case against Microsoft. "Polluted" means "Windows only" the memo explains.

- Microsoft wants to have a product that competes with Java, that ties you to Windows, and that absolutely does not work cross-platform. They want it to have as many good features of Java as possible, but to exclude those that compete with their own technologies. Using it should create non-portable code. This is a good description of J++.

- Give away or bundle everything that ties companies to Microsoft's vision of the Internet: J++, ActiveX software, Internet Explorer, Visual Basic 5

- Lock OEMs into exclusive use of the Microsoft "polluted Java" products. Prohibit and discourage the preinstallation of standard Java with licensing terms to PC and WinCE vendors.

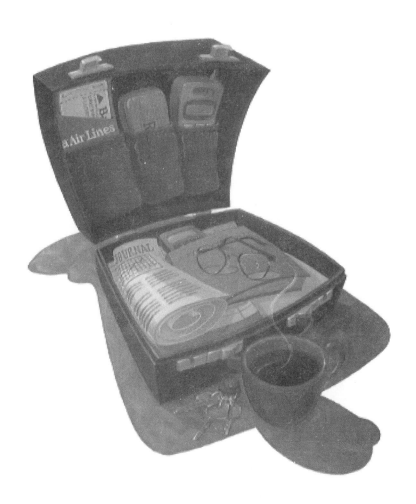

CHAPTER
2

- Internet Origins

- All About the TCP/IP Protocol

- Case Study 1: Using the Internet for Learning

- Summary

The Internet and TCP/IP

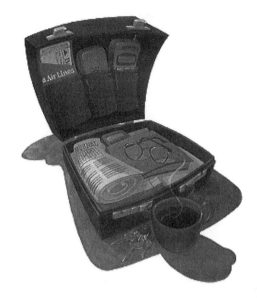

To understand the significance of Java computing and related developments, one needs to appreciate the Internet context, so this chapter opens with a very brief review of the Internet. Although the Internet worldwide computer network has been part of the technical and research computing environment for more than twenty years, it has only recently crossed over into the mainstream. But what a spectacular crossover: one survey suggests that over nine million systems worldwide were connected to the Internet by 1996, providing access for over 50 million people. In 1998, that figure rose to 100 million people.

Starting around 1993 or so, in the course of just a year or two, the Internet was almost magically transformed from an obscure tool exclusive to computer scientists into a strategic asset blessed by politicians at the highest levels. The change was driven by software tools like web browsers that made access trivially easy.

As more people got onto the Internet, it reached the critical mass needed to spur development of new services. Continued growth fed a benign cycle. A bellwether sign was the sudden profusion of books with "Internet" in their title. Stacey's bookstore in Silicon Valley, California, found it was able to fill an entire picture window display with over a hundred different Internet texts, all published within a few months of each other. Finally everyone realized that the "information superhighway" much talked about by politicians would not replace the Internet; it *is* the Internet.

Internet Origins

The Internet came into existence by gradual accretion, not by following some carefully constructed master plan from the outset. It started in a very small way in the late 1960s as the ARPANET[1], a packet switching experiment funded by the U.S. Department of Defense. The ARPANET linked together a handful of computers at a few university and research sites. Everything was done at public expense which is an excellent reason why the public interest, not private profit, should get a fair consideration in determining the future course.

The activity of research relies on the ready exchange of thoughts and ideas with colleagues. The modest cost of a phone data line to the ARPANET instantly enabled the cross-pollination of thoughts and ideas with colleagues throughout the United States who were similarly network connected. These services proved so convenient that universities began to connect other systems and departments, unrelated to network research, to the ARPANET. Figure 2–1 on page 27 illustrates a piece of the Internet with a user transferring files via FTP to the local system.

An important newcomer was the NSFNET, which connected five regional supercomputer centers, each of which had a hierarchy of smaller networks hanging off it, again using IP addressing. The network had become an *internet*—a connected cluster of several levels of networks—and was on its way to growing into today's Internet.

A supporting trend was the rising popularity of local area networks of UNIX workstations in computer science departments in the early 1980s. Companies like Sun Microsystems, Apollo Computer, and Onyx could install workstations linked by Ethernet hardware and IP software. These companies were among the first commercial users of the Internet, and their workstation products were much cheaper than the large, centralized, time-sharing superminis and mainframes they replaced. A few companies experimented with networking personal computers and the NETBIOS software. But at that time, PCs lacked the necessary raw CPU power and were overshadowed by the success of the UNIX Internet Protocol.

Many organizations found it very convenient to connect all their LANs in a wide-area network that could be gatewayed onto the Internet. That way, files could be shared, and e-mail sent across all departmental boundaries. Even better, once on the Internet, an organization no longer needed the expense of a wide-area network to connect all its offices in several different locations. All that was required was to connect each branch office (or campus) to the Internet locally.

---

1.   ARPA—Advanced Research Projects Agency

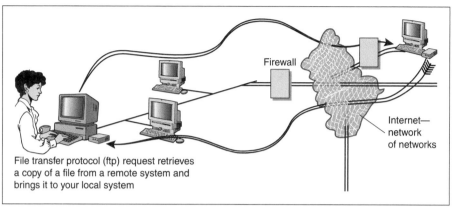

Firewall

Internet—
network
of networks

File transfer protocol (ftp) request retrieves
a copy of a file from a remote system and
brings it to your local system

Figure 2–1

Some early Internet applications are:

ftp: transfer files from one computer to another. FTP was the precursor of a worldwide read-only file system—if you knew the name of a file and host, you could retrieve the file contents.

telnet: use your computer to log into a remote computer.

finger: inquire about the logged-in status of another user, possibly on a remote system.

mail: exchange messages with other users.

Figure 2–2 on page 28 is the historic map of early Internet sites that carried Usenet (back when all the hubs still fit on one sheet of paper). In 1981, these were the main Internet sites in the world, spread out across the United States. The "ucb" sites on the left are at the University of California in Berkeley. The "duke" sites are at Duke University on the East Coast. These organizations were the real Internet pioneers. Fifteen years later, a single-page map like this would only be large enough to depict, not the whole Internet, but just the sites within a few-miles radius of the author's house.

```
From eagle!ucbvax!mark Wed Apr 15 10:45:18 1981
 New Usenet Map      : NET.news
USENET Logical Map, April 15, 1981
```

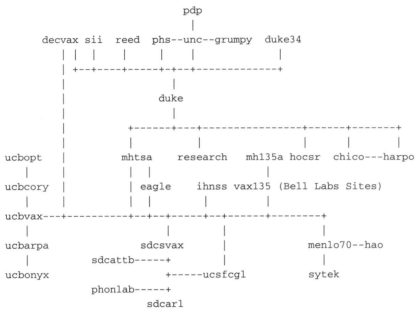

Figure 2–2
The Internet Sites That Carried Net News, circa 1981

Figure 2–3 on page 29 illustrates how a company can connect to remote offices with local calls by routing across the Internet.

Modem communications between different locations could then be placed on the Internet at local phone rates, routed to their final destination across the Internet, and finally delivered again at local rates. Of course, it wasn't really free. In that phase of its life, the Internet was heavily subsidized by the United States government because it was still officially a research project. Today, the costs are borne by all the organizations that are connected to the Internet—in the United States, a little disproportionately by the regional telephone companies. The U.S. Federal Communications Commission regulated Internet backbone tariffs in 1983, letting Internet Service Providers pay only part of the cost of the traffic, with phone companies bearing the lion's share. The idea was to encourage the fledgling industry. After all, the phone companies stand to gain the most from the huge expansion in data traffic. Now the Internet is beginning to provide an alternative to phone companies

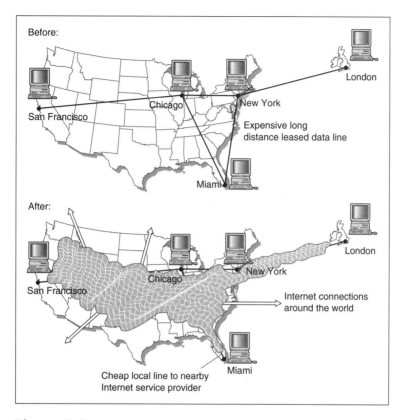

Figure 2–3
Linking to a Company's Remote Branch Offices

(you can even carry voice, somewhat poorly, over the Internet between two PCs), and the phone companies are not happy at all. They are lobbying hard to have ISPs pay more of the backbone bill.

All the early Internet applications were text based, not controlled by easy-to-use graphical windows (those interfaces were not in common use at the time). Worse still, to get successful results, you often had to know what kind of system you were communicating with at the remote end. Another characteristic, only later recognized as a shortcoming, was the absence of any meaningful security. The whole concept was built around the unrestricted exchange of information, so an extra level of complexity to ensure privacy and security was at odds with the basic purpose.

So that's where almost all Internet applications stayed "frozen in time" through to the 1990s: providing elementary file-based applications, mostly in an ASCII-text, batch-oriented manner.

All About the TCP/IP Protocol

One Internet innovation (still a cornerstone today) is that every computer on the net has its own unique address, now known as an IP or "Internet Protocol" address. We'll spend a few pages describing IP because it is the foundation of much that follows, and it's very useful to know the terminology.

An IP (Internet Protocol) address consists of four groups of digits that look like:

```
204.156.141.229
```

All UNIX workstations have IP addressing built into them by default. On a MicrosoftWindows™ system or a Mac, you won't have an IP address unless your system is on a local area net that has IP addressing. Novell's Netware operating system uses IPX—a completely different and incompatible network protocol. Novell is working hard to migrate its customers to IP-based products.

The next generation of IP addresses, known as IPng or IPv6, are 16 bytes long instead of 4, allowing an enormous increase in the number of IP addressable devices—which is already happening. So that old and new formats are readily distinguishable, the eight fields in IPv6 are to be separated by colons, not periods.

A new style IPv6 or IPng address is 128 bits grouped in eight16-bit segments like this:

```
122F:AB02:C5::123:5672:1:127
```

Up to one all-zero segment can be omitted, giving a double colon. Leading zeros can be omitted too. Don't confuse this with similar-looking ethernet addresses.

Giving each system its own unique address allowed any computer to send data to any other computer on the net by wrapping the information in an IP packet and putting it onto the network. Intervening special-purpose router computers were responsible for forwarding the data to the next router closer to the ultimate destination. Lists of paths through neighboring systems, known as "routing tables," were built and maintained automatically.

Once the computer scientists had established IP as a simple, consistent way to send data around in chunks (or "packets"), they built a number of applications on top. They implemented the Transmission Control Protocol (TCP) on top of IP to provide reliable delivery of data packets—when data is sent using TCP, a connection is held open between the two endpoints, just as in a phone call. Data packets are acknowledged, and resent if necessary.

With IP, the data is just "squirted" towards the destination. Different IP packets might travel by different paths across the net, so some may arrive out of sequence or be mislaid entirely. Together, TCP on top of IP forms the TCP/IP acronym that is frequently heard. IP means "big chunks of data are sent by dividing them into several smaller packets," and TCP means "we guarantee the

The great "Ping of Death" saga

In October 1996, the news broke that a programmer had discovered Windows systems could be instructed to send an illegally large ping packet. When the oversized packet arrived at the remote system (anywhere on the Internet, remember) it crashed or panicked the computer. Needless to say, this caused equal amounts of consternation, dismay, entertainment, and diversion, depending on who was pinging and who was panicking. Vulnerable systems included Macs, many versions of UNIX, Netware, Windows 3.11, Windows 95, Windows NT, Tandem NSK and many routers, printers, and other devices with their own IP address.

The problem was actually greater than ping. It's just that ping provides a trivially easy way to send a packet to another system. The buggy Windows software allowed a user to specify a packet size larger than the overall limit of 64 Kb. The packet would be split into several chunks and sent, but would cause problems when it was assembled back into its original size at the other end. The usual failure mode was overwriting whatever lay beyond the packet buffer, causing a kernel panic or hang.

As soon as the problem was known, OS vendors set to work to fix it. One programmer reported that the SGI Irix operating system version 6.2 had been patched to prevent the 64 Kb ping crash from happening. But the SGI systems programmers also retained the hidden ability to send out floods of such pings, allegedly so they could retaliate against evil hackers death-pinging their site. This is not so far-fetched. It is well known that various network sniffers snoop on all TCP traffic up to the firewall at interesting sites. (A firewall is a barrier between the Internet and internal systems.) There is little that organizations can do except keep a strong firewall and institute policies to prevent the outside e-mailing of confidential information.

When the dust finally settled, dozens of computer manufacturers had been obliged to issue emergency patches to their operating systems, while users were turning away ping packets at their firewalls. The problem was severe because it crashed systems, possibly in the middle of doing something useful and because of the ubiquity of the protocol.

Pathological failure cases occasionally happen in every industry, but in the computer industry we have the means to publish the information worldwide immediately. And we do. The same process happened with the Intel Pentium division bug, which eventually put enough pressure on Intel to fix the problem. More information about the Pentium bug is in "MicroProcessor Report," Dec. 26, 1994.

---

reliable delivery of packets in the right order." One of the key advantages of TCP/IP is that it can easily connect hardware systems from different vendors, as long as they both support the protocol.

Another protocol built on top of IP is the User Datagram Protocol (UDP)—see Figure 2–4 on page 33. UDP is a very thin layer on top of IP, and is termed a "stateless" protocol because neither end looks for a response from the other. By way of contrast, TCP makes certain that data gets to the other end by keeping track of it and repeating if necessary, UDP just guarantees the data is sent. UDP

TCP/ IP is the Internet protocol suite. The protocol is an agreement between networks on how they will send information to each other. In the ISO "seven layer" model of networking, TCP covers the transport layer and IP covers the network layer.

For comparison, IBM's System Network Architecture (SNA) is a protocol that has both transport and network aspects. The CCITT X.25 packet switching standard (dating from the 1970s and still heavily used in Europe and Canada) has aspects of both network and data linked to it. Both of these are older alternative protocols on which a network can be based.

The ubiquity of TCP/IP has made it the protocol suite of choice for new networks, where an Internet connection is now generally assumed. Older, established networks, such as those employing SNA, X.25, DECNet, Novell's IPX, and so on, are incompatible with IP. If no Internet connection is required, then the existing protocol can continue to be used, but the systems will be an isolated island in the ocean of telecommunications.

If an Internet connection is required, then the older network must either convert or make some accommodation for TCP/IP. One possibility is to use gateway equipment, perhaps involving protocol conversion hardware. Another possibility is "tunneling," which means wrapping one protocol over another to provide a means of hidden passage. None of the accommodation methods are quite as good as the real thing, but they can save considerable money by allowing a phased period of transition.

is faster than TCP but not guaranteed reliable. UDP might be used to send the ticks of a clock, where timely delivery is more important than going back and repeating dropped ticks. UDP is frequently used for streaming video or audio where dropping the occasional packet is an acceptable price for speedy transmission. Web-browsing is built on the HyperText Transfer Protocol (HTTP) which is built on TCP/IP. You don't want missing words in a web document you browse, so a reliable transmission protocol is a must.

On top of TCP/IP, researchers wrote lots of programs allowing users to access services on other computers. One example is "finger" to enquire about the logon status of users on systems far away. These computer scientists provided the ability to "telnet" to different systems—that is, to log in remotely from one host computer to a different computer located somewhere distant. Another very popular utility allowed files to be transferred from one computer to another. This utility was known as "ftp" because the implementation used a protocol (algorithm) called "File Transfer Protocol" to move the files around.

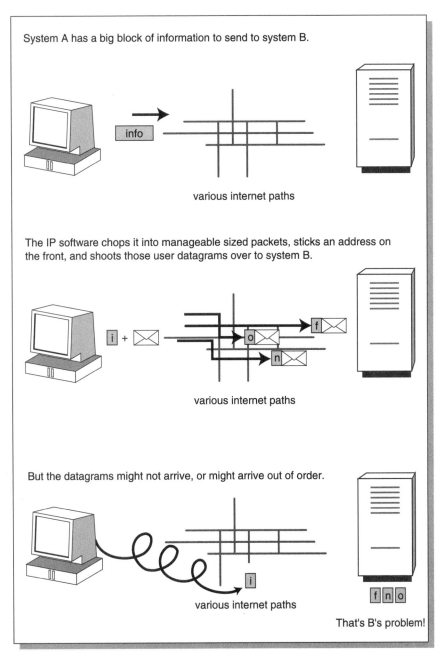

Figure 2–4
The User Datagram Protocol (UDP)

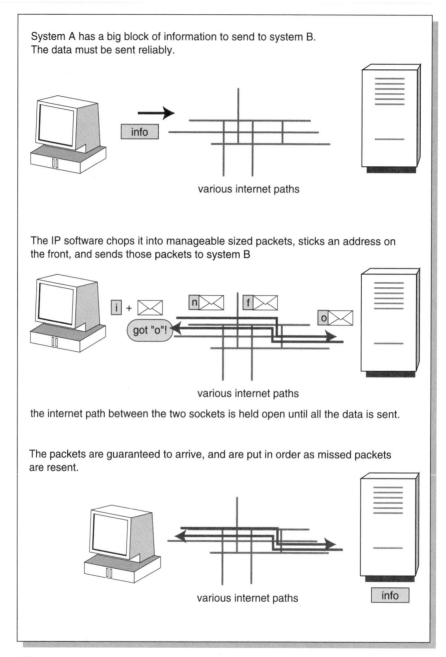

Figure 2-5
The Transmission Control Protocol (TCP)

IP (Internet Protocol) means "**big chunks of data are sent by dividing them into several smaller packets and shooting them over to the destination**"

TCP (Transmission Control Protocol) means "**we guarantee the reliable delivery of packets in the right order, by holding open a path between the source and destination, acknowledging packets and resending if necessary.**" See Figure 2–5 on page 34.

The "seven layer" model of networking is a theoretical model originally intended to define the future of networking. That didn't happen, but the model is still useful in providing a common terminology for comparing different real-world network protocols.

The layers, and typical events each is concerned with, are shown in Figure 2–6. The idea is that each layer is built on the more primitive services offered by the layer below, and in this way, sophisticated services can be supported without every programmer having to be a network genius.

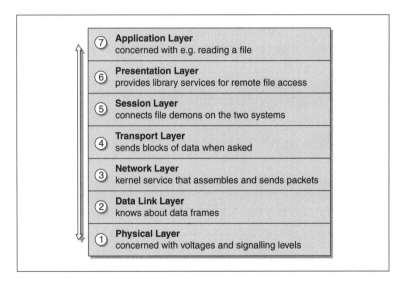

Figure 2–6
The Seven-Layer Open Systems Interconnection Network Model

You had to be quite knowledgeable to use ftp—you needed to specify with various obscure commands where exactly the file was going and whether it contained binary data or ASCII text. Another application was "ping," which has been retrospectively given the acronym "Packet INternet Groper." Pinging a system just means sending it an IP packet and asking for an acknowledgment. Ping is used to help diagnose network connectivity and timing problems. In October 1996 some programmers discovered that Windows 95 and Windows NT did not properly implement IP and could be instructed to send an invalid ping packet that crashed the remote system you were pinging (see details in the The great "Ping of Death" saga box on page 31). News of the "Ping of Death" flew around the Internet like wildfire.

The most popular and widely used application has always been electronic mail. E-mail lets any computer user send a memo to another user. The text message is composed by one user, routed to the recipient's computer (which may be far away on the network) where it is stored until the recipient is ready to read it. It is analogous to the paper mail carried by a national postal service, except e-mail is cheaper, faster, more private and more reliable.

Junk e-mail—unsolicited commercial e-mail—also known as "spam" is getting to be a big nuisance on the Internet, just as junk faxes were a big problem with fax technology a few years ago. Unlike junk faxes and junk postal mail, spam costs the perpetrators nothing to send. Junk faxes were eventually outlawed in the United States. A legislative solution like that would be a little harder to make stick in the case of junk e-mail because of the ease of relocating the offending mail server offshore. Junk fax senders cannot relocate overseas without incurring big phone bills, but there are no long distance charges on Internet traffic (in most countries).

IP networking provides many remote services, each attached to a *port* (a dedicated listening address maintained by the operating system in software). In UNIX, the file /etc/services lists the known IP services, as shown in Table 2-1.

Case Study 1: Using the Internet for Learning

In the early 1980s, another application, distinct from e-mail, file transfer, and telnet, was added to the Internet: network news. Network news, or "Usenet" as it became known, is a phenomenon that is hard to describe if you have not experienced it. Usenet is a computerized bulletin board with hundreds of special interest discussion groups. It provides a great way to exchange informal notes, advice, hints, wisdom, humor, or even insults with a group of surprisingly diverse people.

It was and is heady, exciting, time consuming, and addictive. It greatly expands your field of acquaintances. Today, almost no pastime, interest, or profession is too obscure for Usenet. Every imaginable topic has its own specialized newsgroup devoted to lively (sometimes controversial) discussion. There are a dozen

Table 2-1 The Many Standard IP Services on UNIX

Service	Port number	Protocol	Alternative name
#			
# Network services, Internet style			
#			
tcpmux	1	tcp	
echo	7	tcp	
echo	7	udp	
discard	9	tcp	sink null
discard	9	udp	sink null
systat	11	tcp	users
daytime	13	tcp	
daytime	13	udp	
netstat	15	tcp	
chargen	19	tcp	ttytst source
chargen	19	udp	ttytst source
ftp-data	20	tcp	
ftp	21	tcp	
telnet	23	tcp	
smtp	25	tcp	mail
time	37	tcp	timserver
time	37	udp	timserver
name	42	udp	nameserver
whois	43	tcp	nicname # usually to sri-nic
domain	53	udp	
domain	53	tcp	
bootps	67	udp	# BOOTP/DHCP server
bootpc	68	udp	# BOOTP/DHCP client
hostnames	101	tcp	hostname # usually to sri-nic
sunrpc	111	udp	rpcbind
sunrpc	111	tcp	rpcbind
#			
# Host specific functions			
tftp	69	udp	
rje	77	tcp	
finger	79	tcp	
http	80	tcp	www
link	87	tcp	ttylink
supdup	95	tcp	
iso-tsap	102	tcp	
x400	103	tcp	# ISO Mail
x400-snd	104	tcp	
csnet-ns	105	tcp	
pop-2	109	tcp	# Post Office
uucp-path	117	tcp	
nntp	119	tcp	usenet # Network News Transfer
ntp	123	tcp	# Network Time Protocol
ntp	123	udp	# Network Time Protocol

Usenet newsgroups that I set up in 1997 devoted to Java. A typical posting in the

---

The Java newsgroups

These are the Java newsgroups and their general topics

    comp.lang.java.help — simple programming and setup questions

    comp.lang.java.announce — (moderated) announcements

    comp.lang.java.advocacy — for arguments involving Java

    comp.lang.java.programmer — about programming in Java

    comp.lang.java.security — security issues

    comp.lang.java.machine — JVM and native interfaces

    comp.lang.java.databases — Java access to databases.

    comp.lang.java.softwaretools — editors, compilers, tools, etc

    comp.lang.java.gui — Java windowing libraries and use

    comp.lang.java.beans — software components in Java

    comp.lang.java.corba — (newsgroup added Dec 1997) interaction
between Java and CORBA.

The newsgroups can be read with a dedicated newsreader such as trn, or by using the newsreader that comes with the Communicator browser.

Java programmer group might ask how one does interactive I/O, or how best to round off floating point expressions, or how to use dates in Java.

It turns out that many people like to share their expertise with others (it doesn't hurt that this is a public forum read by tens of thousands of programmers around the world), so such postings often get knowledgeable responses very quickly. A junior programmer who diligently reads comp.lang.java.programmer for a period of 2 or 3 months will very rapidly increase his or her Java knowledge.

Bringing Usenet off the Internet to a news server in-house is a good way to boost the skill of interested staff by giving them the chance to learn from more experienced colleagues in other companies around the world. However, as previously mentioned, Usenet can be very addictive and time consuming, and there are just as many recreational newsgroups as there are newsgroups devoted to computer-related topics. Enough said…

One common criticism of Usenet is "the net has no memory" meaning that the same questions tend to be asked over and over again by different people. To address this problem, many newsgroups, including comp.lang.java.programmer, have compiled a FAQ list.

Just the FAQs, ma'am

The FAQ (meaning "Frequently Asked Questions," but also a pun on "fact") list provides a record of questions that recur frequently in a newsgroup and gives a solid answer on each. A FAQ list is maintained and posted periodically by some public-spirited volunteer on the newsgroup. Not all newsgroups have a FAQ list, but many of them do, and all the FAQs are archived at M.I.T. on the FTP server rtfm.mit.edu and at several other places on the Internet.

You can find out how to obtain the most up-to-date FAQ list for the Java newsgroups or any newsgroup, by sending the e-mail message "help" to the e-mail address `mail-server@rtfm.mit.edu`.

The FAQ list for comp.lang.java.programmer is particularly comprehensive (over 6,000 lines). I wrote it to answer the most common questions that real programmers have raised. The Java FAQ can be read or downloaded from http://www.afu.com. FAQs for any newsgroup tend to be "labors of love," including commentaries from a variety of different people. The Java FAQ was refined and improved over several years, with inputs from some very skilled people. Very few textbooks can boast as much. Finally of course, FAQs are available for free over the Internet to anyone who wants them.

Almost every Java programmer will learn something with their first review of the comp.lang.java.programmer newsgroup and FAQ. In this sense, the Internet offers an important learning resource of direct professional relevance to those in the computer industry. The Java FAQ list will eventually be published in book form for those who do not have Internet access, or for those who do not get the same pleasure from a cathode ray tube that they do from a real, solid book.

At their best, Usenet newsgroups can be a font of knowledge. However, managers should be aware that there are also a small number of newsgroups devoted to dialogue on salacious topics inappropriate in the workplace. You'll avoid needless problems if you ensure that, of the thousands of Usenet newsgroups, your site does not store or forward the few dozen newsgroups whose names begin with alt.sex.

Summary

- The Internet is a loosely organized collection of networks using TCP/IP protocols to packet-switch data to almost anywhere in the world at a very low cost. We are still near the beginning of a global revolution to use it for business, education, and recreation.

How do you...?

One of my team members, knowing of my interest and expertise in the C programming language as well as Java, recently brought me a practical question he had encountered. I didn't know the answer, so I posted the question on the comp.lang.c newsgroup.

```
From:          linden@positive.eng.sun.com (Peter van der Linden)
Subject:       Constant struct: How do you do this?
Date:          1996/11/08
Newsgroups:    comp.lang.c


How do you do this in C?  I have an initialized variable of type struct s1, and a larger
variable of type struct s2 that contains an s1 as a field. I want the s1 field in the vari-
able of type s2 to be initialized to the value of the s1 variable.

I know from the ANSI C standard that only constants are acceptable as initializers for aggre-
gates.  Is there a way to make a constant struct, or can the initialization only be done with
a literal?

struct s1 { int i; int j; int k; int 1; };

struct s1 const s1_var = { 0,1,2,3 };

struct s2 { int i; struct s1 sk; };

const struct s2 s2_var = {
     0,  /* what goes here, to get the s1 field values? */
};

Note: I can do it by making the field in s2 be an address that points to s1 but that isn't
what I want.  I want to say "take the values from const s1 and put them in here".

Note 2: maybe the best I can do is a macro with the literal value in.

--

Peter van der Linden      linden%nospam@eng.sun.com   http://www.best.com/~pvdl
```

- The Internet supports a number of applications that can make computer users more productive: e-mail, telnet, ftp, Usenet news. Originally, users had to be fluent with computers to use these services effectively, but modern web browsers have simplified things to the point where anyone can use them.

How do you...?

My question on the comp.lang.c newsgroup quickly attracted several answers, some right, some wrong. Here is one of the wrong answers. The respondent has misunderstood the question.

```
From:        "Cy Dann" <cd@microsoft.com>
Subject:     Re: Constant struct: How do you do this?
Date:        1996/11/08
Newsgroups:  comp.lang.c

See the C FAQ, Question 2.7.
Since you don't have any pointers in your s1, you can do a direct assignment without worry
of repercussion.  And a const modifier would not help a thing.

> Note 2: maybe the best I can do is a macro with the literal value in.

Nope.  You can do better than that.
```

Luckily, another respondent provided the correct answer.

```
From:        Tanmoy Bhattacharya <tanmoy@qcd.lanl.gov>
Subject:     Re: Constant struct: How do you do this?
Date:        1996/11/08
Newsgroups:  comp.lang.c

Initializers for aggregate or union objects in standard C have to be
constants, or be one expression assignment compatible to it (not for
arrays: an array cannot be initialized from another array, except a
(wide) character array can be initialized from a (wide) string
literal). Note that in C, const objects are merely unmodifiable
variables, and not constants.

So, what you want to do is not possible.

Cheers
Tanmoy
```

The point here is that information on Usenet is unfiltered. Users need to be sophisticated enough and knowledgable enough to determine whether they have been given a correct answer. The amount of confidence with which something is asserted or claimed on the Internet has no relationship to how true it actually is.

CHAPTER 3

- Hypertext

- HTML—Hypertext Markup Language

- Browsers

- Competition among browsers

- Case Study 2: A Basic Commercial Web Site

- Summary

The
World Wide
Web

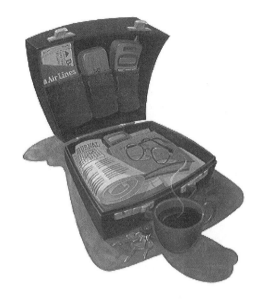

"What a tangled web we weave, when first we practice to deceive."
— Sir Walter Scott

T he 1980s were a period of growing up for the Internet; a period when a critical mass of information was accumulated on line. But two big problems severely hampered general use of the Internet throughout this period. The first problem was the lack of any central index to the wealth of general information that the Internet contained. There were a few inadequate searching utilities, like gopher and archie, that relied on public-spirited sites compiling lists of files, but overall the Internet was like an island full of buried treasure with no treasure map.

The second problem was that you had to be a knowledgeable UNIX operating system user to issue the commands that retrieved information. It was as though expertise every bit as specialized as a private pilot's license was needed to explore the Internet.

That all changed within the space of about a year from mid-1993 onward. The reason it changed was the arrival of some quite simple software that solved both problems at a stroke. This software was the web browser software, and it heralded the notion of the World Wide Web (often called *WWW*). The World Wide Web is the "killer application" that brought the Internet to prominence. Browsers are the "Instamatic®" of the Internet, allowing simple point-and-click operation by everyone.

Hypertext Leading to the Early Web

The whole concept of web browsing originated in 1989 at CERN, the European high-energy physics research laboratory. A programmer there, Tim Berners-Lee, wanted to provide a consistent and easy way for the physicists and researchers to read each other's papers over the computer network. The basic idea was to support a "browser" program and a set of data communication protocols. The browser would let users retrieve a copy of files from any computer system in the organization and display their contents locally, simply by telling the browser the computer and path name where the files were stored. Users could also plant a reference actually inside a document to the location of related documents. The browser and protocols made it easy to follow a link and display the document it pointed to.

When a physicist wrote a paper to share with colleagues, most of the file contained the text of the paper, like any ordinary ASCII file. At each point in the paper where a diagram or picture was needed, there was a special text string that said in effect, "When you display this file in a browser, at this point you should go and retrieve the picture file that you will find at this (specified) location and display it here." Papers intended for sharing and display in a browser contained a mixture of actual text and markup language that located other files. In a diagram, the situation could be represented as shown in Figure 3–1.

Having something in a file that points to a resource elsewhere is the "linking" part of the Microsoft Windows concept of OLE (Object Linking and Embedding). However, OLE operates only on highly structured documents like spreadsheet data files, whereas hypertext brought the idea to simple ASCII text and pictures. Hypertext was thus available to anyone who could use an editor, rather than just to computer programmers.

The CERN browser allowed researchers to tie together all kinds of related information. When one paper referenced another, instead of merely giving a footnote citation, the browser could display a link to it. When clicked, the link would cause the browser to view the linked file. Instead of just knowing the title of the referenced paper, users could directly read its contents.

Important new concept: Hypertext

A computer system supports hypertext when it allows on-line documents to be linked to other documents, so that a person starting to read one document can easily switch to the linked documents and back again at will. This provides a very rich form of reading and study. Figure 3–2 illustrates the difference between documents without and with hypertext.

How hypertext browsing works

A researcher writes a paper that has text and accompanying pictures. The words go in one file, and each image in a separate file. Mixed in with the text are instructions on how to format it for display. The instruction langauge is called "HTML." At each place in the word file where a picture is supposed to appear, there is a reference that allows a browser to locate the picture. The word file looks like this:

The word file is stored in /path/somewhere/paper.txt

The hammer picture is stored in /path/file/hammer.gif

The rocks picture is stored in /path/otherfile/rocks.gif

Someone using an editor to look at the file

/path/somewhere/paper.txt sees the exact text above. Someone using a browser to look at the file /path/somewhere/paper.txt sees the formatted words with the rock and hammer pictures blended together on screen.

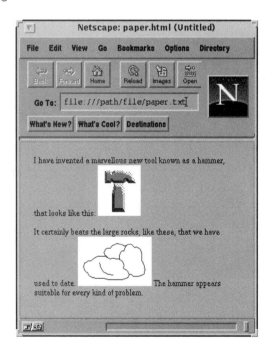

Figure 3–1
How Hypertext Browsing Works

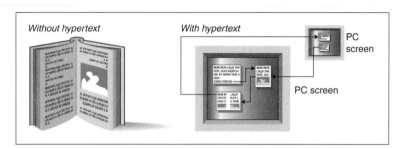

Figure 3–2
Documents without and with Hypertext

So, a file could hold links to other files that contained links to other files and so on, forming a web of related documents. Readers can switch easily among them. This scheme is known as "hypertext." In its first incarnation, the hypertext links were all within one site, but there is no reason to stop at the firewall. A web page can link to (contain information on how to locate) any other web page anywhere on the Internet. When you have a whole world (or Internet) full of web pages with hypertext links to each other, you have the World Wide Web (WWW).

A related term is "hypermedia," meaning that the links need not be restricted to text. Hypermedia means you can link to pictures, audio clips, animation, or anything you can store on a computer system, even computer programs (more about that last one later).

As a concrete example, practically all PC encyclopedia programs support some elementary form of hypertext, allowing you to jump from one entry to related entries. Most of them also support hypermedia, allowing you to run brief animations or film clips accompanying the text. A frequent example is an animation to demonstrate the cycles of an internal combustion engine, linked to the encyclopedia entry on engines. This is true hypermedia—clicking on the text link brings up moving pictures. It provides an enriching experience for the user.

In a conventional printed paper, you can see a reference to other documents in footnotes and the like, but you cannot actually see the documents themselves without physically looking them up. Hypertext overcomes this limitation. Hypertext allows a writer to highlight any words or phrases in an on-line document and link them with other parts of that document or another. A whole group of documents can be linked, forming a network or web of interconnecting hypertext links.

In a browser, the hypertext links are typically displayed in a different color or typeface, and you click on them to follow the link. You thus control how you navigate through a document, and which side topics are followed. The names "browser" and "web browser" follow directly from this.

The CERN system was a good proof of concept, but it lacked a graphical user interface (the first version had a text-only interface), and it lacked the critical mass of users needed to make any communications technology succeed (telephones aren't useful until most of the people you want to call also have them).

Marc Andreessen, an undergraduate at the University of Illinois, who worked part time at the National Center for SuperComputing Applications, had seen a demonstration of the CERN browser and soon set to work to address the limitations. His group released the "Mosaic" browser in June 1993. It could be downloaded across the Internet for free, was available for many different computers, was simple to use, and it really lit the fuse to the explosive growth of the Internet. In 1994 Marc Andreessen and some colleagues from NCSA formed a company that became the Netscape Communications Corporation, selling the Netscape browser. Andreessen and many of his equally far-sighted colleagues are now multimillionaires.

HTML—Hypertext Markup Language

Just as word processors keep their files in their own special format (e.g., Microsoft Word has one format, WordPerfect has another format), web documents have a format known as HTML—Hypertext Markup Language. The HTML format for web documents is thankfully quite simple. People who remember the old troff/nroff/runoff word processor commands will immediately find HTML familiar. HTML consists of the words you want to display, with a few dozen extra text strings, called "tags," sprinkled throughout. The tags tell a browser exactly how to format the rest of the text and specify the hypertext links to other web pages. The text to be displayed together with the HTML tags can be created and modified by any editor that can save text in a straight ASCII file. Figure 3–3 through Figure 3–5 show some example HTML tags. Most HTML tags occur in pairs, marking the beginning and end of the region of text which they affect. When a browser browses an HTML document, it does trivial formatting, aligning the left margin, wrapping words when the line length is reached, bringing in and displaying picture files, and especially showing the hypertext links, and following them when requested.

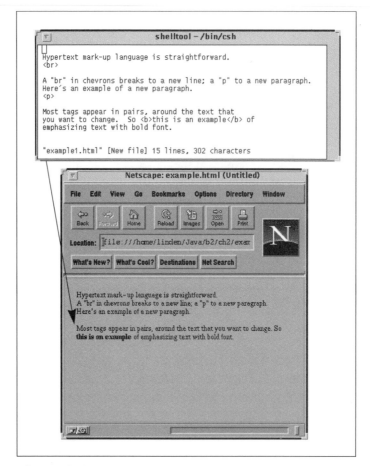

Figure 3–3
HTML Text and Tags

HTML is a very simple markup language that tells a browser how to format the text as it displays it. It is one of the family of languages defined by the large and over-complicated SGML—Standard Generalized Markup Language. HTML is well suited for distributing many kinds of information that require just a little formatting: product data sheets, on-line encyclopedias, recipe books, guide books, and so on. Because the protocol uses ASCII data, it is easy to learn, easy to edit, and easy to transmit. HTML is not suitable for more complicated diagrams and images such as interactive graphics, a "parts explosion" diagram, or anything that changes, like text editing.

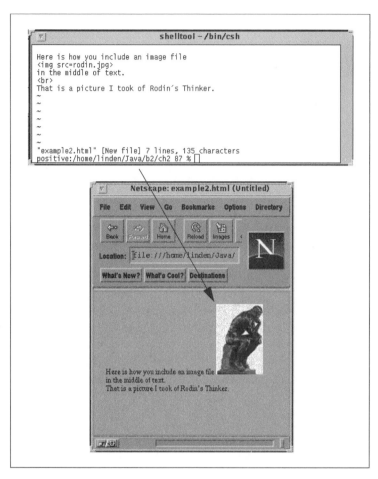

Figure 3–4
An Image Referenced in an HTML File

Browsers

A "web browser" or "browser" is the user interface to the World Wide Web. It is a simple program for retrieving and displaying files and following links to other files, thus supporting hypermedia. A key reason for the popularity of this software has been its utter simplicity to operate—you tell the browser where to look, it looks there and shows the results on your screen.

The Mosaic browser (and all browsers since) are easy to run—you just point and click to read a web document.

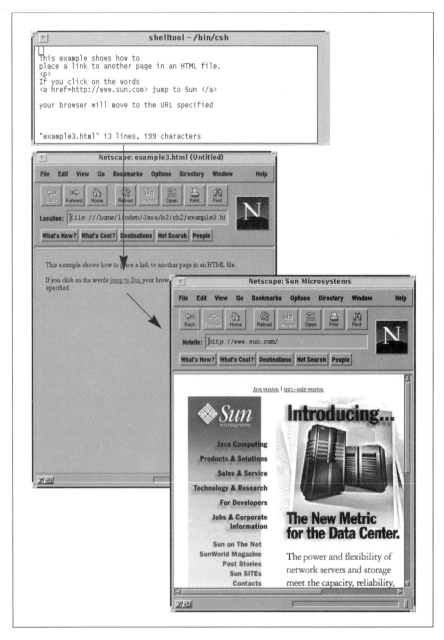

Figure 3–5
A Hypertext Link in an HTML File

On-line Web-Based Business

When an organization gets Internet access, the first thing it does is set up a home page. A home page is a brief web document that introduces the organization and explains its mission. The home page usually has links to other pages giving more in-depth information, perhaps a list of products and ordering information. The home page for an organization started out as just the on-line equivalent of a business card, or an advertisement in the Yellow Pages phone directory. It provides a summary of basic facts and contact information.

Organizations maintain publicly accessible home pages on the Web for the same reason they have receptionists, brochures, and press releases: these are low-cost ways to convey information about the organization and to answer common questions from potential customers. A web site (basic Internet presence) costs about $30 per month paid to an Internet service provider. Cost is not a justification for avoiding an Internet presence. Getting beyond a mere on-line presence to an actual e-commerce site is the hottest area of Internet activity at present.

For the first three years of the web little to no business was conducted on-line through a company's web site. The payment and privacy infrastucture was not there. But the benefits of web-based commerce were so compelling that people quickly worked to provide it. Chapter 6 covers the topic in more detail. By 1997 browsers supported on-demand encryption of data passed back and forth between server and client. This made it possible to send credit card information over the web without the possibility of casual eavesdroppers recording the numbers. Credit cards provide the payment, encryption provides the privacy, and web sites provide the market where buyers come to sellers. But before you can visit a web site, you have to know about it, which is where searching comes in.

Searching for Web Sites

A big problem predating the World Wide Web was searching for information. The World Wide Web solves this in a happily symbiotic manner. A number of enterprising sites have discovered that, if sufficient web surfers visit their pages, advertisers will pay to have material displayed on those pages. An alert and technically savvy company can parlay this into a business by providing automated web-searching services that draw web surfers (readers) to its site. Table 3-1 lists a few of the many sites that you can use to search the Web.

Table 3-1 Some Popular Web-Searching Sites

URL	Description
http://www.yahoo.com	The Yahoo! site. A good place to start looking for something on the Web.
http://www.excite.com	The Excite site. Another well-connected search site.
http://www.altavista.digital.com	A showpiece for the throughput capabilities of DEC's Alpha systems.
http://www.lycos.com	The first site to use web crawler software.
http://www.albany.net/allinone	A search site that lists search sites. There are several others who had this idea too, and I am thinking of starting a search site for indexing all of the search sites that list search sites...
http://www.dejanews.com	A site that searches for the content of old Usenet posts.

The earliest and best known of the search sites was started in April 1994 by a couple of Stanford University students, David Filo and Jerry Yang, as a hobby project to create an index to the Web. They called their efforts "Yahoo!" which allegedly stood for "Yet Another Hierarchical Officious Oracle" (these were graduate students in Electrical Engineering, remember). Filo and Yang are another two "Internet millionaires," created when they incorporated Yahoo! then took it public.

Sites that offer web-searching facilities add to their databases in a couple of ways. They offer readers the opportunity to fill out forms on-line and register interesting sites. Most of their entries are made this way. The second way that they get their links is through automated searching software that looks for new announcements at various places. This kind of searching has been given the poetic name of "web crawling" because the search software follows links from site to site.

When you try to search for something on the World Wide Web using one of the above sites, your search may fail. There can be several reasons for this. You may fail to get the link you want because there is no such information on the Web at all. Frankly, this situation is becoming rarer for any reasonable definition of "information." If there is a topic that someone has thought about, they have usually written down their thoughts and published them on the Web.

Difficulties of Regulating the Web

This seems like a good place to point out something you have probably already guessed—just because something is on the Web does not mean it is legal, decent, honest, or truthful. If you discover someone has published plans for a marvellous new anti-gravity device (or "investment opportunity" or even a cookie recipe, for that matter), don't actually expect it to work. Information on the Web is raw information, and you always need to consider the source from which it is coming. A web site at a university that contains an academic report has a wholly different amount of credibility than a web site at the same university that provides undergraduates with a forum to describe themselves and their interests.

Internet Casinos

Regulation is difficult because sites can easily be based in countries with different, looser laws than the one in which you live. The United States government and individual states are currently very annoyed about web sites that conduct on-line gambling. As long as the web server for a casino is based in places like Curacao in the Dutch Antilles, it cannot be regulated or taxed by the United States. Although some legal officials claim that it is illegal for both parties to take part in Internet-based gambling, in practice it is not so clear cut. There are reasonable doubts about whether serving a web page from the Carribean on demand constitutes a "significant presence" in the United States. The U.S. Senate voted in summer 1998 to outlaw Internet gambling, but it is nearly impossible to enforce laws outside national boundaries. Americans cannot currently be prevented from privately gambling over the Internet any more than they can (or should) be prevented from placing telephone calls to hot chat lines. A search on "offshore casino" finds hundreds of sites.

Of course, it's a complete sucker's game to bet with any offshore casino. Unlike the casinos in Las Vegas where the payout percentage is fixed by law, offshore operations can set the house percentage to be as greedy as they like.

The problem of trying to enforce local laws against the content of international web sites is a more general one. Governments have essentially three choices. They can enact repressive measures and try to enforce them. This approach is the one chosen by France, Singapore, China, and Vietnam among others. They can enact repressive measures, but not try too hard to enforce the unenforceable parts. The United States currently uses this approach. Finally countries can avoid even attempting to regulate outside national boundaries. This pragmatic approach is used by most of the rest of the world. In the long run, international regulatory agreements for Internet communication are inevitable, just as they have been put in place for other kinds of trade and communication.

Returning to the topic of searching, a more common reason for not finding the information you seek is that you just didn't use the right combination of search terms. This is the same problem that all researchers face: you want to be specific enough that you don't get scores of irrelevant or uninteresting references (so you wouldn't search on "tiger," for example). But you don't want to be so specific that nothing at all shows up (so you wouldn't want to search on "the economic effect of white tiger skin trade in Eastern Siberia under the Kruschev regime," either). If your search yields no sites to visit, then try reformulating the query, using different related keywords. There's a big future in cleverer, semantic-aware search algorithms. The Web is bringing Information Science back into the limelight.

Sometimes links don't get added to search sites quickly enough to provide the latest information about rapidly changing events.

In February 1995, many people followed space shuttle mission STS-75 with great interest. This was the mission in which the experiment to reel out several miles of cable failed when the cable broke.

The combination of space shuttle and miles of broken cable flying in low earth orbit (just 180 miles up) proved irresistible, and I wanted to find out all about how the experiment had failed and where exactly I could look in the sky to observe the shuttle. My local newspaper printed some information, but despite intensive searching on my part, nothing of the incident could be found on the Web. The basic shuttle information was all there, but nothing about this new development. The incident was happening in real time, and almost no one had a chance to write and publish informed commentary and get it indexed by a major search site in time for us to see the shuttle in the air. The only organization that did have all the information, NASA, had no interest in highlighting one of their failures. You can read all about the STS-75 mission and its failed experiment now at

`http://www.ksc.nasa.gov/shuttle/missions/sts-75/mission-sts-75.html`

but at the time it was very frustrating not to find any up-to-date information about the hiccup in the mission. A better avenue for finding the information would have been to post a request for information on one of the space-related newsgroups. Searching for static information works best of all.

Sometimes a search will come up with some sites, but when you try to follow them, you experience a delay and then see a message saying "permission denied" or "no data in document." This often means that you are trying to access a very busy site and it can't handle your request right now. Try again once, and if still unsuccessful, set your alarm clock for the early hours when you can make your next attempt. You might want to take account of time zones when you do this and plan your visit for the early hours of the site you are visiting. Sites usually get their peak usage in the mid-morning to mid-afternoon core part of the day, dropping off to next to nothing before sunrise. This has led to the old web adage, "It's always fastest just before the dawn." My brother in London tells me that they try to do all their Web accesses in the morning, before North America wakes up (in its own time zones).

Perhaps the most disappointing reason for a search failure is also the one you can do least about: you are seeking information about something that is too contemporary. Although we joke that "Everything on the Internet happens seven times faster than in life" and talk about "Internet years being like dog years," sometimes, links don't get added to search sites quickly enough to provide the latest information about rapidly changing events.

Competition between Browsers

There was a wide variety of competing browsers for the first couple of years, but the world has now consolidated on the products of Netscape Communications Corporation as the premiere browser. Microsoft's Internet Explorer (IE) is in second place, pushing hard, and will almost inevitably displace Netscape.

Table 3-2 shows market share for some popular browsers.

Table 3-2 Popular Browsers

Organization	Browser Name	% Est. market share (Spring 1998)
Netscape Communications Corp.	Communicator `http://www.netscape.com`	60%
Microsoft	Internet Explorer (a product based on Spyglass's Mosaic)	40%
Opera Software	Opera `http://www.operasoftware.com`	<1%
University of Kansas	Lynx	< 1%

Source: "EWS Browser Statistics, March 1998"

`http://www.ews.uiuc.edu/bstats/latest-month.html`

It's a two horse race in which the front runner has already conceded defeat to the number two entry. Netscape has announced that it recognizes it cannot win the browser war against Microsoft's bundling tactics. So Netscape is adjusting its business model to emphasize server-side products and site advertising instead of browsers. Netscape even put in place a scheme to publish its source code and allow public-spirited programmers to contribute browser improvements.

In Spring 1998, Netscape represented roughly two-thirds of all browsers in use. Netscape used to have a larger market share. A survey in November 1995 by Zona Research Inc, Redwood City, California, reported that Netscape's web browser was the primary browser for 87 percent of users. The same survey of corporate IT sites also found that Microsoft`s Internet Explorer was the primary browser for just 4 percent of users. Microsoft has since been able to force its own browser into the market using a variety of high-pressure tactics that are the antithesis of open competition.

Existing United States laws forbid a company from leveraging a monopoly to snuff out competition in another market segment. In late 1997 the United States Department of Justice filed a legal action claiming that Microsoft had done just that. The Department of Justice further claimed that Microsoft violated the 1995 "consent decree" agreement that ended the previous investigation into the Redmond monopoly. Under the consent decree terms, Microsoft cannot require PC manufacturers to ship a separate product (such as a browser) in order to get a license to ship Windows 95.

Microsoft argues that its browser is not a separate product but an integrated part of Windows 95, even though it did not ship with the first versions of Windows 95. The government argues that Explorer is a separate product from Windows 95 because the company sells versions of it for non-Windows computers. The Justice Department obtained a preliminary injunction against Microsoft. Microsoft appealed the order, and also appealed against the judge's appointment of a Harvard professor as a special master (expert) on the case. Many observers were suprised by the appeal decision in Microsoft's favor. The Department of Justice and twenty individual states filed a much broader anti-trust lawsuit against Microsoft in May 1998, alleging a great many abuses of monopolistic power. The cases are still plodding through the legal system and won't be resolved until long after Microsoft's heavy-handed tactics have ended competition in the browser market.

The pace of browser innovation was very rapid when there was competition. As Netscape and Microsoft battled, each made new feature releases every four or five months. There was also the "perpetual Beta syndrome," where an early test version of the next release is available for downloading soon after the current version first ships. Because browser software is free, users may have more than one browser on their system. For this reason, the market share figures are somewhat imprecise.

How Microsoft increased its browser-installed base by 900 percent

Microsoft was able to increase its browser presence by 900 percent in less than 18 months up to March 1998.

Here are some of the tactics that the United States government says Microsoft used to seize a large share of the browser market. None of these tactics involve "open competition" and "innovation" that are Microsoft's frequent rallying cries. The rather stunning increase in market share was achieved by simpler means: exclusion clauses in licenses, bundling or integration into Win95/98, alleged threats, and financial inducements.

- Microsoft now bundles its Internet Explorer browser with every copy of Windows 95. It has embedded the application as part of the user interface of Windows 98. If Microsoft gives a product away for free, already installed and difficult to remove, few people are going to bother with the effort of getting a different competing product, even if it's also free. Bundling is a method of locking out the competition. When the vast majority of computer users have the same operating system, bundling anything with that OS unfairly restricts competition.

- Key system software updates are shipped with Internet Explorer, forcing people to install the browser to get the latest OS bug fixes and features. Microsoft's Java product won't install unless the user accepts the installation of Microsoft's browser too.

- Microsoft paid domestic American ISPs such as America Online and MCI to bundle the Microsoft browser exclusively. Microsoft paid Apple millions of dollars to bundle Internet Explorer with every new Apple computer shipped. Microsoft also bought exclusive agreements with every ISP in the emerging Russian Internet market, ensuring that competitive products cannot get so much as a toehold in an entire nation.

- Microsoft signed contracts with about two dozen media and entertainment companies to enforce exclusivity. Under the contracts, content providers are featured on the "Channel Bar" of Internet Explorer, and in return are required to promote the Microsoft browser (and no other browser) on their main Internet web pages. After the practice was highlighted in a Senate hearing, Microsoft suspended enforcement of the exclusionary licensing clause in the United States.

- Netscape alleged in April 1998 that three years earlier Microsoft had made them an "offer they couldn't refuse." Netscape refused it anyway. Netscape said that Microsoft proposed to carve up the browser market between them: Microsoft to get Windows, and Netscape the remaining crumbs. Netscape further claimed that Microsoft demanded to invest in Netscape (before it was publicly traded) and when that was turned down, Microsoft threatened to withold technical information about the yet-to-be-launched Windows 95. Microsoft denied these claims. The Department of Justice added the issue to its ongoing investigation.

- In 1997 when Compaq replaced Microsoft's browser with the Netscape browser on its systems, Microsoft threatened the Texas PC manufacturer with the loss of its Windows 95 license. Without Windows 95 preinstalled, a PC is pretty much unsaleable to 99 percent of PC users. Compaq was quickly forced into line. The Department of Justice added the issue to its ongoing investigation. Acer, Gateway and Micron had similar tales.

- When the Department of Justice obtained an injunction requiring Microsoft to offer a version of Windows 95 without Internet Explorer bundled into it, Microsoft eventually complied. But it priced the two versions (with/without IE) the same. PC companies had no cost incentive to seek out a competing browser. All PC manufacturers now bundle the free number two browser (Internet Explorer) in preference to the number one browser (Communicator).

- Microsoft made Internet Explorer available for free download from the start. Netscape had charged $40 for its browser, after a free evaluation period. How does giving a product away for free hurt consumers? Dumping a product ultimately drives all competition from a market. When Japanese chip vendors dumped memory chips in the United States in the early 1980s, it forced Intel from the memory market. Dumping is dumping, even when it only involves domestic companies. A large cash-rich monopoly can wait out competitors for as long as it takes. Netscape was forced to match Microsoft's terms, and no longer charges for its browser. In 1998 Netscape declared a multimillion dollar loss, and laid off hundreds of staff.

Why Browsers Are So Important

Browsers are critically important for two reasons:

- browsers provide an applications programming interface that is independent of the desktop. If people start writing programs for the Netscape browser in large numbers, then the Windows API diminishes in significance. The company that controls the browser may well control the desktop. This is why Microsoft engaged in a fierce struggle with Netscape to wrest away browser leadership.

- The second reason that browsers are significant is e-commerce. The browser is the gateway to the Internet, and hence to electronic commerce. Electronic commerce is growing extremely rapidly in both dollar terms and in significance to the economy. If a single company gained exclusive control of browser software, it would eventually be able to impose a per-bit or per-transaction fee for electronic commerce. That's an unimaginably large revenue stream, like a private tax. This "chokehold" scenario is the reason that the Department of Justice has finally filed suit against Microsoft after years of turning a blind eye to complaints about its practices.

Microsoft is a recent convert to the significance of the WWW, and only reinvented itself around the Internet at the end of 1995. Microsoft's Internet Explorer(IE) browser is based on code licensed from Spyglass, not in-house innovation. Licensing someone else's code enabled Microsoft to come out with a product very quickly after discovering the Internet. Microsoft has integrated the IE browser as the main GUI element of Windows 98. This move forestalls the need to install a browser from anyone else. Microsoft also placed many other IE lock-ins, such as system services and libraries that rely on Explorer being present.

Browsers have led the way to platform-neutral software, originally with HTML alone, then extended with CGI scripts, now with JavaScript and Java. By controlling the browser, Microsoft can ensure its desktop operating system monopoly is not challenged. A good browser looks the same no matter which platform it runs on, so users are less locked into any particular operating system. A browser supports networking, a graphical user interface, and the ability to execute remote programs. It provides an operating environment that is good enough to directly run many simple desktop application programs such as a calculator, a calendar manager, and an e-mail manager. For many PC users, these applications are all that is needed. At that point, the underlying operating system such as MS Windows, the Apple Macintosh environment, or UNIX becomes redundant.

Browsers now offer very similar features:

- Support for simple desktop applications like keeping a calendar manager, sending e-mail, and reading Usenet news.

- The ability to run Java programs. This feature appeared in mid-1995, and just 12 months later was a nearly essential requirement for all browsers.

- The ability to browse hypermedia documents, both within your own site and on other sites anywhere on the Internet.

- The ability to set "bookmarks" that remember a particular site you have reached, allowing you to browse it directly next time.

- The ability to save a local copy of the document you are browsing.

So far no company has come up with a set of browser-based desktop office applications (spreadsheet, word processor, etc) that the market has really taken to heart. Several companies have made a first attempt: Sun Microsystems with Hot-Java Views, Corel, Lotus with e-suite, but the product offerings have yet to hit the sweet spot.

Some companies are standardizing on HTML for basic printed text presentation. It's possible to use HTML for simple documents instead of a word processor. An HTML-based document is publishable and readable everywhere by simple tools. Next generation word processors including MS Word will use HTML or its derivatives as their internal format.

Software "Lock-In" through Unique Features

All browsers originally supported the same HTML language, but over time they started to diverge (although each company races to support everything its competitors offer). The browser suppliers claim they are responding to requests from their customers for richer features. Perhaps, but an additional goal is to build market share by locking customers into a proprietary feature set (a common strategy that works against industry standards throughout the computer world). Browser vendors are very quick to add support for new features that competitors have. As a result, browser features are now converging again!

Netscape invented Frames for version 2 of Navigator. A frame is one of multiple scrollable panels, each with its own URL, that are all displayed on a single page. In other words, frames let you squeeze more content onto a single page. One common use for frames is to split a page into two columns and use the left column for a set of links. When a user clicks on any of them, that page is brought into the right-hand frame. This makes navigation a little simpler. Frames can be useful, so all browsers now support them.

Mitigating the lock-in effect is the fact that popular extensions are soon adopted by other browser vendors. However, the short-term effect of unique HTML extensions is to destroy web page portability and force all people who want to browse the page to use that browser. When you see the words "works best in Netscape" or "looks best in Internet Explorer" on a web page, the page author is attempting to dictate your choice of web browser.

To avoid this undesirable lock-in, users should shun such sites. Web page authors should avoid writing nonstandard HTML features, and they should test their new pages for accessibility by a variety of different browsers. Competing browsers eventually support pretty much the same features, but they still do not support all the "bells and whistles" that some customers demand.

The way to bridge the gap was obvious in hindsight: make the browser provide an Application Programmer Interface that will allow an auxiliary program to "plug in" to the side of the browser, use its screen, framework, and commands, and run independent special-purpose code. The plug-in feature was invented by Netscape and vastly extends the capabilities of the underlying browser. The next chapter addresses the topic in detail.

Case Study 2: A Basic Commercial Web Site

The Campaign for Real Ale, or CAMRA, is a volunteer organization based in Britain whose aim is to keep alive the traditional beers of that nation. From the 1960s on, commercial breweries were merging, and brewing increasingly bland beers. CAMRA was formed to give a voice to educated consumers and to persuade brewers not to drop traditional ales in favor of mass-market, pasteurized products. By all accounts, the Campaign for Real Ale has been very successful, and all major breweries in Britain now feature at least one traditional "live" ale in their product line. With this success under its belt (so to speak), CAMRA has extended its mission to include information and educational activities.

In the second half of 1995, CAMRA set up a web site. It has its own domain name and uses an Internet service provider to administer access to the Internet. The direct cost is minimal: about twenty pounds ($30) a month. The indirect cost of learning the technology and maintaining the web site adds some further expense but is hard to quantify. It also takes time to process incoming e-mail: the web site provides details on how to join CAMRA, including an application form that can be printed out and faxed back. The information submitted includes a credit card number. In 1995 it would have been unsafe to send this kind of information over the Internet, which is why CAMRA uses faxing. Now however a secure server can tell the client browser to encrypt the data before sending it. Credit card data and other sensitive information is routinely sent over the Internet today. Solving this problem was a requirement for electronic commerce so it was quickly tackled by browser companies.

Research assistant Ben Wardle says that the CAMRA web site gets over 1,000 hits each month and brings in half a dozen new members per month from the United States. The cost/benefit ratio is very favorable compared with reaching prospective new members by other media. The cost to process a membership application submitted through forms provided on the Web is about one-tenth the cost of processing a membership application by phone in their old way. CAMRA has made sure that they are listed under "beer" in the major searching engines, such as Yahoo.com.

CAMRA employs a headquarters staff of 13 people, but most of the executives are unpaid volunteers scattered around the country. Some of these people have e-mail access through their jobs and homes, and having CAMRA connected to the Internet allows them to work more closely together and quickly confer with other leaders.

CAMRA doesn't have any real technical expertise on the payroll—and doesn't need to. Everything technical was done by the ISP; all CAMRA provides is the HTML content for the site content. The web site has broadened out from the original concept of just an on-line presence and now forms an alternative avenue for communicating with members. It publishes information about beer festivals, ongoing campaigns, and membership details. The organization plans to buy a scanner to allow them to create their own artwork to further jazz up the site. They have no plans to adopt Java technology yet, unless any technically adept members volunteer to do the work.

The Campaign for Real Ale web site can be found at

```
http://www.camra.org.uk
```

Summary

- Hypertext is a modern idea for intertwining on-line documents so that it is easy to find and read related material. The World Wide Web is an implementation of hypertext that runs over the Internet. Browsers access web pages.

- The World Wide Web was largely responsible for the great explosion in popularity of the Internet. It vastly simplified the use of the Internet, enabling ordinary users to access its communication power.

- Searching on the web sites meant potential advertisers, which meant searching could be sponsored, which lead to good searching tools. This was a benign cycle that greatly helps the usefulness and distribution of information.

- Microsoft has a strategic interest in controlling the browser to protect its desktop operating system monopoly. The United States government has a strategic interest in controlling Microsoft to protect its taxation monopoly.

- Browsers offer the same browsing experience on many different platforms, allowing data centers to maintain software that runs on all hardware and operating systems. We shall build on this topic in the next chapter and describe how Java is the only programming language that offers the capability of securely running a compiled program in a browser.

CHAPTER
4

- How to Say Where to Look: URLs

- Browser Plug-Ins

- Sending Data to the Server: Forms and CGI

- JavaScript

- DHTML, CSS, and XML

- Summary

Programming Techniques in a Browser

This chapter delves into the more technical aspects of browsing. It covers the stages beyond HTML. It describes how naming works on the web, and then covers the technologies used to change browsing from a simple read-only tool into a powerful tool for executing programs. These technologies start with scripting, and also encompass the updates to HTML: DHTML and XML. A scripting language is used when there is a greater interaction with the user. JavaScript is the only scripting language of interest in this context and it is described later in the chapter)

Every web document (or web page, as a document is more commonly known) has its own unique identifying address. You type the web page address into the browser, and it displays the text from that site. Instead of being called a "web page address," it has the rather grandiose name of Uniform Resource Locator—or URL for short. URLs are the mysterious text strings, like

"`http://www.motorola.com/`," that started appearing in the fine print of television and newspaper ads in 1995.

How to Say Where to Look: URLs

A URL is a rather stylized way of saying where to look for something. Just as a file name locates a file on your computer, a URL tells you how to find a resource anywhere on the Internet. URLs are a compact, computer-friendly way of saying "here's where this thing is." URLs generally have three parts to them:

<the kind of thing it is> <the organization that has it> <where it is on that site>

As an example, a web site for the technical books I have written is at

`http://www.best.com/~pvdl` and the URL breaks down as follows.

<the kind of thing it is> <the organization that has it> <where it is on that site>

```
http: //          www.best.com          ~pvdl
```

The "`http:`" stands for HyperText Transport Protocol and tips off the browser about how it should ask the server for the hypertext document. Other possible kinds of protocol that can go here in a URL are "`file:`" when browsing an ordinary file, "`ftp:`" when doing an FTP remote transfer, "`news:`" when accessing a Usenet newsgroup. There are several other possibilities, and these other tags tell the browser to make different kinds of requests. The "`//`" is just a fancy separator between the first and second parts of a URL.

The "`www.best.com`" is the organization that stores this resource, in this case the Internet service provider whose name is "`best.com`". The string "`www.best.com`" is the web site for domain best.com; it resolves to an IP address. You may also see a colon and number at the end of this part of the URL, like this "`:1024`". This is the port the browser should use when talking to the site. A port is like a frequency on a radio station: both you and the transmitter have to agree on the same one to use. The hypertext protocol defaults to use port 80, so most of the time it is just omitted.

Almost all web site names are formed by prefixing "`www.`" onto a domain name. Although it seems superfluous, there are several different services that a domain can offer to the outside world. By naming them all individually, a site has the freedom to allow different services to be served by different computers at its site. There's a movement to change this prefix to the more pronounceable "web." "www" has twice as many syllables as the phrase it abbreviates.

Some of the other services you may see as prefixes on the domain name are: `news.` or `telnet.` or `nntphost.` or `irc.` or `ns.`—these are all network services. The convention is not perfectly thought through, as the protocol part of the

URL could equally be used to direct services to different systems. The redundant design is an artifact of the speed of adoption of web technology. Some things evolved before they were fully thought through.

The last part of the URL indicates where something is, usually by giving a full or relative path name in the file system. A lot of defaults can be assumed for this third part, including omitting it entirely. In this case, "~pvdl" says "in the home directory of user pvdl," and by default it looks there for the file called public_html/index.html. It's even possible to further refine the "where it is on that site" part of a URL and provide a reference to some labeled paragraph inside the document. A longer example is the URL for a long list of all the different browsers, which can be found at

```
http://www.yahoo.com/Computers_and_Internet/Internet/World_Wide_Web/Browers/
```

A nonhypertext URL example is

```
news://comp.lang.java.security
```

Looking up this URL will make your browser start reading the comp.lang.java.security newsgroup. The newsgroup kind of URL is another piece that is somewhat badly designed, because it only has the first and third parts, and the part that is missing (the site on which to look for the newsgroup) has to be conveyed separately, usually by setting an environment variable to specify your news server computer. Another (more serious) problem with the URL format is that there is no good way to say "This is a pool of systems dedicated to serving requests to this URL."

Despite these nits URLs are a practical and extensible naming scheme for locating any resource on the web anywhere in the world. You need to have a basic understanding of the concept, which is really little more than an extension of the path names you use on your computer system to find files on the local disk.

Somewhat Technical Aside

Information scientists love to generalize concepts; although generalization gives greater capabilities, it makes them harder to explain to nonscientists. I sometimes suspect information scientists regard this as being two advantages. The concept of URL has been extended to a "Uniform Resource Name" or URN. URNs are like URLs, but they are applied to resources that are not persistent (that is, resources that exist only while some program is running and are not saved to backing store. Two examples of nonpersistent resources that would be identified by URNs are

processes on another system, and socket connections). The collective term for URNs and URLs is *Uniform Resource Identifiers,* and some of the technical details are still being formulated. In diagram form they look like this:

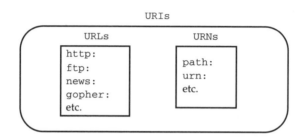

You will use URLs both to start browsing on a particular web page and as embedded text strings in that web page to link you to other pages. A link can be to a file in the same directory or, equally well, to a web page on a different site halfway around the world. These hypertext links are like an entry in a phone book—they simply record at one place the location of another web page somewhere else. Anyone can create a page with as many links to as many other pages as desired. The default configuration allows unrestricted read-only access, but the owner of a web site can password-protect access if desired. If you try to follow a link to a page that is subsequently moved or otherwise made unavailable, the browser will print an error message along the lines of "link not found." This is similar to the phone company's "number unobtainable" message.

Table 4-1 lists the URLs for some web sites you might find interesting to visit. They illustrate the range of different nontechnical organizations that are now on the World Wide Web. You can look up these interesting sites by typing the URL to your browser.

Table 4-1 Interesting Web Sites to Visit

URL	Description of Web Page
`http://www.goarmy.com`	The U.S. Army recruiting home page
`http://www.vatican.va`	The web site of the Holy See—the Pope's own web site
`http://www.fbi.gov/wanted.htm`	The FBI's list of "10 Most Wanted Fugitives"
`http://mendobrew.com`	The home page of Mendocino Brewing Company, a small Northern California brewery
`http://www.ZippoMfg.com`	The home page of the company that makes Zippo lighters

Browser Plug-Ins

One of the important features of modern browsers (again, pioneered by Netscape, copied by others) is the ability to support plug-ins. Plug-ins, as the name suggests, are separate programs that can be loaded into a running browser and make calls into the browser window and library routines. A plug-in will support some extra custom functionality that is not available in the basic browser.

Plug-ins are like the after-market equipment you can buy for a car: luggage racks, sporty wheels, lockable gas cap, fog lights, and so on. Sure, the car manufacturer could supply all that stuff at the factory, but it's better to provide the basic features and let the customers who really want the extras pay for them. The car company usually provides some wiring, fuses, mounting points and switch sites so that fog lights easily fit in the existing framework.

Netscape Communicator 4.05 (the current release in mid 1998) comes with some pretty amazing plug-ins already installed:

- CoolTalk™ (a telephone service over the Internet)
- Live3D™ (for Virtual Reality Modeling Language)
- LiveAudio™ (for playing AU, AIFF, WAV, and MIDI sound files)
- QuickTime™ (for playing MOV format video)
- LiveVideo™ (for playing AVI format video)

Playing video streams is a very I/O intensive operation, and it doesn't perform well on low-bandwidth connections (like modems). So, video signals are usually displayed in a very small window to avoid the frames looking jerky.

Some additional Netscape and IE plug-ins are listed in Table 4-2.

Table 4-2 Netscape Plug-Ins

Plug-in Name	Supplier	Purpose
Java Plug-in	Sun Microsystems	Provide the most up-to-date and standard Java support in a browser.
Acrobat Amber Reader	Adobe	View and print Portable Document Format (PDF) files.
Tcl/Tk plug-in	Sun Microsystems	Tool Command Language/Toolkit embedded scripting language, allowing Tcl/Tk applications to be delivered and run over the Web.
Shockwave	Macromedia	View Director multimedia and animation files in user's browser.
RealAudio	Real Networks	Play good quality audio as it is being downloaded.

Plug-ins are mostly written in C++ at present (because that's how the browser interface is defined), so they have to be recompiled for each platform and the code is not very portable. The plug-ins mentioned above are available on Windows 95, with a smaller choice on Macintosh and UNIX systems.

Some people regard plug-ins as a competing technology to Java, and in one strong sense (bringing third-party executables into a browser) they are. However, there is also a significant difference: Plug-in software extends your browser's capabilities with a big binary application that works only on a specific OS. It's not portable, and it inevitably leads to software application starvation on lower-volume platforms. In other words, software companies write for Windows first, the Macintosh as an afterthought, and usually don't even get to UNIX.

Plug-in technology was a first attempt to improve the client-side execution environment of a browser. JavaScript was a second attempt. Each offered some improvement, yet each had big drawbacks. Java applets are the third attempt to get the right triple balance between power, security, and ease of use.

Plug-ins are inconvenient to set up, and they lack any security, but they are another reinforcement for the concept that browsers are positioned to become the most important application on the new desktop interface. Browsers are already the gateway to the Internet and the emerging world of on-line commerce. Plug-ins extend the capabilities of a browser to the point where it can do anything a stand-alone application program can do.

Executable Content in a Browser: Applets

The most significant development in the browser industry involved the Java language. In early 1995, the HotJava browser introduced a new feature that has since taken the computer industry by storm: the ability to run Java programs that are referenced by web pages. Java programs that run in the context of a browser (like the lightweight office applications that we mentioned a couple of pages back) are known as "applets," meaning "little applications."

Sun Microsystems understands the benefit both to the industry and itself if it encourages the technology to become widespread. So Sun shared the technology widely, licensing it to all, just as it did a decade earlier with its Network File System protocol. All significant browsers now support the execution of embedded Java programs. The ability to embed a Java program in a web page and then run the Java program in a browser that accesses the page is responsible for the great interest in Java. Much of the rest of this book is devoted to explaining the significance and implications of this feature. But first we will describe the remaining browser scripting technologies: Forms, CGI, JavaScript, DHTML and XML. Java applets are fully explained in a later chapter.

Sending Data to the Server: Forms and CGI

HTML has gone through several successive stages of enhancement, as shown in Table 4-3. At first, the information flow across the web was essentially all one-way: from the server to the client. People soon realized how much more useful it would be if there was a way to send some simple data back from the browser to the server and have the server act on it. The HTML "form" tag was introduced to do just that. The server knows how to execute a program based on the form it is sent.

Table 4-3 HTML Feature Enhancement

Feature	HTML 1.0	HTML 2.0	HTML 3.0
Hyperlinks	✔	✔	✔
Images	✔	✔	✔
Lists	✔	✔	✔
Forms		✔	✔
Active Maps and Images		✔	✔
Frames		✔	✔
Tables			✔
Toolbars			✔
Equations			✔

A form gets its name because on the browser screen it looks exactly like some kind of administrative form that you might complete in your handwriting. A form is delimited in an HTML file by the usual `<form>` ... `</form>` tags, and there is a collection of related tags that are put inside a form to specify various formats for fields of data. There are tags to display boxes where you can enter text, pop-up menus, and buttons that you can press to make choices among alternatives. There will usually be a button that you press to submit the form, i.e., send all the information that you entered over to the HTTP server. An example form that lets you make choices about ordering pizza is shown in Figure 4–1.

```
<html>
<head><title>Pizza Menu</title></head>
<body>
<pre>
<h2>Pizza Menu</h2>
<form method="GET" action="http://www.pizzahouse.com/">
This form will send an order to Pizza Palace, 123 Main Street.
Choose from the menu below.
<p>
<pre>Qty          Size            Toppings</pre>
<select name="pnumber" size="1" Maxlength="1">
<option selected>1
<option>2
<option>3
</select>

<select name="psize" size>
<option selected>X-Large
<option>Large
<option>Medium
</select>

<select name="ptop" size=4 Maxlength=3>
<option selected>pepperoni
<option>black olives
<option>extra cheese
<option>sliced tomatos
<option>green peppers
</select>
<p>
<input type="text" size=40 maxlength=40 VALUE="Enter phone and
delivery address
here">

<br>
<p>
<p>
To send your order select <em>Done</em>,
<P>
<pre>
<input type="submit" VALUE="Done">
</pre>
</form>
</body></html>
```

Figure 4–1
Example of Ordering Form

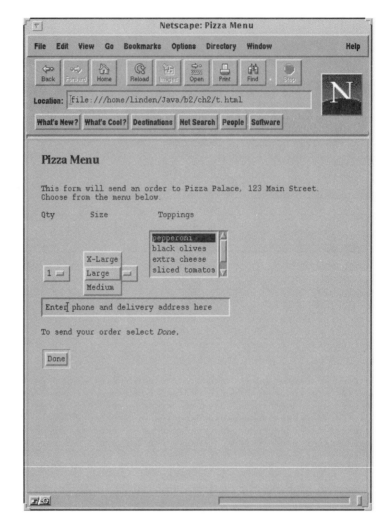

When you browse a web page containing this form, you can fill in the blanks and submit the data back to the server for processing.

Figure 4–1   *(continued)*
Example of Ordering Form

Forms are displayed on the client; they accept information from the browser user and send it to the server. Forms work in conjunction with executable scripts that run on the server, process the information they are sent, and return some HTML text as an answer or response. The script that is activated by a form is called a CGI script and will usually be kept on the same server that served up the form, but because it is a URL, it can be anywhere on the Internet. CGI stands for "Common Gateway Interface," so named because it is a common standard for handling the information returned from an HTML form. It is a gateway in the sense that it allows easy passage of information between a web page and an executable on a server.

Figure 4–2 shows how forms and CGI scripts work. The CGI script can be written in any language that the server knows how to execute. Common choices are Perl, Tcl, C++, or Java. A Java program that runs on a server in response to a client request has been given the name *servlet*, just as an applet is a Java program that is downloaded and run in a web page. Many CGI scripts are simple, but they can get as elaborate as you like and even execute inquiries against an SQL database. This would typically be done by having the CGI script run a program to extract the information and then format the result for sending to the browser.

You may hear the term *cookie*. A cookie is a whimsical name for the technique of a CGI server storing some information in a browser, usually as a placeholder to remind it where it has got to in processing a request from the client. A better name for a cookie would be a "token" or "client data." A cookie is something the server feeds to the client. The browser has to be able to save the cookie and send it back to the server later when asked. In technical terms, cookies represent persistent state on the client side. It might record a file that has been seen or a piece of information from a file.

For a long time CGI scripts and forms were the only way to get full user interaction in a browser. So, the technique was widely used, even though many things about CGI are clumsy, not secure, and expensive in server CPU load. Because CGI was so clumsy (especially in the way it passed data back to the server), many people have written libraries of "helper" functions. This makes processing easier, but also makes CGI scripts less portable because they now rely on an additional component.

Forms are falling from use now that there are much better technologies, namely, JavaScript and Java, so we won't go into more detail. Instead, the next section looks at the JavaScript browser scripting language.

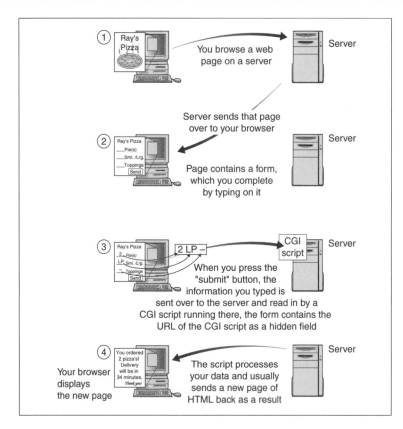

1. When you browse a web page containing a form, you can "fill in the blanks."

2. You then submit the data back to the server for processing.

3. The data you entered on the form is sent to the CGI script on the server.

4. The CGI script runs on the server and processes your data, typically storing some information on the server, and sending some calculated result back to the client browser.

Figure 4–2
How Forms and CGI Scripts Work

CGI scripts can be invoked directly by a browser

CGI scripts don't have to be invoked by forms. A URL is usually an HTML file, but it can equally well be an executable CGI file, in which case the file is executed and the output sent back to the browser.

The output from that CGI script must be in HTML so it will make sense at the browser end. This feature often leads new Java programmers to ask the question "How do I make my Java applet run a program that will create and send me a new web page?" It can be done, but the answer is often that you don't want to do that at all, as it is a CGI idiom. What you usually want to do instead in Java is have the applet calculate how the screen needs to change (perhaps by opening a socket connection to the server and reading some data), and do it itself directly.

JavaScript

There is no universal definition of what constitutes a scripting language as opposed to a regular programming language, and different organizations use the term in different ways. Perhaps a good working definition is to say that a *scripting language* is an uncompiled language in which individual source statements are read and interpreted. In MS-DOS, .bat batch files are written in a scripting language, and the language is the same as that of the interactive command-line interpreter. Running a script lets you issue a series of instructions without using the keyboard or mouse.

Apple has AppleScript, Microsoft has VisualBasicScript (VBS) and General Magic has a TeleScript scripting language. In the context of the World Wide Web, the most significant scripting language is JavaScript, and its clone Microsoft's JScript. The Netscape browser introduced the scripting language to make some HTML-related tasks much easier. JavaScript is much less ambitious than either Apple-Script or TeleScript and addresses a much simpler problem domain: adding some simple local programming capability to a browser. Unlike CGI scripts, the JavaScript language runs on the client, so it has full access to the browser and knows what the user is doing. It also doesn't take CPU cycles away from the server to do its job, which can sometimes be a big issue with CGI.

Netscape defines JavaScript as "an open, cross-platform, object-scripting language for the creation and customization of applications on the Internet and intranets. Complementary to and integrated with the Java programming language, JavaScript can be used by people with little or no programming experience to quickly build complex applications."

Despite the definition, JavaScript has little connection with Java except the name. JavaScript is a good starting point for webmasters who want to take on simple programming tasks but aren't yet ready to make the leap to full object-oriented programming in Java. Just to make sure everyone is clear on the difference:

- Java is a complete, object-oriented, compiled programming language for professional programmers to build entire applications. It also has a mode that allows small programs (applets) to run in a browser.

- JavaScript is a small, simple, interpreted scripting language that runs only in the context of a browser. It is meant for small utilities. If you are familiar with Visual Basic, dBase, or even HTML, you can easily master JavaScript.

JavaScript programs are put in HTML files in source form. They are bracketed by the usual tag pairs, in this case, `<script language="JavaScript">` ... `</script>` tags. As the browser reads the HTML file, it formats the text onto the screen. When it finds a JavaScript tag it starts to interpret (execute) the program that it finds there. This might change the screen contents or text style, or support some interaction with the user. Because it is embedded in the HTML file in source (not binary) form it runs on any and all platforms. It requires no complicated compilation or linking. However JavaScript programs cannot be kept secret. The source is right there for anybody to read and take.

So what can JavaScript actually do? Well, the most visible and obvious feature is the scrolling text display in which a line of text scrolls across your browser, like the old Times Square news bulletin display. However, JavaScript can do a lot more than that. JavaScript enables page designers to access events, such as mouse clicks, and to "glue" together HTML, plug-ins, and Java applets. Figure 4–3 shows the JavaScript source for a simple program. Figure 4–4 shows how the JavaScript program looks when run in a browser. The Netscape documentation suggests that a simple JavaScript might check the time of day and display a background showing either daylight or moonlight as appropriate. Another possibility would be to write a pocket calculator in JavaScript. The language easily has enough power to display buttons of digits and operators and to carry out calculations. Finally, JavaScript originally was very useful for cross-checking the consistency of different fields entered in the same form. However, as Java applets are replacing all but the simplest of forms, this use is diminishing.

An example of a JavaScript program: the currency converter

```
<HTML>

<BODY>

<SCRIPT LANGUAGE="JavaScript">
<!-- hide this script tag's contents from old browsers

function convert(form)
{
   if ((form.dollars.value == "") || (form.forex.value == ""))
   {
       return;
   }
   form.product.value = form.dollars.value * form.forex.value;
}

<!-- done hiding from old browsers -->
</SCRIPT>

<HR>

<H3>
The currency converter
</H3>

<FORM method=POST>
Enter dollar amount:
<INPUT NAME=dollars VALUE=0 onChange=convert(this.form) >
<p>
Enter rate ($1= how much in foreign currency?)
<INPUT NAME=forex VALUE=0 onChange=convert(this.form) >
<p>
The equivalent foreign amount is:
<INPUT NAME=product VALUE="not yet calculated">
<BR>
<INPUT NAME=calc VALUE=Convert TYPE=BUTTON
onClick=convert(this.form)>
</FORM>

</BODY>

</HTML>
```

Figure 4–3
The JavaScript Source for a Simple Currency Conversion Program

Script standardization

When Netscape first launched their browser scripting language, they called it "Live-Script." The Netscape marketing department quickly changed the name to "JavaScript" when it saw how well Java was received. Netscape stock rose $20 on that day. In fact, there is little more connection between Java and JavaScript than there is between Karl Marx and the Marx Brothers. For people who are familiar with UNIX, the appropriate analogy is to say that "Java is to JavaScript as C-shell is to C."

For competitive reasons Microsoft had to support JavaScript in their own browser. So they "innovated" with a version that was an almost identical copy of Netscape's design and called it JScript.

In June 1997 Netscape, Microsoft, and 11 other companies agreed to a common specification for JavaScript as European Computer Manufacturers Association standard 262. The reason for selecting ECMA as the host rather than more obvious choices, such as ANSI or the Open Group, was speed. ECMA could guarantee a voting process within a few months and thence promotion to an ISO standard. The other two organizations have been criticized for taking years to go through the process and for adding undue complexity to simple standards and their testing process.

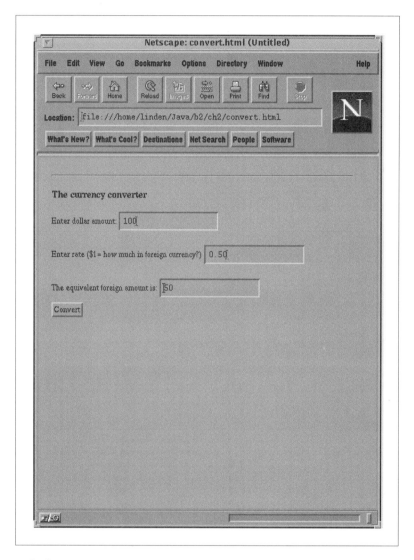

Figure 4–4
A Browser Running the JavaScript Currency Converter Program

For the first year or two, web browsers were simple to use and web pages were simple to create. Now, web browsers offer a much wider range of features, including the ability to run entire applications, and the command languages can take some effort to learn. Creating a basic web page is still easy, but some very elaborate special effects are possible. With JavaScript in particular, it is no longer quite so easy to look at the HTML source for a page and immediately understand how it works. JavaScript was introduced in Netscape Navigator 2.0 and followed by the LiveConnect framework in Navigator 3.0. LiveConnect is a Netscape-specific framework allowing JavaScript, plug-ins, and Java applets to communicate and share data easily with each other.

What JavaScript can and cannot do

JavaScript can:

- Accept input and carry out elaborate calculations
- Define and call its own functions
- Pop up windows and display text
- Change images displayed on the browser
- Play different sound files
- Call and be called from a Java applet in the browser
- Do work on the client side
- Do any of the above in response to events like mouse clicks or screen entry or exit

JavaScript cannot:

- Open files and do I/O
- Communicate with the server or another system
- Do work on the server side
- Make anything happen outside the browser

One example of a JavaScript program would be a function to accept numbers representing monetary values from the user and convert them into equivalent amounts in foreign currency. This could be combined with a CGI script to first read the latest conversion ratios from a database on the server.

As a rule of thumb, if your need involves some JavaScript and a CGI script, it's probably easier, quicker, and cheaper just to write it in Java.

DHTML, CSS, and XML

A big drawback of HTML is that the browser must download another page from the server to change what the user sees on the screen. It can take several seconds to retrieve a new page from across the network, diminishing the "browser as GUI" experience. Simple HTML-based browsing treats the browser like a dumb terminal.

In an effort to endow browsers with greater GUI expressiveness the mark-up language they understand has been updated, enhanced, and extended at a very fast pace. The goal is to offload more of the work from the server onto the client, as well as improving the visuals.

In rapid succession there has been CSS, DHTML and, in early 1998, XML. XML is probably where the buck will stop, at least for a while. This section describes these new mark up languages and what you can do with them. Both leading browsers support CSS, DHTML and XML now.

CSS—Cascading Style Sheets

CSS stands for "Cascading Style Sheets"—an imposing name for an easy concept. A "style sheet" is just a template that can customize the look or appearance (the "style") of an existing HTML tag. For example, if you want all <h3> heading tags to format with a special font and a particular size, you can do it by creating a style sheet for the tag. Style sheets can be in a separate file (included by reference) or at the head of a file, or anywhere in it. The style sheets have a scope which nests, or "cascades" in DHTML terminology. CSS is part of the browser language development known as DHTML.

DHTML—Dynamic HTML

Dynamic HTML (DHTML) makes it possible for a browser display to change without needing to reload a page from the server. The GUI event model is expanded giving the client browser the ability to read mouse clicks and keystrokes. Elements (images, text etc.) can be positioned on the screen in absolute locations and hidden, shown, or moved according to user mousing. You can draw things over around and under the existing text on the page.

In what is termed the "Document Object Model," every image, paragraph, list item, anchor, blockquote, form, and punctuation mark on a web page can be an object with a name. Since these elements are independent objects, they can be addressed and moved around. Font sizes and styles can change as the cursor travels over them. All this is controlled by scripting; either JavaScript or Microsoft's VBS (Visual Basic Script).

The point is that the appearance of a web page is no longer fixed by its file on the server. The page can now be modified dynamically according to input from the user, while it is being shown to him or her. Hence it is termed "dynamic" HTML.

DHTML is just about powerful enough to use to write crude computer games of the kind that involve projectiles colliding with one another with sound effects. The more conventional use of DHTML is to ask for user input, display graphics or further choices based on the answers, then send a summary of data to the server for recording or further processing. Netscape and Microsoft have somewhat incompatible implementations of DHTML, leading to "browser sniffing" where scripts first detect what browser they are running in, and then execute one set of code or another.

XML—Extensible Markup Language

XML was developed to address the Achilles heel of DHTML: it can only change the way things look on the screen, it doesn't actually have any knowledge of what the marked-up text means. Changing fonts, moving, and exposing new graphics is cool but ultimately has more showiness than substance.

What you really want to be able to do is invent your own mark-up tags that describe properties of interest to you. As well as saying things like <table> (put a table here) and <p> (start a new paragraph), you want to be able to define new tags like <total cost> (this field represents the total cost of an on-line order you are placing) and <delivery address> (this field is where to send the goods). That way you can write programs that process the marked up data and extract much more meaningful conclusions.

Enter XML, which is the abbreviation for eXtensible Markup Language. HTML has a fixed number of tags. XML earns the name "extensible" because it allows the web page author to define new tags as they are needed. Then anything that reads the marked-up text cannot only display it, but also get an insight into what the fields represent.

XML still uses matching start and end tags, such as <name> and </name>, to mark up information. This very simple syntax is easy to process by computers and by people. XML supports the programming giving arbitrary names for the tagged data to the scripting language and hence to the client browser. The difference between HTML and XML is that HTML provides a fixed vocabulary of tags and the effect they have on displaying the text. XML merely describes a syntax for markup: it spells out the rules for using angle brackets and other notation to specify a mark-up language of your own design. The tag names and what they actually mean are left for you to choose as appropriate for your application.

XML is really a breathtakingly simple concept (though of course, it is rarely so simply explained) and it relies on scripts to do all the work. Once you have defined your tagnames and marked up your data, your scripts can get at the individual fields and search, total, co-relate or display as appropriate.

The whole family of browser mark-up languages derive from SGML (standard generalized markup language) which is a set of rules for describing how to form markup languages. HTML was a quick but effective hack which didn't really follow all the SGML rules. XML is a natural follow-on development created by browser companies who saw a need. XML follows the SGML requirements, but also tries not to be unduly complicated. It exposes all objects in a file (images, tags, text, etc.) to scripting, based on rules called "the document object model" (DOM) which was brought in as part of DHTML.

Example of XML

An example of the use of XML would be a web site that offered CDs for sale. It could catalog its inventory using XML markup to distinguish fields of interest like title, artist, tracks, and price. Javascript in the web page could easily allow the user to search for particular tracks by particular artists. Conventional searching by matching text could not do this.

Sales descriptions of the products are written in HTML, but some information is also marked up with XML. Here is the HTML information for a web page featuring CDs for sale:

```
<h3>CD Catalog</h3>

<p>

Title / Artist / Year / Price / In stock

<p>

Wish You Were Here, Pink Floyd, 1975, $21, 7 <br>

Some Girls, The Rolling Stones, 1978, $24, 0 <br>
```

That data would probably be placed in an HTML table in a real document, but I'm trying to keep the example simple.

Here is the same information additionally marked up with XML:

```
<h3>CD Catalog</h3>

<p>

Title / Artist / Year / Price / In stock

<p>

<CD title>Wish You Were Here </CD title>,

    <performer> Pink Floyd </performer>,

    <year>1975</year>, <price>$21</price>, <stock>7</stock> <br>

<CD title>Some Girls</CD title>,

    <performer>The Rolling Stones</performer>,

    <year>1978</year>, <price>$24</price>,<stock>0</stock> <br>
```

Remember white space doesn't matter at all in marked up text. With XML, the webmaster can write scripts for users that answer questions like "How much would it cost to buy all the Beatles albums issued after 1969?" or "What is the total value of all the inventory on hand?" These questions cannot be answered by a simple text search of the HTML page.

How do DHTML and XML relate to Java?

DHTML is a document markup language that lets the client browser change how a web page looks after it is downloaded. DHTML can change and move colors, fonts, images, paragraphs, etc. according to keyboard and mouse input from the user. It cannot cause anything to happen outside the browser, such as writing datafiles. DHTML is mostly about clever displays.

XML is also a document markup language. XML lets you label pieces of your text with semantic information. The document can later be browsed by different users who can retrieve the labels and understand more about the data. XML can mark up a document without being stored in it, so you can annotate pages on another web site.

XML is mostly about tagging platform-independent data for later processing.

Java is a general-purpose programming language that is frequently the best way to process complex content on-line. For example, Java easily accesses content that is updated on the server from nonbrowsable sources, such as a database. Java is platform-independent software.

The three technologies, Java, DHTML and XML are complementary rather than competitive.

Even better, if CD sellers standardized on the same XML tags, the way book publishers have standardized on ISBNs, then the same scripts (web pages) could process CD information from any source. Microsoft's CDF (Channel Definition Format) is a dialect of XML tailored toward distributing content including software updates.

Some early adopters in the industry see a great future for XML as middleware that eases the exchange of data between applications, web sites and existing older systems. For example, a spreadsheet datafile could be annotated with XML such that it could be directly read by a browser, allowing easy export of data.

However in spring 1998, XML is still a young technology and yet to be proven by extensive use. Some large pieces of XML remain to be defined. Work on XML continues with two more phases: XLL (Extensible Link Language) which is hypertext link improvement, and XSL (Extensible Stylesheet Language) which is the presentation or screen appearance of XML.

Before readers get too carried away with the benefits of markup language alphabet soup, we should point out the limitations. DHTML and XML are candidates when a task is straightforward and the confines of a browser can be tolerated. But HTML, DHTML, and XML are really band-aid piled upon band-aid. They have a hodgepodge of different syntaxes and different capabilities. They are strung together with scripting languages that lack proper security, and don't scale well for long-term maintenance. Because they are in ASCII rather than binary they are inefficient to read and process.

XML is not a general purpose, distributed, object-oriented programming language. Simple things are simple and quick to do in browser markup languages. Complicated things are best left to more capable tools like Java. XML is advanced web document technology, whereas Java is advanced web programming technology.

Summary

- All web pages are addressed by URLs—Uniform Resource Locators. URLs are text strings, like `http://www.disney.com`, that are seen in many ads nowadays.

- The first browsers just allowed the one-way transfer of information to the desktop. Forms and CGI scripts allowed a two-way dialog with the server. Plug-ins and JavaScript increased interaction with the user. Java programs can run in a browser and replace many of these features.

- Browsers are challenging the Windows32 APIs as the next high-volume desktop interface. Software application companies can write their software to run in browsers instead of writing to an operating system interface. This makes it easier for users to run the software (just browse a URL), and it eliminates maintaining different versions of the product for different operating systems. Best of all, it provides type safety and productivity gains that are missing in Windows and C++.

- HTML has been extended with DHTML and XML to the point where quite sophisticated visual effects are possible. However these markup languages lack the general-purpose nature of Java applets.

CHAPTER
5

- The Java Phenomenon

- Distribution of Executable Content

- Platform Independence

- Who Has Java

- Summary

Java
Applets

The Java Phenomenon

The Java language was first made available for free downloading over the Internet in May 1995. Within a year the language had become so popular that the Java-One user conference at 6000 attendees was as large as the largest other software conference (the annual Microsoft Windows conference). By 1998 JavaOne had more than doubled in size. Some 14,000 people attended the 1998 JavaOne conference and latecomers were turned away as the event stretched the limits of the San Francisco Moscone Center facilities.

Sun Microsystems set up a separate business unit, named JavaSoft, to handle all aspects of developing Java system software products at Sun. JavaSoft is led by ex-IBM executive Alan Baratz, who has been notably successful in spreading the use of Java throughout the technology sector.

Virtually every telecommunications company, every major electronics company, and every computer company has licensed the Java technology from Sun Micro-systems. Java has been adopted by Sony (consumer electronics), by Ericsson (cell phones), by TCI (cable TV), by IBM, and H-P, (computer hardware) and Microsoft, Inprise, and Oracle (computer software) and more than 150 other IT companies. Over three million copies of the Java development kit have been downloaded, and Java is ready to run on millions of computers today. According to the Gartner Group, about 80 percent of higher education institutes currently offer classes in

Java. Given this level of interest, it's not surprising that Java has received the kind of media attention that is more usually associated with the entertainment, not the computer, industry.

A survey released in May 1996 by Forrester Research of Cambridge, Massachusetts, found around 75 percent of large companies were either using or planning to use Java by the end of 1996. Can something apparently so ordinary as a programming language really be responsible for turning the entire computer industry on its head? Yes, a new programming language can be part of a wider movement that achieves this.

The introduction of Java is like the 1982 introduction of the IBM PC.

When the IBM PC was launched, it did not have much that was new or different: it used an existing Intel processor, conservative technology, commodity disks and memory. However in the course of just a few years, it revitalized the entire computer industry and led to a decrease in emphasis on mainframes and the emergence of a whole new model of desktop user computing.

There was nothing fundamentally new or different about the IBM PC; it represented the convergence of several timely and ultimately unstoppable trends that combined to effect these broad changes. A key aspect was that IBM used very little proprietary technology in the PC because they wanted the product out the door quickly and that was the only way to get it done.

If IBM had foreseen the result (that IBM became a niche player in the IBM-compatible world), would they have done it? Probably not. IBM certainly tried hard to get back to a proprietary design with the PS/2 and the MicroChannel Architecture (which has now been supplanted by the PCI bus). In the event, IBM permitted and encouraged other companies to market add-on hardware and software for the PC. And exactly the same kind of open-to-all process is being repeated with the Java programming language right now.

How can one programming language bring about profound changes? By itself, it cannot. The whole panorama of computing is shifting, and Java is at the focal point where many innovations come together. The most significant of these changes are:

- Popularization of the Internet and ubiquity of the Internet, leading to unlimited cheap bandwidth to anywhere. The latest example of the growing ubiquity of the Internet is the WebTV product from Sony and Phillips (Microsoft later bought into the partnership). WebTV is a combined modem and signal converter that connects your phone line and your TV. The TV-top box dials up to an Internet service provider and displays web pages on your TV in a simplified web browser. WebTV is a home appliance that makes web browsing and sending e-mail so easy that the completely nontechnical can do it. The question that is still to be resolved is "Do they want to?"

- The consumer electronics industry blending into the computer industry blending into the telecom industry. These organizations have realized that their growth path lies in mass access to simpler technology. Some examples of this are:

  1. The new IEEE 1394 high speed I/O bus, the physical connectors for which were adapted from Nintendo games (according to industry folklore). 1394 is fast enough to connect video cameras to computer systems.

  2. The DVD standard for storing TV-quality images on a CD-ROM. These DVD (originally meaning Digital Video Disc, now Digital Versatile Device) drives can store around 5 gigabytes, compared with 0.6 gigabytes on the current generation of CD-ROM. DVD players are intended to hold video recordings of entire movies, with soundtracks in several languages.

  3. The 1998 proposed merger between AT&T (the largest phone company) and TCI (a very large cable-tv company). The 1998 $9 billion purchase by Nortel (Northern Telecommunications) of Bay Networks, Inc. is a further example.

- Drive to multimediaize everything. As Windows 95 came out, many PCs did not support multimedia in either hardware or software. Today, full multimedia in the form of sound cards, speakers, video players, CD players, and software is standard, even on laptops and the lowest cost systems. Intel added 50-odd new machine instructions to the Pentium processor specifically to support multimedia. They called these new instructions MMX (Multi Media eXtensions). MMX speeds up some graphics and image processing, but it makes no difference to basic web surfing in a browser. MMX's biggest impact has been on games software.

- Desire for improved software technologies, especially through simplicity rather than increased complexity. As software applications have grown in size, they have also become more complicated to operate. And it is not just applications that have become burdened with confusion. The programming language C++ is not without controversy. Its champions brashly proclaim that if many programmers find C++ difficult to use, the fault is with the programmers, not the tool. On the other hand, proponents of simplicity point out that C++ started out with modest goals, and could have stayed that way. The

crowning achievement of C++, its 1998 blessing as an ISO standard, is also its swan song, as programmers and software tools vendors migrate in large numbers to simpler languages like Visual Basic and, especially, Java.

Java lies at the focal point where all these qualities come together. In the rest of the chapter, we will examine the system features of Java that play directly to these trends. In later chapters, we will summarize the lower-level programming language features.

Distribution of Executable Content: Applets!

The big breakthrough of Java is that it adds "computer program" to the category of browsable hypermedia. When you browse lines of text, they are formatted and displayed nicely for you. When you browse a sound file, it is downloaded to your system and played over your speakers. When you browse an MPEG video clip, the video is run on your screen. And when you browse a Java program, the program is downloaded onto your system and executed. Netscape offers Java-enabled browsers for Windows 3.1, Windows 95, 98 and NT, the Apple Mac, Solaris and many other UNIX platforms. Figure 5–1 illustrates the old way of executing programs; Figure 5–2 illustrates today's Internet way.

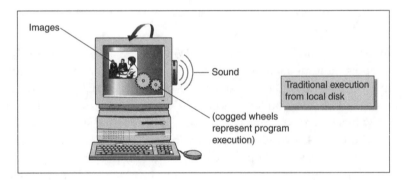

Figure 5–1
Traditional Execution from Local Hard Disk

The way Java works is simple. Unlike ordinary software applications, which take up megabytes on the hard disk of your PC, Java programs or "applets," are little programs that reside on the network in centralized servers. The network delivers them to your machine only when you need them; after use, the client discards what it has been sent.

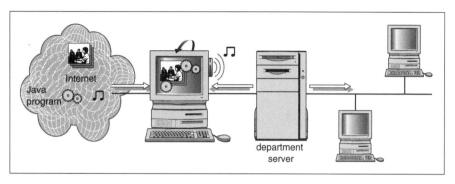

Figure 5–2
Execution from the Internet

It is almost trivially easy to set this up. Chapter 3 described HTML—hypertext markup language—and showed some examples of the special tags used to mark text to be interpreted as a URL rather than displayed literally. There is another special tag that says in effect "This is the URL of an applet." The URL specifies where on the Internet to find the applet, and the tag tells the browser to download and run it.

A Java program that has been written to be downloaded and run in a browser is termed an *applet*. Originally, an applet was considered a little application, but the only size restriction on applets is the download time your users are prepared to endure. Quite large applets exist.

Not all Java programs are applets. You can equally well have a Java program that runs stand-alone (not in a browser). This kind of Java program is termed an "application" just like a program written in any language. There is a lot of interest in applets because they have transformed the World Wide Web from a passive publishing medium into a platform for distributing and running programs.

Why Is It Useful to Run a Program from a Web Page?

Why is it useful to run a program from a web page? The short answer is that

- it allows anyone, anywhere in the world,

- to run your program at any time,

- on any hardware, using any operating system,

- immediately and without having to install anything.

- Even better, this web page program (which you are running anywhere on the Internet) can securely extract data from a server, present and modify according to your commands, and then put the results back into the corporate database.

The old way of distributing software involved creating a dozen different versions to cover different configurations of the three or four top platforms, then mailing a floppy disk with a page of instructions to anyone who might be interested. And trusting that they will install the code on their system, and delete it when they are done or you have an update.

Now you just let users point and click. There are a variety of further reasons why it is useful to download a program from a web page instead of having a local copy, and they mainly have to do with client/server economics. We will look at this in more detail in Chapter 10. For now, note that in addition to the points mentioned above (which are mostly advantages for the user), downloading a program greatly simplifies system administration (one copy of the software on the server instead of 50 copies on 50 clients). Publication of maintenance releases with bug fixes or new versions with new features is easy. The full range of reasons is shown in Table 5-1.

Table 5-1 Why It Is Useful to Access a Java Program in a Web Page

- Anyone on any hardware with any operating system can run the program immediately without installing anything.
- It is simple to start up any program—just browse the web page that it is on.
- The central server greatly simplifies system administration.
- Sharing of disk space and software resources improves. One copy of the software on the server can serve many clients.
- Distribution of software is easier (no more mailing floppy disks).
- The web page can interact with the user.
- The general benefits of client/server, explained in Chapter 10, are realized.
- An applet can be run from any computer on the Internet. It can securely obtain data from a corporate server, present and modify it under your control, then update the corporate database back in the main office.

This is not at all to claim that browsing a program on a server is the total modern replacement for executing a program from your local disk. It is an additional technique that should be used when you need its special advantages. Browsing an applet, and the client/server technique in general, is most useful for medium and large offices, not for SOHO ("small office, home office") users. Web-browsing applets will displace some PC applications, but they may well displace more 3270s, dumb terminals, and X-terminals.

One way to better understand downloading applets is to compare it to using the telephone to learn the current time. When you call the phone company talking clock, the current time information is played for you. This is a client/server model. Other numbers provide the current weather forecast, the freeway road conditions, tidal information, ski news, and so on. By way of contrast, the traditional method of having everyone store the programs on local hard disk is like having 50 clocks scattered around the department, one on each of 50 desks. When people need to know the time, they look at their own desk clock. When they want to know the tide information, they have to look up their own copy of the tidal charts, and so on. This corresponds to everyone having a local copy of each program. Everyone has to be responsible for keeping his own clock accurate, replacing batteries, switching to summer time or whatever. A big company might even employ someone to go around constantly and maintain the clocks. The administration is a lot simpler and cheaper with one central clock. Whether you prefer the "central clock server" model or the "local clock application on every desktop" model depends on whether you see yourself primarily as a broadcaster (distributor/administrator of software) or a consumer (executor of, and tinkerer with, software)

Java on the Client: Applets.

A common question asks of what use are applets. They just do useless stuff like web page animations of steaming coffee cups.

Like many other people, I started out hearing that Java applets were all about toy animations in web pages. I sat down with my team of software technologists and we started to analyze the issue. We quickly realized that movement in web pages was just a tangible and easy-to-program demo.

Instead of an animated coffee cup, think about graphs of your stock portfolio being drawn and updated in real time as share prices change. Think about seeing a route map of a long distance journey with the different flight choices showing costs, times, and durations. Think about a diagram that shows how to test and repair some electronics component: you enter the readings from different points on the board, and the applet dynamically figures out the right subassembly on which to focus.

A less visible but more valuable benefit is in system administration. Existing CGI scripts are run on the server on behalf of the client. When there are only half a dozen clients, that load might not be noticed. When there are scores or hundreds of clients, that number can put a significant load on the server. Java applets run on the client CPU, not the server—a true realization of distributed processing.

A third benefit is the automatic multimedia framework that the web browser provides (yes, the animations, sound effects, coming video, and so on). Finally, the platform independence of Java (discussed in the next section) is a boon to software developers and users alike. Applets make it trivially easy to program the client side of the client/server architecture. The applet concept provides the framework for free without any effort being expanded on programming the underlying network transport protocols. These benefits can be realized by "industrial-strength" applets that do real work, as well as by toy animations.

You may hear the phrase "Java on the client." It just refers to running Java applets in a browser. The browser gets applets from a server or several servers, so the Java software is executing on a client. Some people have raised questions about Java on the client. They wonder if download times may be excessive. They ask if the security restrictions on applets are so tight that nothing useful can be done. They wonder if Java software (being platform neutral) can ever look as polished as a binary designed to run only on one particular system.

These are reasonable questions which the proponents of Java must answer. Fortunately for the Java market, the answer is evidenced by looking at the large number of successful Java client systems. Before highlighting some of those systems, let's explicitly state the answers. The acceptability of software download times depends on how fast your network is compared to your hard disk. The times are not excessive for small to medium-sized programs. An example of a small program would be an enquiry/update against a server database. A medium program would be something like a text editor. A large program would be an entire office suite.

The security restrictions on applets are highly customizable, and are explained in the next chapter. Java is the only system in existence today that allows configurable security for downloadable executables. Microsoft's DNA, since it is based on ActiveX, has no security beyond basic identification so it cannot safely be used on the Internet.

Finally, Java applets adopt the look and feel of the system on which they are running. When running on a Mac, the program looks like any Mac software. When running on Windows 98, the same one Java program looks like any Windows 98 program. If you can program it at all in Java, you get the native look and feel by default. You may not have access to the most specialized GUI elements like, say, balloon help, but there will be an equivalent feature in Java, and it will have the basic appearance of other elements on the platform.

Java on the client seems to be settling into three main areas:

- **Internet Service Provider/Content Provider utilities**

  Yahoo! uses Java applets to run all the games in its games rooms.

  All the conference rooms at Compuserve are implemented in Java, in their new 4.0 web view.

  Microsoft-NBC uses a java applet to provide a ticker tape display of news items.

Microsoft uses a Java applet on the developer portion of its web site for navigation.

- **Commercial applets for Internet/extranet/intranet**

  There is a huge number of applets being developed for internal use only on company intranets. This is a vibrant and fast-growing area, but the applets are generally not published, so lack visibility. Here is a selection of applets that have been published. These applets do tasks that cannot be done by DHTML or XML.

  http://www.quote.com allows real time charting of stock prices. Figure 5–4 shows an example of this applet running.

  http://biz.yahoo.com/f/jl.html is an applet that manages a portfolio of stocks.

  http://www.usps.gov/formmgmt/webforms/—the US Post Office "Hot Forms" software for submitting bulk mailings.

  http://cnnfn.com/markets/9806/02/marimba/index-txt.htm—a description of an investment management tool.

  http://www.cadviewer.com/dwf/asesmp.shtml—a CAD viewer that runs in a browser and understands a couple of AutoCAD formats for computer-aided design drawings. This applet allows you to view CAD drawings without installing any plug-ins. You can zoom in, pan, select layers and more.

  http://www.co-operativebank.co.uk/internet_banking.html is an applet that allows on-line banking, from the UK banking-technology pioneer Co-op Bank. The banking services are written in Java with a little bit of JavaScript glue to tie things together.

  http://www.firstdirect.co.uk/ is another UK bank (part of the HSBC, formerly Midland Bank) offering on-line banking through Java applets. First Direct has a business model that does away with retail bank branches, usually one of the most expensive parts of bank operations. All banking is done by dial-up connection to a secure modem pool, and the Java software is downloaded into the client browser. The bank has been very successful, and taken a large amount of business away from other banks.

- **Complex content-rich applets on educational and research sites**

  http://mars.graham.com/wits/—an applet that provides simulations of the Mars Rover vehicle, and allows some interaction with vehicle control.

  http://fruitfly.berkeley.edu—Berkeley Drosphilia Genome Project

  http://ir.chem.cmu.edu/applets — Carnegie-Mellon Chemical Applets

  http://www.ai.mit.edu/projects/anatomy_browser/index.html — the anatomy browser produced at MIT.

http://www.rmi.de/~gollog/tableuk.htm—an interactive display of the Periodic Table of elements.

http://www.plumbdesign.com/thesaurus/—an interactive visual display of connections between related words. A great way for a student to see the English parts of speech "come alive."

http://home.augsburg.baynet.de/walter.fendt/physengl/physengl.htm—a collection of applets that demonstrate principles of physics for students. The principles include the pulley, lever, pendulum, springs, Ohm's law, light refraction and so on.

http://telerobot.mech.uwa.edu.au/java/applets/usher—an applet at the University of Western Australia that allows users to operate a robot arm.

The http://www.gamelan.com site lists thousands of other applets, often available free for educational use.

Netscape made the Internet look pretty much the same on everyone's machine. Then Java enabled full programs rather than just semistatic web pages, and now it is possible to make all kinds of software that is completely portable and immediately distributable across the entire planet.

Write Once, Run Anywhere (WORA)

If you've been thinking ahead while reading the previous sections, a possible limitation might have occurred to you. You might have noticed when we talked about adding "computer program" to the category of "things that can be browsed" that all the other browsable things (audio, text, video, etc.) are largely independent of computer systems. That is, if I have an MPEG video file, the format is an industry standard and I can generally play it on a Windows system, on a Macintosh, on a Sun workstation, and so on. In contrast, an executable computer program is completely dependent on and totally tied to one specific computer and even one operating system. Thus, we see unique versions of the Lotus 123 spreadsheet specialized for MS-DOS, for Windows 3.1, and for Windows 95. Still other versions are required for non-Intel systems like the Macintosh. If you purchase the wrong version of the software, it is useless to you. The software (up until now) has been tied to the operating system. If you have several different computers, each of them needs its own individual version of the software. So won't it create a problem or fail in some way if you use a PC to browse a program that was written on a Mac and is being served by a Sun workstation?

Amazingly (this is the most significant of Java's key breakthroughs), the answer is no, it won't create a problem. The executable form of Java code is slightly higher level than regular machine code. With the help of an interpreter buried in the

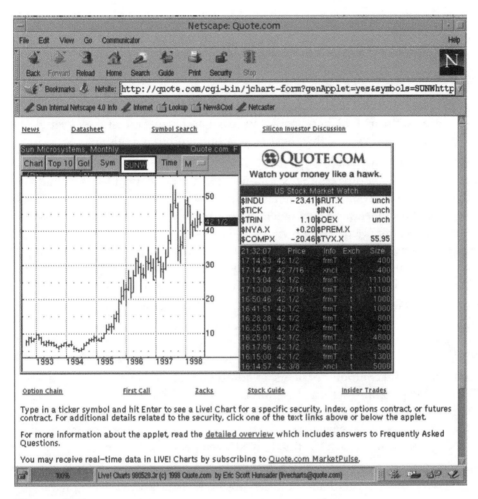

Figure 5–3
Java applet that charts stock price on demand at http://www.quote.com.

browser, a Java applet can easily be executed on any system. The result is that the Java language is platform independent, offering "Write Once, Run Anywhere" capabilities, and reducing the costs of development and deployment.

Consider what this means for your investment in applications software. Java applications allow you to move freely to another operating system or platform *and take your software with you!* In the past, once someone had bought (say) a Mac system and invested $1000 in a dozen programs, they were locked into the Mac. When the time came to buy new hardware, they either had to buy another Mac to keep using their existing software, or come up with another $1000 to buy new software for different hardware. When you use Java software, you just take it with you and the same program runs on any hardware. You don't even have to relearn any commands. If you develop your own software and have had to port it to new systems a couple of times the situation is even better. You can port your application to Java, and that's the last port you'll need to do, ever. You can then spend your future software budget on new feature enhancements rather than keeping up with whatever machine the Physics department is buying this year.

Write Once, Run Anywhere is good news for the skill sets of your staff, too. It typically takes a skilled programmer six months to a year of patient learning and practice to become competent on a new kind of system. Now, anyone who invests that same effort in learning Java will be a fluent programmer on *all* systems on which Java is supported. In my own case, I have specialized in UNIX systems for two decades and my skills did not apply to the Macintosh. While learning Java, my earliest programs ran with equal facility on the Macintosh, and Windows 95, 98, NT, Sun's Solaris version of UNIX, and a dozen other operating systems.

The skills of Java programmers apply to a wider range of systems, opening up a wider variety of job opportunities to them. Instead of mastering one set of libraries, such as the Microsoft Foundation Classes, and being forever typecast as a "Windows-only" programmer, programmers can learn the Java libraries and be productive on all computer systems. In addition, Sun has announced a Sun Java Certification program, designed by Sun Educational Services to professionally validate customers' Java expertise. Programmers can demonstrate their Java knowledge by taking the basic Sun Certified Java Programmer examination, and then the more detailed Sun Certified Java Developer qualification.

Platform independence is equally good news for employers: they can now choose from a wider pool of candidates for each position. ISVs (Independent Software Vendors) love platform independence because they need only write and maintain one version of their products. No more "Lotus 123 for Windows," "Lotus 123 for MS-DOS," "Lotus 123 for UNIX"—one program binary will run on all systems. In fact the only company that doesn't like platform independence is Microsoft. It is not in Microsoft's interest for customers to be able to move their software to different systems. Microsoft is working very hard to undermine Java portability by flooding the market with incompatible versions of Java.

The 1998 Federal antitrust case against Microsoft revealed a Microsoft internal memo saying that the company had a strategic goal to pollute cross-platform Java. Software developers who are interested in portability will avoid Java products from the only company in the entire computer industry worldwide that is seeking to undermine cross-platform Java.

The Java Plug-In

Equally as problematic for users of standard Java, Netscape fumbled its software development efforts in 1997 as its core markets were devoured by Microsoft. Netscape was late to market with a JDK 1.1 compiler, hampering the progress of Java.

To enable customers to enjoy standard Java regardless of browser choices, Sun came out with a Java Plug-In product. The Java Plug-In is a browser plug-in like the Cool-Talk or Real Audio plug-ins mentioned in an earlier chapter. The Java Plug-In lets applets run in a standard JVM instead of whatever JVM is built into the browser.

The Java Plug-In requires a modification to the HTML that invokes the applet. The different HTML ensures that the plug-in JVM is called. The plug-in comes with a utility to convert existing HTML files to use the new tags. The Java Plug-In is probably most useful in the controlled environment of an intranet, rather than for home or general Internet use. The plug-in can be downloaded from

```
http://java.sun.com/products/plugin/index.html
```

Enterprise customers particularly have embraced the Java Plug-In. It allows MIS departments to deploy applets with the most up-to-date features, and know they will run reliably and consistently even when the browser is updated or changed. Future releases of the Java Plug-In will keep up with future releases of the Java Language, providing an easy way to keep your old browser but update your Java support. The Java Plug-In is available without charge,

Platform Independence

Platform independence is the main goal of Java and it has been achieved, so this is an important section to understand. The level of platform independence is essentially 100 percent perfect today for the language and for most of the libraries. There is really only one area where it falls a little short: the windowing library. In the first version of Java, window support was a layer built on top of the native window system. It was thus subject to all the native window system quirks and differences. JavaSoft is hard at work tackling the issue to make Java windowing as cross platform as the rest of the libraries. It has rewritten windowing support in Java to eliminate platform differences.

Some software users may take the view that software portability doesn't matter to them. They may be quite happy using a Windows 3.1 system forever, and see no reason to consider Java. Obviously, software users can make choices for themselves. The point is that Windows 3.1, or any operating system, will not be here forever. Take a moment to think about the different operating system versions that Microsoft has had in five years up to 1998 as shown in Table 5-2.

Table 5-2 Microsoft OS Versions since 1993

OS	API
MS-DOS	Various incompatible APIs for the non-GUI system
Windows 3.11	Win16 16-bit API
	Win32s 32-bit subset API without threads or long filenames.
Windows CE	The consumer electronics OS, mostly a subset of WinNT, includes the threads API missing from Win32s.
Windows 95	Windows 4.0 bundled on top of MS-DOS 7.0.
	Has the Win32 API except for security and other APIs.
Windows 98	Maintenance release of Windows 95.
	Win32 on Win95 + IE4.0 APIs.
Windows NT	Microsoft's opportunity to offer a product with a feature set comparable to the UNIX operating system.
	NT 3.5 doesn't have the Win95 shell API.
	NT 4.0 is missing some APIs that are in Win95. NT 5.0 has many new APIs. NT 6.0 will offer the Win64 API for 64-bit processing.
	The future, object-oriented release of NT is code-named "Cairo." It has remained vaporware since it was announced in 1992 for shipment in 1994.
WinTerm	API for remote terminal access to NT.

Even if you are committed to using just Microsoft software for ever and ever, software portability affects you in these ways:

- There are different APIs on different OS's (e.g., Win16, Win32s, Win32). Applications are not portable across these different APIs.

- Installing a new Microsoft application frequently installs new system libraries (known as "DLL's"—dynamically-linked libraries) which can affect, and even break, other applications.

- Because of bugfixes in unpublicized new OS releases, different versions of the same OS sometimes have different APIs. Windows 95 had an A version, a B version, and several OEM versions. You couldn't tell which you had except by installing it and querying through the control panel. Some applications (e.g., networking code) would run on one version but not on another.

- Its revenue model requires Microsoft to force software updates into the market regularly. Two years after buying Office 95, many sites have to buy Office 97 because of deliberate data incompatibilities between the two programs. It's not hard to make software upwardly compatible with data; this was done over multiple revisions of HTML. Premature software obsolescence has no advantage for users.

It's hard enough to write an application that runs well on just Windows 95 and NT. Microsoft promised a unified API across its OS products, but has not been able to deliver it. Worse, there are plenty of places where Microsoft has introduced a hidden (undocumented) API for its own applications, giving them an advantage over independent software vendors (see Table 5-3). The Amazon on-line bookstore lists half-a-dozen books that explore these hidden APIs. Even if programmers restrict themselves to the subset of common and published APIs, there are cases where the same API call does different things on two OS's. Assuring porta-

Table 5-3 Microsoft's Undocumented APIs

Product	Undocumented API use
MS Quick C/Windows 1.0	Uses at least one undocumented API, and the product will not run under Win95 or WinNT. Will not even install.
Visual C++ v4.0 on	The product includes a utility pstat.exe which uses undocumented APIs from ntdll.dll to retrieve information about processes and threads,
Web server	The Microsoft web server uses special APIs that were added to NT 4.0 to speed up performance. The APIs were not documented to the public until many months after the Microsoft product was shipped.
Exception handling	The Visual C++ run-time library source omits exactly the source file needed to document the OS interface for supporting exception handler chains. This interface is needed by competing language products that need to be compatible with Visual C++.
Password handling under NT 3.1 and 3.5	One of the most requested APIs for NT was an application call that would validate a password. Microsoft had such an API but claimed it was reserved for the OS group. Then MS SQL Server 4.21 came out, and was completely integrated into the NT security system, including use of the supposedly reserved password API. No other applications vendor had the opportunity to use the LsaLogonUser call.

Table 5-3 Microsoft's Undocumented APIs *(continued)*

Product	Undocumented API use
Win95 socket library	The upgrade from Win3.1 to Win95 removed the old socket library, leaving Microsoft Network as the only working Internet application on the desktop. Navigator did not work; Compuserve and AOL access did not work. Microsoft used the new socket API in its own products but did not release the API to competitors for many months.
Windows 3.11	Microsoft put some code in the 3.11 beta that created incompatibilities with DR-DOS. Specifically, Microsoft added the DOSMGR callout API to Windows which made a number of undocumented DOS calls. Microsoft changed the interface to the XMS (eXtended Memory Standard) memory manager, the interface to Loadhi VxD, and changed the use of the processor's "nested task flag."
	All these interface changes were made in incompatible ways. The beta version of 3.11 issued an error message when it detected it was running on DR-DOS. The code is still in the FCS version, but turned off by a flag.
	Some of the code was encrypted so it was not easy to reverse engineer it and learn why the window system would not start.
Internet Explorer	Internet Explorer versions 1 and 2 make heavy use of undocumented Win95 functions provided by SHELL32.DLL. Netscape chairman Jim Clark, says that when Netscape asked Microsoft for information about undocumented Win95 APIs, Microsoft in return asked for a 20 percent stake in Netscape (Reuters, September 27, 1995). IE version 3 increased the number of undocumented APIs used.

bility across successive Microsoft OSs is next to impossible for nontrivial applications. But if you make portability one of your key software requirements now by specifying Java, you are protecting your investment for the future.

Volume Drives Everything

It's a basic business principle that the more customers you have, the better. Everything else being equal, this principle leads companies to supply large markets (where there is a large amount of demand) in preference to smaller ones. It is particularly true in the software industry, where the cost of product raw materials (a CD or floppy disk) is very low and an extra copy of a product can be manufactured very cheaply. Once the cost of development has been recouped, every additional sale is almost all profit. This is not true for a product like a car, where the biggest part of the selling price represents the cost of the raw materials and machining and assembly of the vehicle.

The availability of application software for a platform is directly proportional to the installed base of that platform. The higher the installed base, the greater the amount of available software. The economics of software (high development cost, very low product copy cost) motivates software vendors very strongly to seek out high-volume markets and ignore low-volume niches. Because the marginal rate of return is so high, a rational software vendor will prefer to saturate an existing market before seeking a new market.

Most software vendors produce a Windows version first; they may produce an Apple Macintosh version afterwards. Only a very small number of software companies port or write applications for UNIX, and those applications are expensive. Today, the new highest volume platform is Java. It encompasses all the systems shown in Figure 5–4.

The lack of applications software on low-volume platforms contributes to a vicious cycle: Developers don't want to supply low-volume platforms, so applications software is sparse and expensive, which in turn is one important factor that acts as a brake on platform sales. Pretty early in the PC revolution, buyers cottoned onto the concept that they should choose their favorite application software first, and then buy the hardware that it ran on. By the way, "low volume" is a comparative term. The estimates for installed base on desktop clients by the end of 1998 are shown in Figure 5–4.

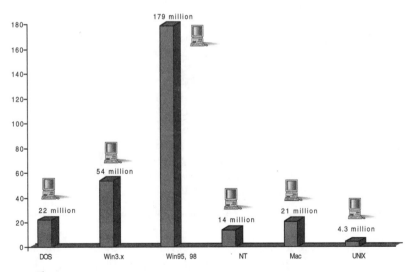

Figure 5–4

Total Estimated Installed Base of Desktop Operating Systems in 1998
Source: IDC report "Client Operating Environment Review and Forecast" July 1997.

In the past, vendors of lower-volume platforms have had two main approaches to getting ISVs to port their applications:

- Make the port easy by providing standardized languages and libraries, and access to porting centers with hardware to borrow

- Pay the ISV to port their product to your hardware

Most computer hardware manufacturers preferred the first method, whereas most ISVs preferred the second method. Which actually happened depended on the changing dynamics of strengths and needs.

Bearing the costs of porting software

In the late 1980s, one software company had a very lucrative business selling a COBOL compiler for the PC. Several UNIX vendors felt they needed to offer a COBOL compiler, too. Each paid the compiler company up to a million dollars for a port to their hardware, and more in annual prepaid royalty fees for per-copy sales.

An unusual clause in the contract stipulated that the unearned portion of the annual prepaid royalties would expire at the end of each year. In other words, the contract might specify annual prepaid royalties of half a million dollars each year for five years and a royalty of $100 on each compiler sold. At the end of the first year if only 250 compilers had been sold, then only 250 * 100 or $25,000 of the prepaid $500,000 had been earned. The clause meant that the unearned $475,000 already paid could not be carried forward to set against compiler sales for the following year. Instead, a further $500,000 had to be paid.

This unusual licensing term should have raised a warning flag to the UNIX vendors. Whenever there's a term in a contract for which you don't understand the reason, you need to dig a bit deeper. In fact (as the compiler vendor knew all along), the volume market for business data processing using COBOL on UNIX workstations didn't exist at that time. The compiler vendor made a very large amount of money regardless. They made all the money from charging the UNIX hardware manufacturers to port a product that hardly anyone wanted or bought.

In an ironic twist of fate, this vendor completely missed the shift in industry focus to networking and the Internet and is now suffering financial turmoil, while the UNIX workstation vendors are doing very well. By doing away with the need to port software, Java also does away with sharp business practices like this one.

The pressing need to make it easy for ISVs to port to their platforms has led the UNIX vendors to provide full support for many programming languages that have been standardized. Some examples are shown in the Table 5-4.

Table 5-4 Some Standardized Programming Languages

Language	Standards body	Standard
C	ISO	ISO/IEC 9899-1990
Fortran 77	ANSI	X3.198-1992
Fortran 90	ISO	ISO/IEC 1539-1991
COBOL	ANSI	X3.23-1985(R1991)
Pascal	ISO	ISO/IEC 7185-1990

Java will be the subject of an international standard, too. In March 1997, Sun Microsystems applied for recognition as a Publicly Available Specification (PAS) submitter by ISO/IEC's JTC 1. The ISO/IEC JTC 1 (International Organization for Standardization/International Electrotechnical Commission Joint Technical Committee 1) is the top computing standards-developing group in the world. Microsoft and Intel led a campaign to try to prevent Sun standardizing Java this way, but their campaign failed. The great majority of computer companies could see the value to the industry of standard Java.

The PAS process is JTC's "fast track" allowing for rapid decisions on proposed international standards. The fast track and the technology submission direct from Sun are both essential, as a protracted standardization process would be the worst of all worlds. C++ took about a decade for ANSI adoption. A lengthy standardization process would allow Microsoft new ways to move on its stated objective of undermining portable Java. Now that ISO has accepted Sun's PAS application, the next step is for Sun to publish the roadmap describing what APIs will be submitted and when.

Portability through API and ABI Standards

A standard for the programming language and libraries (known as an API standard) goes only part of the way to making a platform attractive to ISVs.

The Microsoft Windows interfaces and the Apple Macintosh interfaces are de facto standardized. These operating system interfaces are only available from a single supplier, so there is no opportunity for differences in either of these worlds.

The UNIX market is an open one, meaning no one vendor controls the operating system, and the product is available from several sources. In theory, this openness promotes competition and thus benefits users. In practice, because of the economics of software described above, the availability of many slightly incompatible versions of UNIX fragmented the market, lowered the volume of each, and made UNIX an unattractive platform for software vendors. Sun's executive leadership realized that software portability was the key to retrieving the situation, and this is why Java is readily licensed to all without partiality to any.

What is an "open system"?

The terms "open system" and "proprietary system" are thrown around a lot in the industry in ways that debase their meaning. Here is the definition of the term "open" from Scott McNealy, CEO of Sun Microsystems.

An "open system" has:

- Interfaces that are published. Different vendors can review the interfaces to see all the features that are supported.
- Interfaces that include fully documented specifications. As well as the API being public, there must be a specification saying what each function does when it is called and how it modifies its parameters.
- Interfaces that are free of licensing fees and are open to all to use. If there are per-copy charges or royalty fees, then it is not an open system. The system must be unencumbered by third-party tariffs or royalties.

If the interfaces meet these criteria (as does Java, for example), then it is an open system or an open technology.

It is important to distinguish between the specification of the interfaces and some implementation of that specification. An individual implementation built upon an open interface can be proprietary and can be licensed or sold without affecting the status of the interface as being an open one.

Why Source Standards Aren't Much Help

Standards for a language and library API are a step in the right direction but fall short of solving the problem of software availability on low-volume platforms. APIs benefit software vendors. If the source of a program conforms to an API, that program will compile on any system that supports the API. The biggest problem is that *source* standards offer only the assurance that the software need not be *changed* to run on a different platform, just recompiled. However, if the ISV wants to support his product on ten different platforms that each support a source standard like POSIX, he still needs to build, test, and ship ten different versions. Since ISVs still have to sustain multiple versions of the product, they don't get the benefit of high volumes.

The second half of the picture is the Application Binary Interface. An ABI is a promise to users that all programs that adhere to the standard will run on their system. Some example ABI standards are shown in Table 5-5.

Table 5-5 Three Examples of ABIs

ABI Standard	Computer System
Common Hardware Reference Platform (CHRP)	Motorola/Apple/IBM Power PC
SPARC Compliance Definition	Sun Microsystems SPARC
The Java Virtual Machine Specification	All systems

An ABI describes the environment that a program can rely on while it is executing. It includes things like the addressable space that a program can use, the dynamic library interfaces, register usage for argument passing, and linkage conventions that you need to match when you run the code. The ABI will apply to all programming languages and is not bound to any one of them. An ABI means that software vendors can supply shrink-wrapped software for all implementations of that platform. ABIs benefit users. If a program conforms to an ABI, it will run on two different systems that support the ABI.

What do "API" and "ABI" mean?

There are two kinds of standards in the software world: API and ABI.

An **API (Application Programmer Interface)**, also known as a source standard, is a promise to the implementor. An API lists the libraries and system calls a programmer can use. In the past, these have varied widely between Windows, the Apple Mac, and the 57 varieties of UNIX. However, if the API is standard, the code can just be recompiled and it will run any system that implements the API. In theory, this could really reduce porting costs to just the cost of recompilation.

An **ABI (Application Binary Interface)**, also known as a binary standard, is a promise to the user of software. It says that any programs that adhere to the ABI will run on the user's system and can be linked together. The compiler writer is bound by the ABI. An ABI is intended to promote a "shrink-wrapped software" market when several different vendors are selling hardware using the same underlying chip.

Compliance to an ABI also allows a hardware clone market to exist. A program that conforms to a system's ABI will run on any processor that complies with the ABI, regardless of who built the system (original manufacturer, clone maker, or OEM).

The lack of a common i86 ABI is the reason that MS-DOS programs won't work under UNIX on Intel, and vice versa. If there were such a standard supported by both environments and if there were a common library API, then executables would work under either. Heck, if there was a common UNIX-on-Intel ABI, then

The guilty secret of C++

All compilers for a given hardware system should follow a common ABI. Among other virtues, it means that binary files from different compilers can be linked together. It turns out that there are so many implementation choices that different compilers will not have the same ABI unless it is set in advance as a design goal.

One language that particularly suffers from different ABIs is C++. Like UNIX, C++ had an informal beginning, with a widely shared reference implementation available from Bell Labs. Also like UNIX, it began to diverge rapidly as numerous software companies felt they could provide a cheaper or better implementation or support their own favorite features. Eventually, C++ started on the road to ANSI standardization, a notoriously lengthy process that can stretch over six or seven years or more. Without universal agreement on the API and language semantics, it is not surprising that the ABIs of the different compilers also diverged. What this means in practice is that you cannot generally link together files generated by different C++ compilers. This is especially noticeable in the case of software libraries written in C++. Library vendors are obliged to support different versions of their product for each different C++ compiler that a customer might use!

For all the grand-sounding talk of "code reuse" and "code portability" that C++ is said to offer, in practice it actually represents a step backward. Few people seem to know about this guilty secret of C++, and the news ought to be more widely disseminated. Lack of binary compatibility is seen in the Windows world as elsewhere. Microsoft used to use Intel Object Module Format (OMF) but switched to Common Object File Format (COFF) in their 32-bit compilers. Borland still uses Intel OMF even in their 32-bit compilers. So even Microsoft and Borland C modules can't directly be linked together (there are various tedious workarounds). However, the Windows C industry doesn't explicitly promote code reuse quite so much as the C++ folks.

---

you could buy shrink-wrapped UNIX-on-Intel software for Linux, SunSoft, UNIXWare, AT&T, Unisys, Sequent, SCO, and all the other vendors with UNIX-on-Intel operating systems.

Lack of a common ABI or even API has give IBM the problem of a fragmented user base. IBM sells six different types of computers and operating systems:

- Mainframes like the IBM ES9000 series
- Minicomputers like the AS/400 range
- UNIX workstations like the RS6000 range
- OS/2-based PS/2 range
- PC Windows-compatible systems
- network computers

Despite attempts like SNA (Systems Network Architecture), none of these are compatible with the others. But now that IBM has enthusiastically embraced Java across its whole product line, customers will be able to use one version of applications software anywhere. The situation looks like the diagram shown in Figure 5–5.

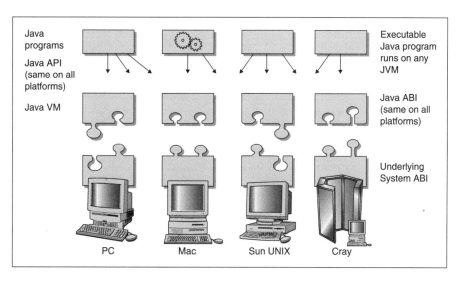

Figure 5–5
Write Once, Run Anywhere

Holier than the Pope: more IBM compatible than IBM

The de facto ABI for Windows systems is "Does it run Windows applications?" In the early days of the PC industry, the critical ABI test was running the Flight Simulator program. To squeeze the last drop of performance out of small systems, Flight Simulator directly manipulated the graphics hardware and so was an excellent hardware compatibility litmus test. This led to an anomaly when PC clone vendors started upgrading from the Intel iAPX186 to the Intel 286 chip: the Compaq 286 system could successfully run down-rev versions of Flight Simulator, but the IBM 286 PC system could not. The Compaq system was more IBM-compatible than the IBM system. This was the point at which IBM started to become marginalized in the IBM-compatible market.

The binary code that comes out of a Java compiler will run on any processor and operating system. For example, I can compile a Java program to obtain the object code (termed "bytecode" in Java terminology). This object code, or bytecode, will

The Java Virtual Machine

The Java Virtual Machine (JVM) implements the "Write Once, Run Anywhere" portability goal. The concept of API and ABI that we have examined at length in the previous section is the reason Java programs are so portable.

- An API says in essence, "These libraries are available." Java has one API that is the same on all platforms.
- An ABI says in essence, "All systems that support this interface will run your programs." Java has the same ABI on all platforms. Not just on all platforms using the same CPU chip, but all platforms regardless of processor!

With its API and ABI concepts put together, the Java language has the same libraries and features on all systems, and the code that comes out of any Java compiler on any system runs on all systems.

run on a Power PC, on an OS/2 system, a Pentium-based system under Windows 95, a Macintosh using MacOS, a JavaStation using JavaOS or a SPARC-based workstation running UNIX SVr4.

The ABI that Java uses wasn't for any existing real system. It describes an idealized virtual machine, whose instructions are the Java bytecode instructions. This idealized virtual system is even called the "Java Virtual Machine," to highlight the difference between the design and a physical machine. With all the interest in Java, a number of companies are now working on creating real hardware that actually uses the Java bytecode instructions as elementary assembly-level instructions. Such a processor (obviously heavily microcoded) would directly run Java programs.

The JVM design is not exclusively tied to Java. Noticing this, some people have suggested that if the compiler for their favorite other language was retargeted to the JVM, then programs in their favorite other language would be as portable as Java programs. One company, Intermetrics, has modified one of their Ada compiler products to successfully target it to the JVM. Now their Ada programs run on any Java interpreter. The product is called AppletMagic, and more information is available at the Intermetrics web site at http://www.intermetrics.com. Some languages like LISP, Scheme, and yes, COBOL are a good fit for the JVM. The two obvious choices, C and C++, are poor candidates for both the JVM and for automatic translation into Java (which is equivalent, because Java can then be compiled for the JVM). The problem with C and C++ is their unconstrained access to memory and their ability to turn integers into memory addresses. Java and the JVM do not support turning integers into pointers, so one would have to do something like declare a very large Java array that represented C's view of memory. The array could be manipulated the way C and C++ manipulate memory, but it would be slow.

Running other languages on the JVM

The Java Virtual Machine can run any program that consists of valid bytecodes. Here is how some other languages map onto bytecodes. It is quite straightforward to retarget a compiler to output bytecodes instead of native machine code. When you do that, all your programs compiled by that compiler become as portable as Java itself. Those programs also have access to all the Java libraries for windowing, networking, and more.

Language	Match for JVM?
Ada, Ada 95	YES, Intermetrics has an implementation.
COBOL	YES, PERCobol Enterprise Edition is a fully ANSI 1985 X3.23b compliant COBOL development environment which generates Java source code. See http://www.Synkronix.com. It provides an easy path for MIS staff into the modern world of client/server Java distributed processing.
Perl	YES
Forth	YES
Smalltalk	YES, IBM is reported to be working on this.
LISP, Scheme	YES, may require adding one or two instructions to JVM.
APL	YES, the unique character set used by APL is problematic, but otherwise the JVM supports APL. The APL market is small, but access to execution environments on all platforms could give it a new lease on life.
Visual Basic	YES, except for "pass by reference" parameters (can be solved).
FORTRAN	YES, except for "pass by reference" parameters (can be solved).
C, C++	NO, too lax in access to memory. A restricted subset could be supported.

In the late 1970s the UCSD-Pascal variant of Pascal used the same idea of compiling to a low-level, machine-independent form (known as p-code) for later interpretation on any system. In the late 1980s the Open Software Foundation tried to bridge the binary compatibility gaps between its members by using ANDF (Architecture Neutral Distribution Format). The OSF ANDF initiative failed because they didn't think of providing an interpreted environment. Worse still, they didn't support a common API on all platforms. Fear of performance problems made them instead require each customer to do a final compilation from ANDF to native binaries. Customers don't like to buy software on a "some assembly required" basis, and the ANDF venture collapsed under its own weight.

Figure 5–6 illustrates how the JVM looks on different platforms.

The practice of "Write Once, Run Anywhere" is so desirable, and so far from current industry practice, that the slogan has been trademarked by JavaSoft. A number of other new terms have been coined to describe the process of compiling a

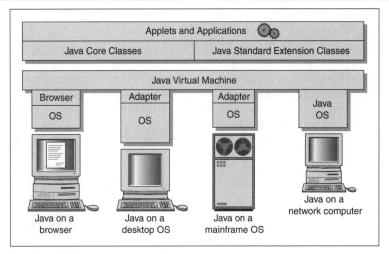

Figure 5–6
JVM on Different Platforms

program on any system and being able to run that program on any other system. People talk about "architecture neutral" and "platform independent." Figure 5–7 explains these terms in detail.

"Architecture neutral" and "platform independent" mean the same thing. A Java program can be compiled on any system, and the resultant object code executed on any other system. This is an incredible breakthrough for ISVs, because their potential market is no longer just their chosen niche, but literally every computer system on the planet. This is an incredible breakthrough for vendors of lower-volume platforms, because the problem of scarce expensive software is resolved. This is an incredible breakthrough for computer users, because they will now be able to choose from a universe of software.

At present, if you go into a retail software outlet, you will see walls of software for Windows, a few shelves of software for the Macintosh, and usually nothing at all for any other kind of system. Imagine how much more choice everyone would have if every piece of software in the store was written in Java and would run on all computers! That is the tremendous promise that Java holds out and is the reason for the unique level of interest in the language.

The main organization that loses out by "write once, run anywhere" is Microsoft. Java reduces Microsoft's highly profitable monopoly on the desktop API. In a Java world, Microsoft can still dictate when new operating system revisions appear, but these revisions are of minor interest to many programmers and computer users. The API of interest has shifted upwards from the OS, first to the browser,

Software terms

Architecture neutral   "Architecture neutral" is another way of saying that Java expects the same ABI on *all* systems. Since different computers vary greatly in the binary interface they support, Java smooths over this by having another layer that fits on the actual system ABI at one end and offers the "Java Virtual Machine" interface at the other end. This Java Virtual Machine is just a fancy name for an interpreter—a program that runs the Java bytecodes.

Platform independent   Java was designed with Internet applications in mind. That means heterogeneous (mixed) systems, with different software libraries and features. "Platform independent" means the software runs on all computers, regardless of hardware or operating system. Before Java, platform independence was regarded as the Holy Grail of software—highly desirable but unattainable in practice.

Write Once, Run Anywhere   This slogan describes platform independence from an ISV's point of view. Once the program is compiled, that binary version can be executed on any computer system. It is no longer necessary to port the software and support say, "Lotus 123 for Windows 3.11," "Lotus 123 for Windows 95," "Lotus 123 for Solaris UNIX," "Lotus 123 for Hewlett-Packard UNIX," and so on.

Backward compatibility   A system is "backward compatible" if newer versions of the system continue to run old software. Backward compatibility is extremely important to computer users to safeguard their investment in software. Backward compatibility is usually provided by newer releases of operating systems.

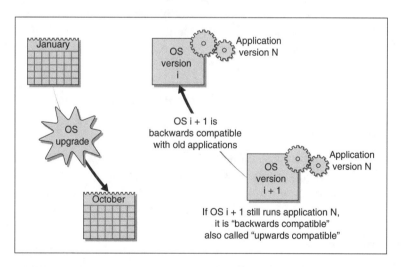

Figure 5-7
Backwards Compatibility

Upward compatibility   The term is a synonym for backward compatibility. When you refer to the older software, you say "upward compatible;" and when you refer to the newer software, "backward compatible" is the term. The JDK 1.0.2 is upward binary compatible with JDK 1.1. That means that class files built with the 1.0.2 compiler will run correctly on 1.1 systems.

Forward compatibility   "Forward compatibility" is rarer in the world of software, because you need to predict the future (or not make any big changes) to make it work. A system is forward compatible if old versions of the system can run newer software. JavaSoft's policy is that bug-fix releases (so called "dot-dot" releases, like 1.0.1 and 1.0.2) will have both backward and forward compatibility. So, class files built by a 1.0.2 compiler will run on a 1.0.0 system. There may be forward compatibility between 1.1 programs that do not use any new features and the older 1.0.2 version of the JVM. "Downward compatibility" is a synonym for forward compatibility when referring to the newer software.

and now to Java. Microsoft can still optimize its own applications for Windows, but a large number of ISVs will prefer to use Java and access a potential market that is the entire world of computer systems.

Microsoft uses a combination of carrot and stick to get people to buy into new features of future products. Because of the common Java API on all platforms, Java programmers won't be able to take advantage of Microsoft-only facilities, some of which some users may actually want. And if not using the features means losing Microsoft's support in marketing and selling your product (like the Win95 branding program), some vendors will still follow Microsoft's lead. There is a threat here to Microsoft, but it's difficult to predict how long it will take to get to the end result of the majority of applications being written in Java.

Who Has Java?

By now all leading computer companies have licensed the JVM software from Sun and are bundling it with their OS products. The vendors that have signed license agreements include Apple Computer Inc., Hewlett-Packard Company, Hitachi, Ltd., International Business Machines Corporation, Microsoft Corporation, Motorola, Novell, Inc., The Santa Cruz Operation, Inc. (SCO), and over 150 other organizations.

Sun also offers the Java Runtime Environment (JRE) which is the set of libraries needed to run (rather than develop) Java applications. Users can install the JRE on their systems to make them Java ready immediately while they wait for the OS vendors to catch up with a bundled release of the JVM. The JRE is just the JDK without the development tools (compiler, debugger, etc.). It is the smallest set of components from the JDK needed to execute Java programs. The JRE is now available for Solaris, Windows 95 and NT.

Summary

- Java is a new programming language designed by Sun Microsystems. It has been universally adopted since its release in mid-1995. Java is popular because it is "web friendly": Java makes it simple to communicate with Internet protocols.

- An *applet* is a Java program embedded in a web page. When a browser looks at that web page, the applet is downloaded onto the system with the browser and executed on that system. This means the applet is using local (client) computing resources, and all the server need do is serve up the page (send the file contents over the network). Unlike CGI scripts or DHTML, Java applets can interact with the user in real time.

- Applets offer a cross-platform solution to the client part of client/server, with no installation required. Applets also bring true interactiveness to a web page.

- Java was designed to be "Write Once, Run Anywhere," meaning that the binaries run on all computers. By using Java, end users can retain their investment in software while upgrading or changing or staying with one operating system.

- The availability of application software for a system is directly proportional to the installed base of that system. The higher the installed base, the greater the amount of available software. All major OS vendors now bundle Java in their products, giving Java a huge installed base. Over time, the number of applications will follow.

- Java changes the economics of the business by supporting "write once, run anywhere." Software companies that use Java can expand their market by selling their products for any computer. Low-volume hardware platforms can run the standard binary of the latest Java applications without any custom porting.

- Java is also a good general purpose programming language for those who do not want or need client/server access.

CHAPTER 6

- How the Internet Runs

- Connecting Your Company to the Internet

- Evolution of On-line Commerce

- On-line Commerce Today

- Case Study 3: Web-Based Retailing

- Summary

The Internet and E-Commerce

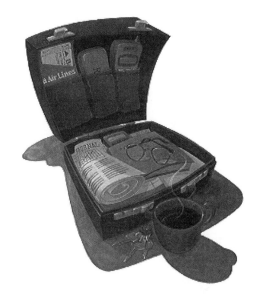

In a way, this is the single most important chapter of this book because it deals with the area of the Internet that will have the largest financial impact: E-commerce. On-line commerce, web-based commerce, e-commerce (electronic-commerce) are all built on the same foundation: using the Internet as a channel for business transactions. The concept has little that is new: Television has displayed tempting ads for years, and business has been conducted by phone for even longer. E-commerce has existed from the point where companies first started accepting payment by taking down a credit card number over the phone. This kind of payment is universal in the United States, though still a novelty in most of Europe.

The difference between phone orders and web-based commerce is simply this: with web-based commerce there is now a computer at both ends of the transaction. The computers allow automated searching, comparison shopping, two-way flow of data, just-in-time inventory reordering, automated payment, speed, accuracy, throughput, automated record keeping and order dispatch, links to related transactions, and a host of second order benefits like order profiling ("what made this customer place this order exactly?") and improved accessibility ("please display the fine print larger"). The beauty of on-line commerce is that it may be a revolution in terms of Internet use, but it is merely an evolution of existing business processes. It may be new to an individual company, but business and customers in general are used to it. That familiarity is a considerable driving factor speeding up the adoption of on-line commerce.

What e-commerce means is that people have found some practical ways to blend their business needs with the Internet's unique communication advantages. Without doubt Java is the Lingua Franca of on-line commerce. It provides a consistent end-to-end implementation language with all the right features of portability, browser capability, database access, graphical capabilities, security, and privacy. Let's start by summarizing how the Internet itself is organized, how it is administered, and how its services are paid for.

How the Internet Runs

Internet sites (which double as World Wide Web sites as soon as a site starts running the software) are divided in the United States into six top-level domains that classify the site's purpose as commercial, educational, governmental, and so on (see Table 6-1). Other countries use different domain schemes, and there's a lot of pressure to introduce a wider variety of top-level domains in the United States. One proposal involves using five letters to specify the top domain names and introducing 7 to 31 new top-level domains.

A notable aspect of the Internet from its earliest days was that it was not planned; it just evolved to meet the needs of its users. There was no central direction, no governing president, and no elaborate bureaucratic procedure. If you found its basic communication services useful, you simply went out and leased a data line or dial-up connection to route your own network onto the nearest Internet system that would agree to a connection. Usually, multiple connections were in the interests of both parties, as it aided overall net connectivity.

Distributed Administration

Lacking central bureaucracy to push in other directions, the Internet has been a model of market forces in action. Those services that people found useful, like net news and web browsing, stayed around and were developed. Those services that were too hard to use, like first generation searching tools, never had a poular following and eventually withered away.

There is an Internet Engineering Task Force that is solely concerned with the implementation aspects of keeping the Internet running. That is, they do not set pricing guidelines nor approve new connections. They concern themselves with matters like recommending new protocols and usually set up a subgroup for each new challenge to face. The IETF reports to the Internet Activities Board, which blesses new standards but also has no say whatsoever in who gets on the Internet.

Table 6-1 Internet domain schemes

Domain Name	Purpose of Site	Example Site Name
.com	Commercial organizations	afu.com
.edu	Educational institutions	cs.yale.edu
.gov	Government-related bodies	nasa.gov
.mil	U.S. military groups	chinalake.navy.mil
.net	Groups providing nonprofit net access	texas.net
.org	Other nonprofit ventures	kidshealth.org
There are also domains used in other lands:		
.uk	United Kingdom site	ox.ac.uk
.ca	Canadian sites	freenet.carlton.ca
.jp	Japanese sites	twics.co.jp
and so on, for about 40 countries		

In February 1997, the Internet International ad-hoc committee announced seven new top-level domain names in the United States, and ended the Network Solutions monopoly by allowing other bodies around the world to register new Internet addresses. The proposed new domains are:

.arts	artistic organizations, such as galleries, theatres, etc.
.firm	commercial organizations (some overlap with .com)
.info	organizations dealing with information (newspapers, media)
.nom	nom de plume—for personal domains
.rec	recreational entities, clubs, etc.
.store	companies offering on-line sales catalogs
.web	web-related organizations and groups

The organization that actually hands out IP addresses and oversees the Internet Registry that associates domain names (like sun.com) with IP addresses is the InterNIC (meaning Internet Network Information Center). InterNIC is about the only centralized administrative activity on all the Internet, but it looks like its task of handing out IP addresses and domain names will soon be decentralized and spun off to more nations and more competitors. InterNIC is a cooperative activity between the National Science Foundation, Network Solutions, Inc., and AT&T. The term InterNIC is used to describe both the consortium that provides the registration services and the services themselves. InterNIC services are often called the "white pages" of the Internet. The InterNIC site at http://www.internic.net/ds/about.html is a good place to start looking if you want to get the latest net statistics or register your own domain name.

Connecting Your Company to the Internet

Internet access always comes by renting access through an Internet Service Provider that is already connected. In most urban areas, there are several alternative providers to choose from (more consolidation of ISPs will inevitably occur). An organization can select the appropriate point on the price/capacity curve, ranging from cheap dial-up service using a modem and a PC, to an expensive, leased T3 trunk line carrying 44 megabits of data per second. Table 6-2 lists the performance of typical technologies for networking connections.

Table 6-2 Network Technologies

Net hardware	Speed	Description
modem	56K bits per second	Typical modem speed (in 1998)
ISDN	128K bits per second	ISDN phone line
10baseT ethernet	10M bits per second	LAN technology : the number is the speed Mbaud. The "base" means baseband signalling (not moduated on a carrier wave). The "T" means the signal is on twisted pair wiring.
100baseT ethernet	100M bits per second	
T1 trunk line	1.544M bits per second	WAN leased line: this is the most common connection between networks on the Internet today.
T3 trunk line	44.736M bits per second	WAN leased line connection. This is fast enough for full screen video. More typically used for inter-LAN connections.
FDDI—Fibre Distributed Data Interface	100M bits per second	A standard for transmitting data on optical fiber cable. Usually used on a LAN. The British spelling of "fibre" is usually used.
Gigabit Ethernet	1000M bits per second	Emerging technology to run LAN connections 10 to 100 times faster than classic ethernet.

The ISP connection brings the Internet into your organization; you then have the task of administering the computer system at your end of the connection, configuring it for the appropriate blend of services and security, distributing it on your internal networks, and keeping it all working. Doing this takes, well, work. How much work depends on what you choose to do. Most organizations choose to invest in having this computer expertise in house nowadays. Figure 6–1 illustrates the components that make up a typical network and how the network connects to the Internet.

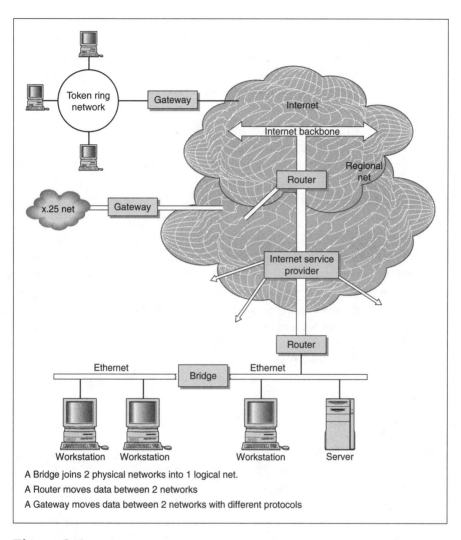

Figure 6-1
Internet: Layers of Connected Networks

The point has now been reached where essentially all businesses should be on the Internet, at the very least for sending and receiving e-mail. Not being on the Internet now is like not having a telephone. Even if you can get by without the service, you will appear eccentric and old fashioned to most of your customers. Computer companies in particular, and MIS departments of any organization, must ensure their staff are familiar with Internet applications just to stay in the game.

It is now clear that we are at the start of a new industrial revolution. In the first industrial revolution, blacksmiths had to adapt from working with horseshoes to working with horseless carriages, or go out of business. In the information revolution, computer professionals need to adapt from a culture of centralized information with expensive communication, to the new paradigm of low-cost, decentralized information processing.

Jim Clark, the chairman of Netscape Communications, likens the Internet to the phone network only for data, meaning that it is widely available, widely used, cheap, and fast becoming a basic utility. When Clark first said this, it was a bold comparison. Today it is increasingly taken for granted as a near-obvious truism. The analogy holds true on several other levels, and we will return to it.

In January 1994, the FBI posted its Unabomber material on the Internet for ftp retrieval and offered a $1 million reward for information leading to an arrest. This was a little surprising, as the Unabomber had made it clear all along that he eschewed technology, and, in fact, he was ultimately turned in by a member of his family. Nonetheless it was representative of the way established organizations were updating their communication policies. By the start of 1997, seven percent of people in the United States were using the Internet (source: Mark Magillivray, quoted in IEEE Computer, January 1997). By 1998, 100 million people around the world were using the Internet, and some experts were predicting that figure would grow tenfold within seven years (source: Morgan Stanley US Investment Research, Internet Retail report, May 28 1997).

Web Meets Net

One of the biggest problems with the early Internet was that it was all so unorganized. The key strength, decentralization, was also a key weakness. Certainly, you could download a copy of a file from anywhere on the Internet—if you knew that it existed and where it was. The Internet was like a vast library that had no central index. There was a treasure house of information out there, but the trick was in finding it. People passed on information by e-mail, word-of-mouth, and news postings. There were some crude text-based searching utilities, but text-based Internet programs were basically stop-gap solutions to the wrong problem. We didn't just need better *searching*, we needed an entire, better *user interface* to the Internet.

There was a real grass-roots recognition that the growing base of information was greatly handicapped by the lack of any central index. There was an ocean of data out there, but no charts highlighting the fishing grounds. To get its start, on-line commerce had to use tools that were simple enough for anyone to learn. The catalyst was a remarkable development from Europe known as web browsing.

The World Wide Web offers a simple, consistent, universal naming scheme, and web browsers provide a very simple, window-based front end to Internet applications to look for things by that name. Because browsing is simple, it opens the door to use by a wide range of noncomputer experts. Many of these people were first attracted to the Internet by the net-news and e-mail applications. The development of the web browser interface made Internet use so simple that they stayed around and added to the critical mass of users.

Web browsers to the rescue!

A web browser is a simple, window-based program that provides a friendly front end to programs that retrieve information across the Internet. In recent times, the browser has taken on more and more capabilities while retaining the same look and feel on multiple platforms (Netscape looks and works the same whether you run it on Windows 98, the Mac, or UNIX). Because of its role as platform-neutral software that bridges a client computer to the Internet, the browser has become one of the most important desktop applications.

Simple interfaces mean more users, which means more potential customers, which leads to the viability of on-line commerce.

Evolution of On-line Commerce

When people talk about the commercialization of the net, they generally mean the presence of companies that are not in the computer industry on the net, either for self-promotion or for trade. Companies started out with just a simple informational web site, and many are now making the easy step into on-line retailing from their web sites. Hundreds of thousands of organizations, ranging from a bead shop with a web site that the author discovered while on vacation in Prescott, Arizona, to pretty much all the Fortune 1000 companies, now have an Internet address and presence.

On-line commerce is growing by leaps and bounds in a way that makes it seem like a new California Gold Rush. Because it is growing so fast, it's almost pointless to quote statistics. Here are a few numbers anyway: on-line sales in 1997 totalled more than $3 billion, while information that was read on-line influenced a further $4.4 billion of purchases, according to market research firm Cyber Dialogue. Direct on-line sales were $8 billion in 1998 (Forrester Research). International Data Corporation (IDC) predicts that United States businesses will buy and sell $208.5 billion worth of goods on-line by 2002. Note, that is *billions* of dollars, not million. Forrester Research gives a higher estimate for the same period: $327 billion. (Source: "The Emerging Digital Economy" U.S. Dept of Commerce Report, 1998).

How many computers are there on the Internet?

There are about 30 million computers connected to the Internet, according to figures provided at the start of 1998 by Network Wizards Inc. Each of those computers may have many or just one person using it. Figure 6–2 summarizes the growth from 1991 to 1998.

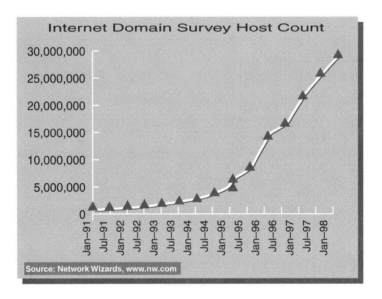

Figure 6–2

These numbers were estimated by pinging 1 percent of all hosts, which is an intensive way of ensuring data accuracy. The survey data was produced by Network Wizards and is available at http://www.nw.com.

The entire U.S. economy has a gross domestic product of $7,600 billion (1996 est.) so you can see why people are excited about the prospect of 5 percent of the economy moving to a different paradigm within five years.

You can also understand why the Federal government will not allow any single company to own a chokehold on the whole sector.

Stages of E-Commerce

E-commerce didn't start with the internet, but that looks like the place where everything is rapidly heading. The variety of e-commerce techniques can be broken down as follows.

Non-Internet-based e-commerce. This covers such staples as bank ATM networks, and business-to-business EDI (Electronic Data Interchange) systems. EDI is a 1970s standard for exchanging data between companies, sometimes simply by mailing a magnetic tape, more typically over a private link known as a Value-Added Network (VAN). The cost of a private VAN is prohibitive compared with the cost of Internet connectivity and this segment is moving to Internet transport. Banks originally experimented with on-line services by providing their customers with a dial-up connection direct to the banking systems. Again, this is now moving to a more general web-based model. E-commerce allows a bank to gain new customers outside its traditional geographic area, but is unlikely to provide a long-term competitive advantage because the service will soon be a feature of all banks.

Informational web site. It is so quick and easy to set up the initial web presence that there is no reason for an organization not to do this. This is termed a "front office system" as it involves direct interaction with the public. The web site showcases basic information about the organization, its products and services. If the organization has a strong brand image, customers may be able to find its site directly. If not, they will need to be referred from one of the search engine sites, so owners will want to make sure their sites are catalogued there.

Search sites will sooner or later charge all companies to be listed there, just as the Yellow Pages charges for an entry. This is why people have bid up the stock price of Yahoo! and Excite to giddy heights.

Retail operations. The stage beyond mere advertisment is to take orders on-line. This can be done with a forms interface connected to CGI scripts or Java servlets running on the server. The next step up in sophistication is then to automate "back office" processing of customer data, connecting it to related systems such as billing, inventory control, service operations and the like.

This kind of application is the new "high ground" of e-commerce, and furious competition is under way to become the leading provider of e-commerce software. Lotus has some strong product offerings, as does Netscape. The financial rewards will be very high for those companies that can offer the best turnkey solutions here. Less than one percent of retail businesses sold on-line in 1998, which means 99 percent of the market is still open.

Business to business. This category is a specialization or outgrowth of the previous one. It involves companies using the Internet for commercial transactions with their business partners. At its simplest, that can be just buying and selling. But it also includes making status information available to web-based enquiries, selectively exposing data (such as account information, or product documentation), and even allowing business partners to directly update your live data.

Business-to-business Internet communication is described by a special term which did not exist before 1997. Just as using Internet protocols to access data within a single organization is termed "intranet access," so business-to-business communication is termed "extranet access." One company that is making extensive use of extranet technology is PC-supplier Dell Computer Corporation.

On-Line Commerce Today

The crucial enabler for on-line commerce was support for encrypted transmission between client browser and server. The IETF was slow to provide secure IP services (it is still finalizing the definition of IPSec—IP Security—protocols in 1998). Netscape introduced the Secure Sockets Layer (SSL) in 1996 with Navigator 3.0, and Microsoft then added the feature for the 3.0 release of Internet Explorer. HTTP messages travel over open networks, so it is essential to use encryption when you want to send financial information like credit-card authorizations. SSL is the minimum enabler for on-line commerce by letting a client and server talk privately. IPSec will make the net more secure in more and different ways.

Computer vendors were among the first to see the value of direct sales from a web site. Dell Computing, a "top-three" worldwide vendor of PCs (along with Compaq and then IBM), has been particularly successful with web-based sales. Apple is emulating them with on-line sales of Macintosh equipment, but Apple has to be careful not to undermine its distributors. Dell always sold direct to customers rather than through retail channels, so on-line ordering was a natural evolution.

Dell introduced commerce through its Internet site in July 1996. Just two years later the web site was generating direct sales of $4 million per day, about ten percent of Dell's total sales. Any prospective customer can get immediate price quotes, then place orders electronically, and later check the order status and delivery dates. High volume customers also get password-protected extranet access to the Dell web site. There they can browse and place orders for custom system configurations, with prenegotiated discounts, and specialized management reports. Dell's web site is open for business 24 hours a day, and is cheaper than taking orders by phone. One limitation is that Dell will only accept e-commerce orders for addresses within the United States.

Selling PCs is a cut-throat, narrow-margin business. Look at it this way: PC "manufacturers" are really just component integrators. They buy complete motherboards from Intel, the operating system from Microsoft, disks from Seagate or Western Digital or one or two others, and all remaining parts from the lowest bidder. The assembly used to be done in East Asia for $5/hour, now China does it for less than $1/hour. Since the assemblers need no R&D expertise, anyone can get into the business with front money of a few million dollars, and lots of people do.

The big players really need an "edge" to distinguish their products from all the other nearly identical ones. Compaq has built a name for sturdy construction, IBM has a prestigious brand name, H-P offers solid support and great printers. Alone of the major PC vendors, Dell has no in-house service or support organization (it subcontracts out the work to Wang and Unisys). So offering easy on-line sales is perhaps the key competitive advantage for Dell. However, it is not likely to remain unique to Dell for long. Any company can move into on-line sales, and a number already have. The networking company Cisco Systems gets about 50 percent of its business on line. Book vendor Amazon Inc, the subject of the case study at the end of this chapter, conducts 100 percent of its business through the Internet.

E-commerce is obviously convenient for customers, but vendors get some big benefits too. Booz-Allen & Hamilton estimates that a banking transaction handled by a teller at a branch bank costs more than one dollar. The same transaction using the Internet costs the bank about a penny. The Air Transport Association of America showed in November 1997 that the cost of processing an airline ticket purchased through a travel agent could be cut by a factor of eight when the customer booked the ticket direct with the airline. The saving can be shared with the customer or taken directly to the airline's bottom line.

Products Best Suited for E-Commerce

The simplest products to buy and sell on-line are those which have no tangible form, so they can be delivered as well as ordered on line. Goods which can be sent later by mail are also good candidates for e-commerce. This means:

- Banking services. The banking industry is notoriously slow to embrace change of any kind, but in this instance they may end up being driven rather than led. In the U.K. a couple of banks, such as the Co-op Bank, already offer web-based personal account banking. Customers like the ease of access, and the bank loves the lowered transaction cost. See the URL at `http://www.co-operativebank.co.uk/internet_banking.html`. The system was written in Java.

- Payment of bills. For a couple of years now, the Holy Grail of e-commerce retailers has been finding a way to submit bills to consumers electronically, and have them paid the same way. Electronic payment is much cheaper, faster and more secure than sending bills through the mail, or even direct debit at your bank. E-commerce is the main reason that WebTV is interesting. If it catches on, it provides a low cost way to submit bills on line, and allow customers to authorize payment.

- Any kind of a product that can be delivered electronically: stocks, insurance, loans, financial transactions of all kinds.

- Audio/video for entertainment, training, education, and the like.

- Buying tickets for future events, travel or entertainment. Today, you can search for airline tickets and optimize your flights for cost, convenience or dates, using the SABRE reservation system at
  `http://www.travelocity.com`

- classified advertising. There are several web sites with car ads on line (e.g., see `http://autoconnect.com` or `http://www.traderonline.com`).

- Anything that can later be sent by mail, like books, PCs, or any catalog product.

It is worth pointing out that Microsoft is leveraging its desktop operating system monopoly and its deep pockets to establish a significant presence on every single one of these "ripe plums" of e-commerce (see Table 6-3).

Table 6-3 Microsoft Blanket Coverage of E-Commerce Ready Sectors

E-Commerce sector	Microsoft venture
Banking services	Microsoft offers the "Marble" server product to allow bank web sites to support some encrypted ATM transactions, and is actively embracing on-line banking in other ways including joint ventures with Wells Fargo Bank, and First Data Corp (the world's largest merchant processor for credit cards).
Payment of bills	Microsoft bought partial ownership of WebTV in 1997, paying $425M, which works out to an astonishing $60,000 per customer. Understanding WebTV as a gateway to e-commerce for on-line bills makes that investment more understandable. The Justice Department failed its duty to the public by not scrutinizing this takeover.
Financial products	Microsoft has a venture that includes an investment web site. The web site also offers real estate, mortgage services, and insurance products. The site is apparently subsidized to provide the kind of quality content that draws in more individuals.
Entertainment products	Microsoft has numerous partnerships for on-line entertainment around the world. In the United States, Microsoft has partnered with news network NBC to form MSNBC, has launched the MSBET service in partnership with Black Entertainment Television, and operates the on-line magazine Slate.
	Microsoft owns the digital rights to such content as Ansel Adams' photographs, Leonardo da Vinci's notebooks, and the 16 million photo Bettmann Archive—one of the largest and most important collections of commercial photographs.

Table 6-3 Microsoft Blanket Coverage of E-Commerce Ready Sectors *(Continued)*

E-Commerce sector	Microsoft venture
Ticketing	Microsoft's Expedia on-line travel service booked $100M of travel transactions in 1997. Internet Explorer has built-in links that take users directly to the Microsoft subsidiary.
Classified ads	Microsoft's CarPoint site charges car dealers $1000 per month plus a commission on sales. Microsoft also runs the city-by-city information sites known as "Sidewalk," and the "Board-walk" venture specializing in real estate advertising.
	Several newspapers had initially cooperated with Microsoft based on promises from the company not to move into classi-fied ads, yet within the year Microsoft broke those promises and struck out on its own account.
Catalog goods	Microsoft recently took a stake in Comcast Cable, which in turns owns the QVC home-shopping cable channel.

One commercial activity that the web handles very well is brokerage: bringing buyers and sellers together. Already 90 percent of real estate listings in California are available on the web, and this is a portent for the future in other places, too. But selling real estate is a very "people-oriented" activity. Savvy real estate brokers provide a lot of value-added services like inspiring confidence, marshaling legal paperwork, lining up mortgage lenders, and handling negotiations. So real estate brokers, though their business may change, will not be replaced by on-line services.

Stockbrokers have a problem however. The activity of "making a market" in a stock is hardly needed when on-line services can more efficiently match buyers and sellers automatically. People are already submitting stock trading orders via e-commerce. Charles Schwab has about one third of the total on-line trading market, and the sector grew by 25 percent in the first three months of 1998. Investors placed an average of 192,000 on-line securities trades each day during that period. Trading stocks on-line has some benefits (e.g., automatic graphing and portfolio recording) but is not fundamentally different from any discount brokerage. The real user benefit will be doing the brokering activity electronically, cutting out the middleman.

In fall 1998 the US Pacific Stock Exchange introduced an intranet-based trading system that by-passes traditional brokers. Nasdaq plans to follow in 1999. E-commerce is rapidly changing the world around us, and affecting everyone either at work or as a consumer.

Table 6-4 Advantages of Web-Based E-Commerce

Seller advantages:

- Lower operating costs. Compared with retail, the vendor has essentially no overhead. For example, costs of public premises, demonstration models, and sales staff go to zero.

- Middleman markup is eliminated.

- Web site is open 24 hours a day/7 days a week including holidays, and can easily cope with seasonal fluctuations in volume.

- Sites can be customized for preferred purchasers.

- Web site presence is unrelated to the size of the company, allowing smaller players to compete just as effectively as industry giants.

- Sales and customer data is automatically available on line for analysis and exploitation.

- Sales literature and catalogs are easy to provide and update. The customer bears the cost of printing. Service manuals can also be put on line.

Buyer advantages:

- Shopping is much more convenient and quicker than visiting stores.

- Comparison shopping without committment is fast and easy.

- Dealing direct with the manufacturer ensures the most up-to-date products and information.

- Retail customers do not have to carry bulky purchases around for the rest of their shopping trip.

Newspapers, too, face a real threat as their lucrative classified and display advertising is displaced by on line services (see Table 6-4). I recently looked for a used car on line, and was only mildly surprised to see that one web site could serve up, free to me, a long list of classified ads for the vehicle in question, each with a picture, and the whole list sorted by vehicle age, price, or distance from my house. I could even leave my phone number and have the sellers contact me if I chose. Purchasers cannot get that kind of service from reading newspaper ads. The Newspaper Association of America reported in a 1996 study that newspaper publishers could lose as much as 50 percent of their classified ad income in the next five years.

After I bought my car, I wanted to choose a personalized (vanity) license plate for it. You can now do this on line in California, by browsing the Department of Motor Vehicles site at `http://plates.ca.gov/search`. You can search for a license plate that you want, see existing similar plates, and apply for any plate that isn't already taken. After choosing a plate, you can shop around for insurance and a car loan for your new vehicle on line, too. Many government services besides vehicle regulation are moving on line. Some cities now allow building permits to be applied for over the Internet. The Federal government just announced that the patent and trademark database will be moved on line, and the Securities Exchange Commission already offers this kind of access to company filings. Finally, the art of software development itself and the distribution of the finished product can move on line. Perhaps computer programmers in a few years time will all be independent contractors working from their homes without ever having to commute. Perhaps software in the near future will be purchased on line and all automatically downloaded and installed on your system.

If programmers all work from home, and deliver software via the Internet, they can be located anywhere, including countries like Russia, Singapore, or Ireland with educated populations and low wages. But every software job that is transferred overseas takes a little bit of the nation's intellectual capital with it, as well as diminishing opportunities in the United States. Telecommuting is a double-edged sword.

Build It and They Will Come—Not!

Unlike shopping in real life which involves a conscious decision to travel to the mall, on-line shopping can come to you. This is almost (but not quite) a "push" technology where the latest data is sent to you instead of you asking for it. But only the strongest product brands can expect "build it and they will come" web sites. For most businesses, the web site must go to the customer.

That means making sure the site is listed in the popular search engines, if necessary by paying placement fees. Sites can also increase their web presence by encouraging other sites to link to them, and providing a financial incentive to do so. Usually this takes the form of a percentage referral fee for any orders placed by the referred browser. All of this costs money, and there are real fears that a small number of "funnel" or "portal" sites will dominate Internet access. Certainly Microsoft realizes this, and invented a special screen area called the "Content Bar" so it could control the on ramp for the information superhighway. Microsoft is using its desktop operating system to leverage a presence in e-commerce and direct users to sites that Microsoft wishes to favor.

The funnel effect is why investors are buying up the search engine sites. It's not for the direct advertising revenue, though that is nice, it is for the future referral and listing fees search sites can charge once the market shakes out.

Challenges Ahead for E-Commerce

E-commerce is happening now on a global basis, no matter what. The economics are too compelling to ignore. The anxiety that participants have is rooted in the uncertainty of government regulation. Most players want governments to create a predictable legal framework, to enforce existing laws against a monopolist taking over everything, and then let the operation of fair competition work out all the rest. The problem with a monopoly controlling everything is that it supresses the free competition needed to make the capitalistic system work. It would be especially tragic if e-commerce fell under one giant thumb right from birth.

Most particularly, players do not want content regulation (censorship), localized distorting influences (substantially different e-commerce laws in country A versus country B), encryption restrictions, or discriminatory taxation. Alas, we already have the first three of these (censorship, differing national laws, and encryption limitations). It remains to be seen how long politicians can resist the temptation to pull extra taxes out of e-commerce participants on the net.

E-commerce has a few drawbacks too. The customer needs to sell himself on the benefits of a product without the tactile experience of seeing and touching the real thing. The selling is passive rather than active, and the buyer needs to have some idea of what he wants. The United States federal policy on encryption hampers international trade. Countries like France that deny the use of encryption to their citizens are moving themselves to the back of the e-commerce line.

There are social challenges ahead. As with the first Industrial Revolution, change is accompanied by upheaval that can be hard to anticipate. There will be a shift away from employment in some sectors, into others. Public policy needs to anticipate social effects that may be far reaching, and plan for them.

Case Study 3: Web-Based Retailing

Amazon.com is perhaps the best known and most successful of the on-line booksellers. The company is pretty much the "poster boy" of web-based retailing. Unlike other booksellers, Amazon conducts business exclusively through the Internet (see Figure 6–3). It does not have any retail premises, and attracts all customers by aggressive advertising, word of mouth referrals, and links from other sites.

When Amazon started, it didn't even have book storage facilities of its own. It used "just in time" inventory control to call down books from publishers stocks as they were ordered, and send them on to customers. That lack of traditional inventory led to good operating efficiency—and much rancor with traditional booksellers. When Amazon ambitiously labeled itself as the world's biggest bookstore, Barnes & Noble actually filed a fruitless lawsuit against the on-line fledgling. Today Barnes & Noble has adopted the "if you can't beat them, join them" approach and has its own on-line sales outlet at
`http://www.barnesandnoble.com`.

Figure 6-3
Amazon's Home Page

Amazon opened up its web site for business in July 1995, with a goal of offering the widest possible selection of books. Today, it has sold books to two and a half million people in more than 160 countries, and offers three million titles. However, Amazon's highest goal is customer service. It built its business on the simple premise that if you treat customers better than your competitors they will come back to you. When you order a book from Amazon, the order is filled and sent very rapidly.

Customer service extends to other areas too. Amazon.com has been very creative with its web site, and allows any customer to annotate the on-line description of a book with mini reviews. I was finally able to provide the feedback to paleontology author Stephen J. Gould that the prose in his books is way too flowery. The feedback may or may not have reached him, but I certainly felt better for expressing it. Customers really like being able to read extracts from books and comments from others.

People can search for books by author, title, general subject, keyword, ISBN and more besides. The web site uses cookies to recognize returning visitors by name, and to suggest new titles related to past purchases. Amazon uses a lot of clever on line marketing, including suggesting related titles to customers. You can even sign up to be notified periodically by e-mail of new books in your field.

They have branched out into music CDs, and my guess would be that when the technology arrives for on-line product downloading of software, video and music, Amazon will be in the vanguard. They have already bought the Internet Movie Database (`http://www.imdb.com`) which is a noncommercial storehouse of movie and television information on the Internet. An obvious enhancement for Amazon to offer, in due course when the technology gets there, is to send on demand the audio for an extract from the text. This might be either the author reading his work, or a machine-generated voice for a passage chosen by the customer. Finally, when you buy at Amazon, you don't have to carry heavy parcels on the rest of your shopping trip.

Buying a book on-line from Amazon

This is the process of buying a book from an on-line bookseller. The first time through there is a "name and address" form to fill out. On subsequent visitis this is how you buy a book.

1. You go to the bookseller's site and search for the book you want, by topic, by author, title, etc, then follow the link to the book's description, where you click the button marked "buy now with one click."

2. The book arrives by mail a few days later.

Each stage of the process is just a single click, or some simple typing. The steps in the process have deliberately been made idiot proof, and similar to a in-person book purchase.

I recently ordered a book from Amazon by e-mail on Saturday night, to my surprise, I got an e-mail confirmation of the order on Sunday night. When I came home from work on Monday, the book was waiting for me. That kind of service is hard for bookstores to compete with.

In a process known as "affiliate marketing," Amazon pays other sites to link to them, and remits a percentage of book purchases that are made from such a link. This makes impulse purchases very easy. You're browsing a web site to do with some aspect of a hobby, and you follow a link marked "this book explains the technique in detail." The link takes you directly to the book's entry in the Amazon catalog. You find that the book has a moderate price discount which pays for the shipping. Sold!

Amazon is a savvy and innovative company. Its business model is amazing. It charges a customer's credit card on shipping a book, and gets the funds from the credit card company within a day. It doesn't pay the book distributor for a month or two. So Amazon has free use of its suppliers' money for 45 days. Very few other companies can achieve this. It is already the third largest bookseller in the United States, on line or off line, and it is expanding into Europe. Currently it is working on localizing its site, so customers in France can read sales literature in French, and buy French products. Annualized turnover was about $360M in 1998, all from on-line trading. Amazon is a new company and currently reinvests all its income in growing the business. The business plan predicts the company will become profitable within a couple more years. The number of active customers grew 50 percent in the first quarter of 1998, and the majority of these were repeat customers, so the prospects are bright for this e-commerce retail pioneer. The Amazon on-line retailing site runs on a Sun Microsystem Starfire server.

Summary

- The Internet has always been a successful example of self-regulation. It has grown and adapted to meet market needs.

- The Internet is essentially "dial-tone for data"—a transmission medium for (mostly) nonvoice communication. It has expanded exponentially in recent years and some industry experts predict that it will outgrow the phone network within a few years.

- Now that the security and privacy infrastructure is in place, the hottest growth area on the Internet is web-based commerce. Since there is a computer at both ends of an e-commerce transaction, a wide variety of automated processing becomes possible, such as comparison shopping, inventory control, and order fulfillment.

- Microsoft is establishing a strong presence in all areas of e-commerce, in both framework and content. Society's interests will be better served by open competition for e-commerce business, rather than early domination by a single vendor.

- E-commerce is a natural evolution of existing business methods like TV advertising and placing orders by phone. It combines these elements with the Internet as a communication channel. On-line retailing is a lot cheaper and quicker than other methods of displaying and selling goods.

CHAPTER

7

- What Is Security?

- Web Site Security Measures

- Java Security Measures
  - Language
  - Sandbox
  - Code signing

- Security Comparison: Java, ActiveX, Plug-Ins

- Case Study 4: Lack of Security with DNA

- Why DNA's ActiveX Is Unsafe for Internet Use

- Finer-Grained Security

- Other Security Issues

- Summary

Distributed Processing Security Issues

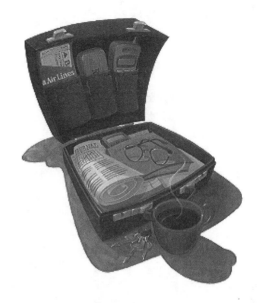

What Is Security?

The term *computer security* means controlling access to the resources of your computer system: the files, screen, peripherals and CPU cycles. Even on a single-user system, like Windows 98, security is an issue because the user may inadvertently bring a computer virus onto the system and destroy valuable work. Proper computer security relies on being able to grant or deny access based on who an individual is. Computer security is considered to have three aspects:

- **Identification / authentication**
  "Are you who you say you are?"

- **Resource control / confidentiality**
  "Do you have permission to view/modify these bits?"

- **Integrity**
  "Can I ensure that the right bits are there and that no one else has changed them?"

Before we examine what these aspects mean in the context of Java, we need to place computer security in its overall context. As is often said, there is no such thing as 100 percent security. Locks can break, guards can be bribed, disaffected employees can tape the conversations of executives, and doors can be left open by the cleaners. Computer security is one aspect of the overall assurance of an organization, and it should match the level of care taken by the rest of the organization. This is the "a steel door doesn't secure a straw hut" maxim.

There is a trade-off in cost versus benefit for all security measures. Each organization needs to decide where it is along that curve and institute the appropriate security policies, including computer security policies. Figure 7–1 illustrates the trade-offs.

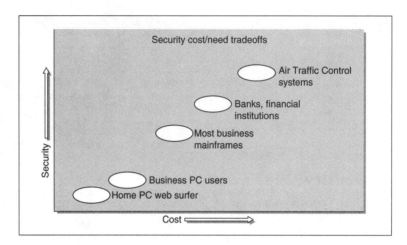

Figure 7–1
Security Cost/Need Trade-offs

An individual PC user who goes web surfing for fun will generally prefer the most open kind of access. This kind of user should be able to download everything that takes his or her fancy, without constantly being bombarded with warning messages and restrictions. At the other end of the spectrum, the government computers that implement air traffic control need to be highly secure, both physically and logically. People's lives depend on the ready availability of accurate information to the authorized system users. This kind of system should probably be isolated from the main corporate network.

In terms of existing computer systems, the default, out-of-the-box product security mechanisms vary across the spectrum, as shown in Figure 7–2. Windows NT is the first Microsoft operating system to offer any appreciable support for security, although it is not configured that way out of the box. Windows 95/98 have no built-in security mechanism, and cannot have any imposed on top because the OS framework is not there. A basic level of security is essential for cooperative distributed systems.

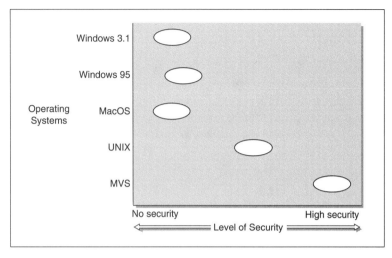

Figure 7-2
Security Spectrum

Web Site Security Measures

A web site is a company asset, and it needs to be protected like any company asset. The protection must cover two fronts. First, a system administrator needs to make sure that the web site doesn't provide a conduit for unauthorized access to the internal computer network. Second, the administrator must make sure that the web site itself is secure against unauthorized changes.

Securing a web site is not rocket science. It just takes diligent and continued application of a few simple procedures. Alas, most web servers do not come configured for security by default, and it's all too easy to overlook some of the necessary steps. The first and most obvious precaution is to set up a firewall. The firewall, named after the panel that separates car passengers from the heat of the engine, is a system that examines all incoming IP requests and passes through harmless ones (like retrieval of a web page from the server) while refusing unauthorized requests (like remote login to a system behind the firewall).

In December 1996, computer security consultant Dan Farmer published the results of a security survey that he conducted on the Internet. He examined several thousand sites, including government organizations, worldwide banks, credit unions, media organizations, and other on-line businesses. These were all sites that by the nature of their business should be expected to be more secure

than the average site. Farmer looked for specific vulnerabilities to known loop-holes, and he published the results of his survey at
`http://www.InfoWar.Com`.

Farmer found that over 60 percent of the sites he examined had some vulnerability that would allow unauthorized access or file removal. Worse still, Farmer found that these financial and federal organizations were potentially twice as vulnerable as the sites in a control group of 500 randomly selected sites. In other words, the sites that most need to protect themselves are least effective at doing so.

Farmer estimated that 10 to 20 percent of the sites he examined could be pene-trated by using techniques like:

- NIS attacks (anticipating and sending out fake replies to network enquiries)
- Packet capture or "snarfing" (eavesdropping on packets that are routed through a site)
- IP spoofing (sending out forged packets)
- Subverting other trusted hosts and other techniques.

These figures don't include nontechnical means of subverting security, like insider attacks. Nor do they include simple denial of service attacks like the ping of death.

The value of Farmer's findings is twofold. First, it's clear that many sites are ill-informed about the large number of potential security problems on their Internet gateway systems. And second, despite this, their systems function anyway. A lot of press coverage has been given to some high-profile, and highly embarrassing, web site changes, but most organizations are more worried about getting the word out than they are about crackers modifying their message.

Like any powerful tool, Internet communications can be used for good or bad. No less an organization than the U.S. Central Intelligence Agency found this out the hard way in September 1996. Angry over a court case in their country, Swedish crackers electronically broke into the web site of the United States government's spy agency and changed it to slam the Swedish prosecutor Bo Skarinder, urging him to "stop lying." The CIA web site used to look like Figure 7–3(a).

Why does a spy agency have a web site? Well, they have phones don't they? Per-haps the question is better phrased as why there are still organizations which don't have web sites. The renegade Swedish programmers focused world atten-tion on their grievances (and gave the CIA a bad case of embarrassment) by changing the web site title to "Central Stupidity Agency" and modifying the con-tent to look like Figure 7–3(b).

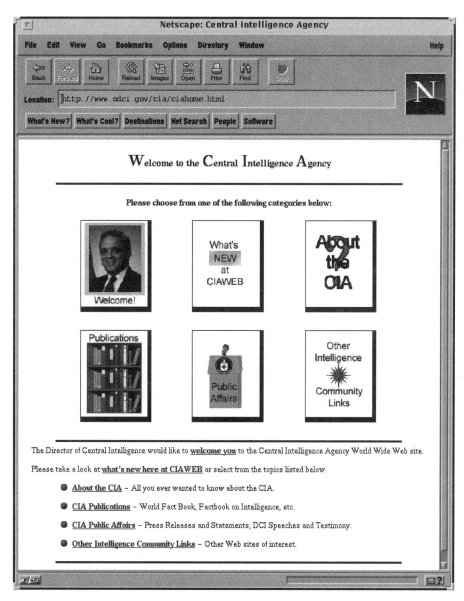

Figure 7–3 (a) CIA Web Site

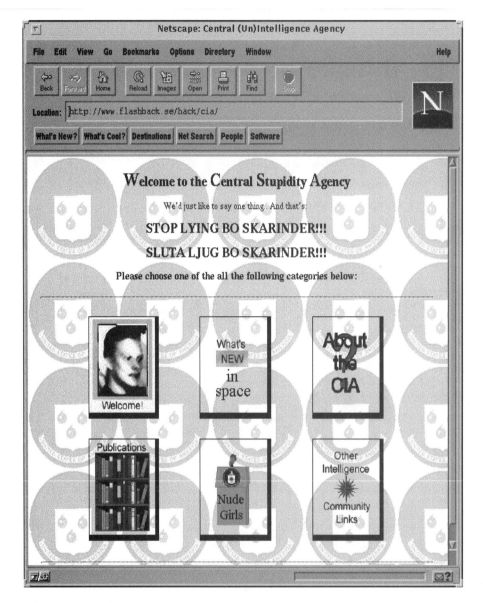

Figure 7–3 (b)
CIA Web Site After Modification by Swedish Crackers

The modified CIA page was on line for about 12 hours before the CIA learned of it and pulled the plug. A CIA spokesman emphasized that this system was not connected to any internal CIA systems and there was no breach of national security.

Was the prank juvenile? Certainly. Wrong? Of course. But these Swedish programmers also highlighted the lack of security on the Internet. A month previously, a different group had modified the U.S. Department of Justice home page to read "U.S. Department of Injustice" among other changes, in a protest against the overzealous Computer Decency Act of 1996. That law was later ruled unconstitutional by a federal court.

The present state of web site security is that there is too much complacency and not enough competency. Any new technology that we add needs to go in the opposite direction: to bolster computer security, not add to the problems.

Java Security Measures

When Java programs run as stand-alone applications, they do not introduce any new or special considerations of security. The same issues of good computer security apply equally to Java applications and to applications written in any other languages: Secure the equipment physically, make regular backup copies of the data for the application, don't give an application more privileges than it needs to run, don't acquire critical software from sources you do not trust, and don't leave confidential data files in publicly accessible places.

The single-user do's and don'ts of computer security
- Do secure the computer equipment physically.
- Do make regular backup copies of data and programs.
- Do keep your password private.
- Don't install software from sources you do not trust.
- Don't leave confidential data in publicly accessible places.
- Don't give an application more privileges than it needs to run.

Security for Java Applets

Java applets, like any framework for remote distribution of executables, bring up issues of computer security that must be addressed. When you browse a web page containing an applet, you implicitly invite that applet to come over to your computer system and start executing in your environment. This is rather like throwing open the front door to your home and yelling outside "come on in" to anyone who happens to be passing.

As we have already seen, a web page with an applet can be anywhere on the Internet, and the applet could have been written by anyone. You automatically start that applet running on your system simply by browsing the web page that contains it. There may not even be a visible indication that there is an applet on that page! Without serious attention paid to the security aspect, Java applets (or any remote distribution scheme, such as ActiveX) would be too risky to run except in controlled circumstances on private nets because the executable could be an innocent and useful program, or it could contain destructive bugs, or it could even have been written with malicious intent.

Security Measures for Applets

Fortunately, the designers of the Java system realized the need for security, and designed it into the Java system from the outset. They carefully put strong protective measures in place to allow applets to run without compromising a system. The protective measures applied to applets are of three major types:

1. Language
2. Sandbox (disabled access to features)
3. Code signing

The goal is to allow browsers to safely run untrusted applets on a trusted system.

The first line of defense: Language

Java is inherently more secure than many older languages because it is more rigorous in many areas. In particular, in Java:

- Array accesses are checked to be within bounds at run time. Deliberately overrunning an array in C to overwrite the stack was the basic method of attack used by the November 1988 Internet worm. It was also the vulnerability discovered in many PC mail programms in summer 1998. This cannot happen in Java programs.

- Only legal type conversions are allowed. The compiler will not permit an object to be converted to any arbitrary type. This restriction ensures that private data stays private and prevents access to variables of the run-time system.

- Java programs do not use pointers explicitly. C++ programmers often use pointers to access strings and arrays, but these are both supported as built-in classes in Java, and error-prone, low-level techniques cannot be used. The Java programmer cannot create or modify physical addresses, ensuring that a Java program cannot tamper with memory.

- The compiler enforces the rule that constants cannot change. In C and C++, constant data can be modified through a pointer.

- All method calls are checked to ensure that the method is being invoked on the correct type of object.

These language rules mean that there is no way to "trick" a Java program into inadvertently subverting the system. However, it does not provide full protection. A Java compiler could be written that did not enforce these rules, or a program could be written that overtly destroys your data by deleting files. This case is prevented by the second line of defense: the sandbox. The sandbox protects against illegal bytecode modification by examining the bytecode before running it.

The second line of defense: Sandbox
A browser runs an applet in what has come to be called a "sandbox"—meaning a rigidly constrained environment that does not have access to your system resources. The name comes from the image of little children playing, each playing independently in his or her own sandbox. Whatever structures one child builds and knocks down has no effect on any of the others.

You can think of the applet sandbox as being like the firewall that separates and protects your internal systems from the Internet. The sandbox is like a firewall on your system built around any applets that you import from the Internet. Thus, even if someone put malicious code in an applet, the sandbox makes sure it cannot access your disk to read your confidential data and transmit it off site.

When an applet is retrieved over the network, the bytecode is examined before it is executed. This process has been given the grand-sounding name of "verification." Verifying an applet means ensuring that it is not able to replace any of the installed run-time components. Then, the bytecode is checked to make sure it adheres to all the restrictions mentioned above. The verifier ensures that each operation has the correct number and type of operands and does not leave the stack in an inconsistent state. Doing most of the checking as the code is loaded (rather than as it is run) is a potential weakness in total security but has not proven a problem in practice. It is done for better speed at run-time. Stack overflow and underflow are checked for as execution proceeds. Finally, the sandbox restrictions are imposed.

Some people have criticized the Java sandbox as rendering applets useless. They say that if a Java applet can't read or write files, it is useless. The criticism is inaccurate because it is an oversimplification to say that Java applets can't do file I/O. The ability to control I/O has been delegated to the browser. A Java class called SecurityManager is part of each run-time system and sets the policy. The browser vendor provides a default version of the class, and the class controls whether remote applets can write to files. So, the browser user (or the MIS department providing the browser configuration files) sets the policy on applet I/O.

A sandbox is like a room built out of firewalls. Applets are executed inside a sandbox by default, so they cannot access the private or vulnerable resources of your system. This is a representative but not exhaustive list of the restrictions on remotely accessed applets.

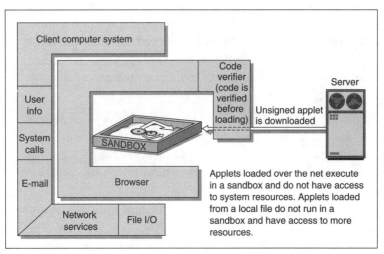

By default, an applet accessed over the net:
- cannot read or write files;
- cannot open a socket connection, except to the server that it came from;
- cannot start up a program on your system;
- cannot call native (non-Java) code.

Applets accessed from a local file system (rather than over the net) are allowed more privileges. They can only be on your local file system with your permission, so it is presumed that you trust them.

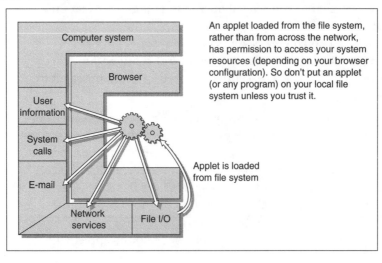

One common choice is to make the browser pop up a dialog when the applet requests I/O. The user can decide whether to allow it or not, based on the kind of page he or she is browsing.

As an example of the different policies, you can do file I/O (on the client) from within Sun's appletviewer, but the same applet fails from within Communicator and Explorer. There is some pressure for browser vendors to make the `Securi-tyManager` class more configurable by the user.

The other way that Java applets can do file I/O is indirectly, by communicating back to their server. This is standard procedure, and trivial to implement. It requires a file system process running on the server that served the applet to listen for requests from applets and act on them. This does not break security, as the server that served the applet can be assumed to know what the applet is doing.

The third line of defense: Code signing

The Java security goal has been to start with a conservative approach and then add features as secure ways to accomplish them were devised. Accordingly, the JDK 1.1 release (which shipped in February 1997) introduced code signing. Code signing is a way of applying a digital signature to an applet. This signature uses crypto-graphic techniques to assure the downloader that the applet comes from the organization it claims to and that it has not been changed or corrupted in transmission.

The goal is to be able to tell if an applet is trusted or untrusted. We want to allow trusted applets access to our computer systems, but we must still ensure that untrusted applets cannot steal or damage information on a computer running a Java-enabled browser. Users can configure their browsers with a list of organizations that they trust to have nondestructive code. Applets from these organizations can then be run automatically with more privileges, including file access.

The signed class scheme uses a public key encryption scheme, which centers on codes that take two keys. One key encrypts a message, and a second, different, key decrypts it. The clever part is that knowing one key does not provide any hint about what the other key is. It's like encrypting things is done by translating them into Martian; the encryption key is an English-to-Martian dictionary, and the decryption key is a Martian-to-English dictionary. So the key used for decryption can even be made public (hence the name "public key"). You pick up the decryption key from a source you trust to give you the right one, perhaps reading it off the company's annual report.

A "signed class" has all the files, images, sound files, etc., that make up the applet bundled together in a single file, known as a Java Archive or "JAR file." Then, an identification string and some other data are stored in the class in encrypted form. Anyone can decrypt the class by using the public decryption key and check that the

encrypted values match the plain text values. If they do match, the class has not been tampered with, and hence we can trust the class as coming from where it says it comes from, which is the first of the three security essentials. As a side effect, code signing prevents a software virus from being added to a program. The changed bytes would mean that the class no longer matched its encrypted signature.

Are Java applets vulnerable to viruses?

No. Java applets are not vulnerable to viruses. There has never been a known instance of rogue Java code secretly traveling from system to system. Although Java applets travel from server to client systems, Sun has invested a lot of effort into making sure that Java has a strong security model, precisely to avoid the kinds of viruses that are common in the PC world.

In the case of applets, they are run in what is called a "sandbox"—meaning a rigidly constrained environment that does not have access to your system resources. Thus, even if someone put malicious code in an applet, it cannot access your disk to modify or delete files. Java applets are therefore not vulnerable to computer viruses. MS Windows viruses rely on code being executed automatically, either as part of a boot sequence or a word processor macro initialization. These opportunities don't exist in the Java world.

Java supports "signed classes" for applets and applications. These are classes that are cryptographically guaranteed to be tamper-resistant. Users can let these classes access some system resources, secure in the knowledge that the origins of the class are guaranteed. Both forms of security (sandbox and signed classes) are needed.

I recently browsed a web page in Belgium which mentioned "Java viruses" as though they existed (they don't). Puzzled, I sent e-mail to the webmaster to ask for more details. It transpired that the web site was created by a 14-year-old Belgian boy who had misunderstood the terminology used in press reports (English was not his first language). The Web is like any other media: just because you read something doesn't make it true. You need to ask intelligent questions, consider the source, and check facts for yourself.

When you decrypt something by using the Sun decryption key, it will only make sense if it was encrypted with the Sun encryption key. Any other key produces gibberish. Hence when the class loader of your browser decrypts something and it makes sense, the browser can be sure that the material comes from where it says it comes. An evil hacker cannot make changes to a class and wrap it up with its signature again. No one except Sun has the ability to encrypt a class with Sun's secret encrypting key.

Code signing provides a guarantee about the origin of an applet. It is like buying shrink-wrapped software in a retail store. The printed label says who produced it, and the shrinkwrap shows that the product has not been tampered with since it left the factory. But code signing does not provide any assurance about what the applet does. It does not guarantee that the applet will not format your hard drive and send your e-mail file to the *New York Times*. It does not protect you against the author of the applet making some mistake that erases your data, or worse.

Note that the sandbox and the verifier depend on bytecodes. If software is translated into native code, not only does it lose platform independence, but it can no longer be inspected for security. This is the flaw that makes ActiveX an inherently nonsecure technology.

The JDK 1.2 release brings easier access to the security API and the ability to have a finer level of control over access to system resources. It is easier to configure security policy, and the policy can be applied equally to Java applications as well as to applets.

Early History of Security Attacks

When Java was first launched, the source code was also made available free to anyone who wanted to look at it (there was a charge if you wanted to build it into a commercial product). This meant that universities could easily examine the applet security code, looking for weaknesses and mistakes. A team at Princeton university was particularly adept, and a number of bugs were found by them and other researchers in early versions.

When bugs in the Java implementation were found, they were quickly resolved. From the outset, Java engineers had the goal of safely allowing users to download and run code from anywhere on the Internet. Essentially no security goals were set for earlier systems like Windows 3.1 and Windows 95 and these systems have no security architecture. The various browser plug-ins have no security at all. Users who are interested in security should consider the system they are currently using and ask what security policies they are following. Anyone using Windows on a PC, or a browser, or MIME-enabled e-mail software, or a word processor that reads in and executes macros by default, is already running a system with multiple security loopholes. Increased use of Java generally increases system security, although as pointed out at the beginning of the chapter, a steel door will not secure a grass hut.

A key distinction to make is between "model" and "implementation." Implementations are written, refined, changed, found lacking, and improved. When implementation bugs are identified and fixed, the security works as planned. But a security flaw that remains in the model would be very bad news indeed, as it would mean that secure implementations were just not possible. Fortunately, computer scientists are convinced that is not the case, though the media are often confused in their reporting of this critical point. With the JDK 1.2 release, there are no known security flaws in the Java language or its security design. It's possible that more flaws will be uncovered in the programming, though the most recent weaknesses have been of the type "If I can plant this file on your system, then this applet can take advantage of it in this way."

Security Comparison: Java, DNA, Plug-Ins

Let's compare the Java security model, the security model for DNA from Microsoft, and security for browser plug-ins. (DNA is a family of Microsoft technologies including the ActiveX framework for remote execution of MS-Windows code; ActiveX was itself the new name for network OLE). Table 7-1 compares the three essentials of computer security for the three models.

Table 7-1 Security Comparison

	Java	DNA's ActiveX	Plug-Ins
• Identification and authentication	YES, code signing	YES, code signing	NO
• Resource access /confidentiality	YES, sandbox	NO	NO
• Integrity	YES, verifier	NO	NO

As you can see, plug-ins offer no computer security whatever. The plug-in is a binary program that has complete access to the same computer resources that you have access to. It can delete files or copy them to a remote system. What makes this freedom acceptable is that you always know when you are running a plug-in, and (unlike applets and DNA ActiveX controls) a plug-in doesn't appear on your system unless you explicitly ask for it.

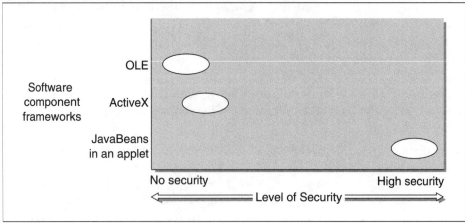

Figure 7–4
Out of Box Security

As described earlier in this chapter, Java offers a full range of configurable security measures, with features to support all three elements of a security architecture. You can safely use Java on the Internet and on local networks without fear of revealing private data, or otherwise compromising your systems.

However, it is a different story with Microsoft DNA. DNA supports only the part of a security architecture that authenticates a user, which by itself is inadequate for computer security, and does not support the concepts of a fine-grained access control, nor data integrity. Let's examine the implications.

Even with code signing, DNA security is all or nothing: either the feature is totally disabled or it is totally enabled and all the resources of your system become available to the DNA (ActiveX) control author. When used on a single-user system such as Windows 95 or 98, the ActiveX part of DNA opens even worse possibilities—it allows the malevolent to create fake audit trails, cover up tracks, and generally operate under concealment. Figure 7–4 shows the level of security for different software frameworks.

Case Study 4: Lack of Security with DNA

In August 1996, computer consultant Fred McLain dramatically demonstrated the security problems with the ActiveX part of DNA. He created a web page that, when browsed from a Windows system, shut down and powered off the computer! He called this the "Internet Exploder" parodying Microsoft's Internet Explorer browser. McLain created the control to counter Microsoft's claim that ActiveX was secure.

The web page contained an explanation about the dangers of ActiveX, along with a link to the page with the control. If you followed the link, it provided a further warning, and then powered off your computer system using the Energy Star power management feature in the BIOS. Microsoft tried to rebut McLain's demonstration by pointing out that he did not use the code signing feature.

So McLain applied for and automatically received a Certificate of Authority from Verisign. Verisign is the Mountain View, California, company working with Microsoft on ActiveX security. He then signed the control, using Microsoft's ActiveX Software Development Kit, which can be downloaded from Microsoft's web page. Verisign's certificate, when combined with Microsoft's Authenticode technology, tells users who published the ActiveX control, and makes the code tamper resistant. Users can then choose whether to let their browser download the control. Now, naive users believed "Internet Exploder" was harmless because it was digitally signed, but it still shut down their systems in exactly the same way.

DNA security is a "blame assignment" architecture

Computer security has three aspects:
- identification and authentication
- resource access and confidentiality
- data integrity

The ActiveX part of DNA was originally marketed as providing computer security, but it supports just one of the three essentials (identification) and lacks the other two.

ActiveX supports user identification by code signing, which tells you where a piece of code originated. But if that piece of code is buggy or carries a hidden virus, or is deliberately malicious and destroys or publishes your files, code signing doesn't help one whit. Code doesn't even have to be deliberately malicious to bring down your system. The ping of death was a simple buffer overrun bug that was discovered by accident.

Computer consultant Glenn Vanderburg comments that because of its shortcomings, the ActiveX security model is best considered a "blame assignment architecture." After something has gone badly wrong, it might tell you who did it, but it doesn't protect you from something going wrong in the first place. Since the "Internet Exploder" and the "Bank Robbery using DNA's ActiveX" incidents, Microsoft has soft-pedaled the ActiveX name, reverting to OLE in some cases. However the technology is still very much in use, and is a central part of the DNA initiative introduced in spring 1998.

Large companies that care about security usually prohibit ActiveX. According to a February 3, 1997 story in Network World magazine, Lockheed Martin Corp has banned ActiveX on its intranet. Boeing Corp has similarly decreed that ActiveX is not to be deployed or used on company systems.

"ActiveX controls can perform any operation that Windows can. It can wipe your hard disk with no record, look up your TurboTax records and e-mail them to someone, or install a virus that doesn't go off for a year. Even though you may have a signed control and have seen the certificate, it's a dangerous technology. I advise people not to use Microsoft Internet Explorer—it's too dangerous," McLain said.

McLain concluded wryly, "This effectively addresses Microsoft's rebuttal to my claims of a security hole in their implementation of ActiveX." The Internet Exploder was intended to profile the risk inherent in using ActiveX. As such, McLain chose a harmless but dramatic demonstration of powering the system down. An actual attack could be more subtle and could cover up its tracks so you would not know where to assign the blame.

Lawyers acting for the Redmond monopoly swooped down on Fred McLain, and forced him to take the ActiveX control off line (the argument was that he had allegedly broken a clause in the Verisign license agreement promising that a control will not do anything that damages users). If he had been based outside the United States, there would have been no practical way to force the control off the Internet.

Why DNA's ActiveX Is Unsafe for Internet Use

You can be sure of the origin of an ActiveX component, but you have no way to judge the safety of running the component. Will an unexpected bug trash your file system or crash your system? Will a malicious programmer plant a sleeper virus that only becomes effective months later? Will the ActiveX control secretly send your corporate data to an e-mail address in Panama? ActiveX has no way to safeguard against these problems. DNA's ActiveX offers only the same kind of security as shrink-wrapped software, except that if a retailer sells you software with a virus you have recourse against the store. If your system is trashed by an ActiveX control downloaded from a web site in Bulgaria, there is little you can do.

Browsers can be configured to refuse all ActiveX code, to pop up a window asking if it should be accepted, or to accept it without interaction. This model works fine for low volumes, but it is inadequate with normal use of a browser. Rather than be bothered with the frequent repetition of a question they don't understand, most users will select the configuration that allows code to run without the question being asked. The key issue is the more-or-less automatic downloading of executable programs. People might install half a dozen shrink-wrapped software packages on their PC in a year. They might encounter and run several thousand ActiveX controls while web surfing in the same 12 months. Even the company firewall provides no protections, as an ActiveX control can compromise anything accessible from the PC inside the firewall. The Authenticode code signature only tells you "who did this" after the fact.

Most computer security experts recommend that companies totally disable the use of ActiveX over the Internet. It simply cannot be made secure. Even when using ActiveX on a company's internal intranet, precautions have to be taken to guard against "time bombs" and other unauthorized changes by insiders. Before ActiveX existed, code that was written on one system stayed on that system unless physically transported elsewhere. With ActiveX, code is pulled to other systems by web browsing. This means that denying people physical access to systems with confidential data is no longer adequate. You must now deny users of those systems access to "potentially dangerous places," including internal places

ActiveX used for Information Super Highway robbery

In February 1997, CNN reported that a group of German crackers had created an ActiveX control that could transfer money from unsuspecting web browsers. The Chaos Computer Club of Hamburg demonstrated on German TV how to use ActiveX to transfer funds out of an individual's bank account. When a user browses the web site containing the ActiveX control, the control is downloaded to the user's system where it looks for the popular Quicken financial software. A Java applet cannot be used to break system security this way because it runs in a sandbox and cannot access other parts of the user's system. If the ActiveX control finds Quicken, it puts a funds transfer order on the Quicken list. The next time the user dials up to the bank, that false order is automatically carried out along with any real ones.

Microsoft's manager for Internet platforms acknowledged "ActiveX will get a bad rap here" and classified the issue as one of user education.

that might have controls written by malcontented employees. One security model that avoids all these issues is to avoid using ActiveX altogether. Another is to mandate the use of Java in place of DNA.

Finer-Grained Security

It should be clear at this point that "all or nothing" security models are inadequate. The only way you can be sure that ActiveX won't compromise your system security is not to use it—to disable it completely. Java applets in the sandbox are better—you can run them with safety, but they cannot access any of your files and so are of limited value.

What are needed are some intermediate points between "anything goes" and "confined to the sandbox" access. With a sandbox in place, signing code is the next step. The way that signed applets work is shown in Figure 7–5. With the origin of code known, the sandbox can provide different levels of privilege on demand or on checking with the user. One level of permission may be "This applet can write up to 10 Mb of data and use up to 6 minutes of CPU time." A simpler approach might link the permission to the intended use of the applet.

For example, an applet might ask for "typical word processor privileges." This access would give it the right to read all files with a certain extension and to create new ones of that type. It could look at and import image files but not delete them. Another permission level might be "games privileges." This access allows reading and writing of a single file in a special, user-defined, game-scores directory, and users know that they won't be putting themselves at major risk. Because of its

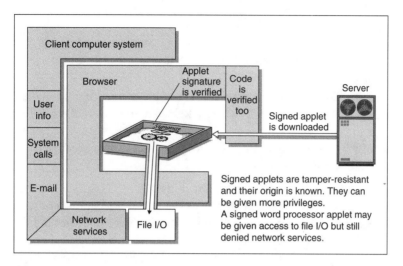

Figure 7–5
Signed Applets Have More Privileges

reliance on native code, there's no way for ActiveX to offer similar levels of access control. Fine-grained levels of security and simpler configuration came in with the Java 1.2 release in fall 1998.

Other Security Issues

There are a number of other computer security issues to be aware of. These are of lesser significance than the issues already outlined, but still important.

Decompiling

Java class files (the output from the compiler) are rich enough that a determined effort can reconstruct the Java source. The process of examining a binary to regenerate the source code, known as "decompilation," has always been possible (and has always been done) for all programming languages. Investigators were looking at C source code of the 1988 Internet worm within hours of isolating the binary program. Java makes it a little simpler to decompile by embedding more information like data names and types in the object code.

Many different kinds of software have been decompiled, from Microsoft Windows (by ISVs looking for the undocumented system calls) to the Forth interpreter in Postscript printers. One engineer even decompiled the software in an Apple Newton, and published his own API manual. Enterprising students have written various decompilers for Java. Even more enterprising people sell software tools that foil decompilers. You cannot prevent attempts to decompile any software product, but you can make it more difficult. The best protection for software ultimately lies in the proper use of the legal system to protect patented works.

Denial-of-Service Attacks

A "denial-of-service" attack is one where the malefactor steals intangible computer resources like CPU time, rather than tangible data. The ping of death mentioned earlier was a denial-of-service attack. When your system crashes, it is unavailable to you for the time it takes to reboot. Denial of service means that some part of your system resources are not available to you because they are being diverted by a third party.

It's very difficult, if not impossible, for a web browser to completely prevent denial-of-service attacks. The Java applet system does not claim to prevent denial-of-service attacks; indeed, no comparable system claims to prevent denial-of-service attacks. One scenario involving denial of service is to publish an attractive web page, say, an applet with a popular computer game like Doom or Quake. As well as the game applet being downloaded, a second applet is sent over that (say) calculates a million digits of pi and sends the result back to the server. The applet author has stolen some computer time from you. In the extreme case, the applet might put a big enough load on your system to make it unavailable for use by you.

Encryption

Computer encryption is a controversial issue in the United States. The concept is straightforward: encryption means transforming information into a meaningless bit stream that can later be changed back if the correct key is held. Encryption allows computer users to keep secret information secret. Even if a cracker gains access to the files, in encrypted form they yield no information.

The controversy centers around the United States government's desire to regulate encryption so that people use only codes that the government can easily break. Some governments, like that of France, prevent their citizens from using encryption altogether. Similarly, the British government recently drafted draconian regulations to require providers of encryption software to operate under government license, and to place a copy of all the secret keys in escrow. In the United States that restriction would be unconstitutional, and thus not merely illegal but against the fundamental principles on which the nation was founded. To get around this, the United States government over several successive administrations has taken the position that strong encryption software is a munition, like machine guns, tanks, and artillery pieces. Software that includes strong encryption, like the

Netscape Navigator browser and the UNIX operating system, can be sold domestically, but sales of the software overseas are subject to the International Traffic In Arms Regulations!

It is inconvenient and expensive to maintain two different copies of a product, so most software vendors just use weak encryption (which can be exported, since the United States government can break it easily) in all products. The software export ban does not actually prevent any countries overseas from having strong encryption. There are plenty of non-U.S.-based suppliers to fill the gap. The practical effect is to discourage the use and adoption of strong encryption inside the USA. And that, say some commentators, is the real agenda. This belief is bolstered by other evidence.

The United States government has tried several times to impose a standard for other encryption equipment (telephones and the like) sold to federal agencies. The proposed standards (the Clipper chip was the best known) all provided some way for the United States government to read the encrypted traffic. As the purchaser of equipment made to this standard, the government would already be able to read its own traffic so it must have been intended to make other domestic traffic crackable. Industry watchers say that the United States government was trying to use its purchasing muscle to impose a single domestic standard that had the "crackable" feature it liked. In December 1996, a federal judge in San Francisco ruled that the United States government's restraints on software were an unconstitutional limit on free speech (another basis of American culture). The saga is still unfolding.

The other effect of banning the export of strong encryption software is that United States software companies lose all overseas sales. This hurts, and for a period of several years, software industry groups have been negotiating with the United States government to have the ban lifted. So far the results have been inconclusive. The government is adamant that it wants to be able to crack American codes that are used overseas, and it has made a number of proposals involving "key escrow" schemes. These involve a third party who holds a copy of the secret key and will hand it over to the Feds on receipt of a United States court order. So far the gulf between the government and the industry has not been bridged yet.

Trade on the Internet would really benefit from a standard, common, globally accepted, strong encryption protocol. That stands little chance of happening while the United States government maintains its current position. The Council of European Professional Informatics Societies (CEPIS), an organization with nearly 200,000 professional members in its 20 member societies, issued a policy statement on this topic. CEPIS states that governmental restrictions on encryption actually put security at risk.

The CEPIS statement summarizes the issues well, and calls on all governments to remove restrictions on the use of encryption.

Netscape's SSL

Finally, you may hear the term *SSL* in a security context. SSL is Netscape's Secure Socket Layer—the software encryption protocol behind the Netsite secure server and the Netscape Navigator browser. It is a security protocol that prevents eavesdropping, tampering, or message forgery over the Internet. (So it's the big three again: privacy, integrity, and identification.) The current version was released in March 1996. Microsoft soon copied Netscape's work, and added a compatible copy of SSL to Internet Explorer.

SSL is a layer above TCP/IP and below the application layers, so you can transparently add SSL to anything that uses sockets: telnet, ftp, mosaic, httpd. You need it at both the client and server end. It uses RSA data encryption and relies on signed digital certificates from a trusted third party.

If a URL starts with https:// instead of http://, it is coming from a secure server. Netscape wants to make it a standard, and they developed an ANSI C library reference implementation called SSLRef, which they submitted to the IETF. If you use Netscape Navigator 3.0 or later as your browser, you automatically have access to SSL when you browse secure sites. There's a web site at `http://psych.psy.uq.oz.au/~ftp/Crypto` with a public domain implementation.

Internet Security versus Openness

The Internet was designed for the open exchange of information, and despite the lack of a security infrastructure, it remains a force for great good. On December 8, 1996, the *New York Times* reported that when Serbian president Slobodan Milosevic tried to muzzle journalists in the country by shutting down the independent Belgrade radio station B-92, he spawned a technologically based backlash. Tens of thousands of students, professionals, professors, and journalists immediately connected their computers to the Internet, and the radio station switched its output to a live audio feed across the Internet. And the radio station continued to use its web site to report (at `http://www.xs4all.nl/opennet`) on the protests that were sparked by the government's annulment of local elections won by the opposition.

A similar situation occurred in China during the Tienamen Massacre in 1989. After protestors were killed by the Chinese security forces, the Chinese government imposed a news clampdown. Chinese computer science students raced to their computer terminals to e-mail their friends and colleagues in the West with

Council of European Professional Informatics Societies (CEPIS)
POLICY STATEMENT
Governmental Restrictions on Encryption Products Put Security at Risk

Worldwide, there is a political debate regarding the virtue or otherwise of a control of encryption, in particular whether the import, export, and production of cryptographic tools and their use should be restricted. In several countries legal regulations exist, in some others steps are undertaken towards such regulations. At present an OECD Committee is drafting guidelines on cryptographic policy.

But there are concerns; the Council of European Professional Informatics Societies (CEPIS) —with nearly 200,000 professionals in its 20-member societies, the largest European association of professionals working in information technology (IT)—has agreed to the following statement:

Should one wish to employ electronic communication as the main vehicle for commercial and personal interaction, then one ought to be assured, and be able to prove, that messages are

- not disclosed to unauthorized recipients (confidentiality),
- not tampered with (integrity),
- shown to be from the senders stated (authenticity).

It has always been an aim of secure reliable communication to comply with these requirements. The more the information society becomes a reality, the more enterprises, administrations and private persons urgently need the absolute assurance that these requirements are met.

To achieve this, so called "strong" cryptography is available. Several tools based on strong crypto-algorithms are in the public domain and offered on the Internet, others are integrated within commercial products.

A different technique for confidential and even unobservable communication is to use steganography, where secret data are hidden within larger inconspicuous everyday data in such a way that third parties are unable even to detect their existence. Hence there is no way of preventing unobservable secret communication.

To enable surveillance of electronic messaging, many criminal and national security investigators, such as police and secret services, demand access to keys used for encrypted communication. In order for this to be effective, escrowing (bonding) of these keys is advocated. However, for the reasons given above, key escrow (i.e., depositing copies of the keys with a "trusted third party," including back ups) cannot even guarantee effective monitoring. Moreover, key escrow already constitutes a risk for the secrecy of the keys and therefore for the secrecy of the data. This risk is exacerbated in cases of central escrowing.

Besides, the burdens of cost and administrative effort as well as the loss of trust in communications could be significant and are prone to deter individuals and organizations, especially small business users, from gaining the benefits of modern information and communications systems.

Effective electronic surveillance of digital networks is difficult and time consuming, and requires extensive resources. In particular, closed groups such as criminal organizations might even use steganographic techniques to avoid any detection short of physical access to the terminals they use. Thus restrictions on encryption may be of very limited help in the fight against organized crime. On the other hand, the essential security of business and private communication may be seriously imperiled and economically hampered should they be subjected to insufficiently secured key escrow.

On these grounds, CEPIS recommends the following:

(1)   The use of cryptography for identifying data corruption or authenticating people/organizations should be free of restrictions and encouraged by governments.

(2)   All individuals and organizations in the private and public sectors should be able to store and transmit data to others, with confidentiality protection appropriate for their requirements, and should have ready access to the technology to achieve this.

(3)   The opportunity for individuals or organizations in the private and public sectors to benefit from information systems should not be reduced by incommensurable measures considered necessary for the enforcement of law.

(4)   The governments of the world should agree on a policy relating to their access to other people's computerized data, while seeking the best technical advice available in the world on:

(4.1) whether and which access mechanisms to computerized data are an effective, efficient and adequate way to fight (organized) crime and mount effective prosecution of criminals, and

(4.2) how to implement the policy whilst minimizing the security risks to organizations and individual citizens.

(Evaluation and implementation of the policy will require regular review as the technology evolves).

Further Information:
Council of European Professional Informatics Societies (CEPIS)
7 Mansfield Mews
GB London W1M 9FJ
United Kingdom

Tel/fax: +44 171 637 5607
E-mail: cepis@bcs.org.uk
URL: http://www.bcs.org.uk/cepis.htm

The CEPIS Legal & Security Issues Network
URL: http://www.wi.leidenuniv.nl/~verrynst/cepislsi.html
E-mail: Kai Rannenberg (kara@iig.uni-freiburg.de), Secretary

1996-10-20

up-to-the-minute news of the massacre. For a period of several days, eyewitness reports from ordinary people distributed on the Internet formed the only news coming out of China.

Colombian government defeats rebel web site

The Revolutionary Armed Forces of Colombia (FARC) is a group of left-wing insurgents that has fought the Colombian government for over 30 years with roadblocks, armed attacks, and civil disobedience over agricultural landholdings. FARC has denounced the Colombian government for having links to drug trafficking, and the Colombian government has made the same accusation about FARC.

In 1995, FARC became the first guerrilla group to have a web site! FARC's home page contained on-line copies of their political magazine, *Resistencia*, and was hosted on a server in Mexico City. (No word yet on whether one of the new top-level domains blessed by InterNIC will be ".rev" for revolutionaries, insurrectionists, and mutineers.) The FARC site existed for about a year until the URL was published in El Tiempo, Colombia's biggest daily newspaper.

The very next day, the Mexican web site was abruptly pulled by the service provider without explanation. According to a Reuters press report of September 25, 1996, FARC's spokesman in Mexico City, Leon Calcarca, called it "an attack on freedom of expression" and blamed the censorship on pressure from the Colombian government.

This incident is highly unusual, not just for a guerrilla group having a web site, but also because a government was able to reach across national boundaries and persuade another government to shut down that web site. FARC won't be permanently deprived of a voice—all it need do is find a server in a less-pliable host nation a little further away. There are plenty to be found.

The story gets even more unusual. The Colombian government has been negotiating with the Fuerzas Armadas Revolucionarias de Colombia (FARC) guerrillas for the return of 60 Colombian soldiers held captive.

The negotiations were being done via personal meetings of intermediaries, which was slow and risky for all involved. In January 1997, the Colombian government suggested instead negotiating via e-mail! To everyone's surprise FARC declared that it was under the impression that it was already corresponding with the government in e-mail. The e-mail which claimed to be from the Colombian government is thought to have been sent by a right-wing faction trying to sabotage the dialog.

Governments generally have little power to regulate this kind of information dissemination. They can forcibly shut down web sites inside their national borders, but in the case of radio station B-92, the web site was located in Holland, which wasn't afraid to stand up to pressure from Belgrade. The web site was updated by the radio station from Belgrade by modem. The Serbian government would have had to shut down international phone service to prevent updates to the web site.

But even then, the people would find other ways to physically transport data out of the country. Society is changing in ways that do not allow despots to continue their tyranny in the dark.

The Internet imports local cultural values from all corners of the globe and places them under a bright light on your computer screen. Sometimes remote local values are different from our local values, and a kulturkampf (struggle between outlooks) occurs. The government of Singapore (a one-party state) requires all individual Internet users to be filtered by a proxy server at the ISP gateway. The law is phrased in terms of providing highbrow intellectual content and is administered by the city-state's broadcasting authority (`http://www.sba.gov.sg/`). But to foreigners it looks like the Singapore government is attempting to censor its citizens from adult and political content that it deems undesirable. The Singapore proxy server can block direct access to www.playboy.com, but it cannot prevent users from telnetting to a public access site in the United States or searching on the Deja News archive and reading all the forbidden information there.

In a famous remark, John Gilmore noted that "the Net interprets censorship as damage, and routes around it." The government of France passed a law in 1994 banning adverts in foreign languages, and the law has been applied to web sites in France. In 1997, a lawsuit was filed against the Lorraine, France, campus of Atlanta-based Georgia Tech University. The French campus has a web site (`http://www.georgiatech-metz.fr`) in English, and the University was sued to try to compel it to provide a French translation. Regulations like this seem repressive and ultimately self-defeating, but perhaps they just appear that way because of our local values. English is the undisputed language of Internet, just as it is the language of air-traffic control. The French are not immune to outside influences on their language. Reuters news agency reported in January 1997 that the government of France has changed the name of its elite airborne troops from the "Commandos de Recherche et d'Action en Profondeur" (Long-Range Search and Action Commandos) to "Groupement de Commandos Parachutistes" (Parachute Commando Group) because the new GCP acronym is better received outside France. Apparently, the French authorities were fed up with provoking mirth every time they threatened to hurl their CRAP at an enemy.

Mass electronic communication can now bring extraordinary influence to bear on governments and private companies alike. Pressure from the Internet forced the Intel Corporation to back away from its initial position that it would not replace defective versions of its Pentium processor. Early versions of the Pentium P5 chip had a faulty division instruction that gave inaccurate results for some operands. Intel was forced to acknowledge the problem in October 1994 when the finder, Professor Tom Nicely of Virginia, reported it on a newsgroup and the report was widely forwarded. Intel stonewalled for a couple of weeks, but public anger forced Intel to make a series of limited concessions, eventually offering a free replacement CPU chip. This cost Intel $475 million according to the San Jose *Mercury News* (Dec 26, 1995), and an untold sum in public good will. The crisis was an object lesson in how not to conduct public relations in the era of the Internet.

Summary

- Connecting a computer system to the networks of the outside world is like knocking a new doorway into your office building. Some care has to be taken that only authorized users carrying authorized data pass through the portal. Just browsing a web page sends over any embedded applets and executes them on your system. So some form of applet security check is required. Without a security check, an applet could, either through maliciousness or poor programming, corrupt your files or transmit the contents to points unknown.

- Java addresses the security situation by supporting several levels of resource access control. Some of Java's security is user-configurable, and some of it (to avoid a breach of security) is set by the system.

- Special attention has been given to the security aspects of downloading and executing code automatically. This ensures that the same kind of malicious viruses that occur in the Microsoft Windows world cannot occur in Java.

- Microsoft's DNA technology uses ActiveX which supports only identification and has no provision for the other two aspects of computer security, resource access control and system integrity. Therefore, ActiveX cannot be safely deployed to bring in executable content from the Internet. It can be used on networks within a single organization with appropriate safeguards, but will still be vulnerable to bugs or malicious code.

- Java offers all three elements of computer security and thus can safely be deployed in an intranet or to bring in executable content from the Internet.

CHAPTER
8

- The Java Philosophy

- Object-Oriented Programming

- Language Features: Uniform Data Types

- Case Study 5: USPS Use of Java

- Summary

Java
Language
Specifics

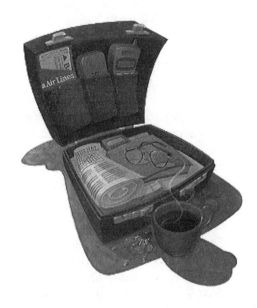

The Java Philosophy

"C++ will do for C what Algol 68 did for Algol."
— *Dave Smith, programming consultant*

New programming languages are not especially rare. They come along every couple of years, sometimes blossom for a day in the sun, and then usually fade away. However, it is unprecedented for a new language to engage the entire computer industry's attention, to sustain it, and move into widespread use. And far rarer still for the language to engage a vast array of *other* industries. For programmers to get excited about programming languages is to be expected. For computerphobes everywhere to start getting excited is astonishing. Readers with long memories might recall the early days of two other programming languages that are today quite widely used: Ada and C++.

Ada was designed by committee, or rather, by several committees. In the late 1970s the U.S. Department of Defense wanted to contain its huge spending on software by consolidating and rationalizing the languages it used. Not finding any one existing language suitable, it asked for bids on a universal, real-time control language. Four competing compiler companies submitted designs matching the specifications, and eventually one was chosen. Here's where practice and theory parted company. The paper language design turned out to be much harder to implement than anyone had anticipated. Early Ada compilers were huge, buggy, and slow. The first implementation for the PC needed an extra memory card to give the compiler the megabytes of memory it needed to run. Several parts of the language were hard to understand as well as hard to implement. Despite the elaborate military procurement process (cynics would say "because of"), the language had some useability problems. The best thing you could say about Ada was that it was an improvement on the Babel of obscure languages the Department was using before. Largely because of its size and complexity, Ada never crossed over into mainstream use and today is mostly deployed only on projects where the contract mandates it.

In contrast to the "design by committee" origin of Ada, C++ started out as the work of just one man, Bell Labs researcher, Bjarne Stroustrup. In the mid-1980s, Stroustrup wanted a mainstream language to provide the kind of object-oriented support that he had used in Simula-67. Finding nothing suitable, he set to work modifying and extending C. Because backward compatibility with C was a design goal, Stroustrup called his language "C++," which is a pun on the C arithmetic operator that adds one to its operand. The work took place over several years, gradually involved more and more people, and shifted from being an internal project to an industry-wide initiative. Although the original goal was simple ("add support for object-oriented programming to C") the resulting language grew more and more complicated as the progenitor and others piled new features on top of new features.

C++ was finally approved as an ISO standard in July 1998. It had taken about a decade to get there. Although C++ failed to meet its original goal of backward compatibility with C (there are some C programs that are not valid C++, and there are some C programs that do different things when compiled by a C++ compiler), C++ is compatible enough with C that it is in wide use. But the path has not been smooth for C++, and the language has many detractors who criticize it for over-complexity. Programmers seem to either love C++ or hate it, and either way they express their opinion with passion.

Some of the complexity in C++ is due to its "kitchen sink" approach. If a few well-placed people argue in favor of including a feature such as templates, the feature gets included in the language. After all, the protagonists argue, if you don't like the feature you don't have to use it. Unhappily, all programmers pay the cost of a language feature whether they use it or not. Compilers become larger and slower, and other tools such as linkers and debuggers are affected. Code maintenance is made more difficult because those maintaining code have no say in what features are used. The language itself is harder to define and standardize. No one feature in C++ is impossibly complex, but several of them in combination are daunting.

Language generations

Some people classify programming languages into generations, using these definitions:

1st generation: Machine language. The programming was done using numbers to represent directly the instructions and contents of memory.

2nd generation: Symbolic assembler. Short text words could be used to represent instructions and memory locations. Programming thus started to be done symbolically rather than exclusively in numbers.

3rd generation: The procedural languages starting with FORTRAN, Algol, COBOL, LISP. These languages became popular in the early 1960s and were the first high-level languages, meaning they dealt with more abstract concepts than low-level details of a computer's registers, interrupts, and memory model.

The 3rd generation includes the newer procedural languages such as Pascal, Modula (and its descendants), C, C++, Ada 95, and Eiffel.

4th generation: The distinguishing characteristic of 4th generation languages is that they are nonprocedural. Instead of describing the data manipulations that are needed, a programmer using a 4th generation language (the term was coined by computer industry guru, James Martin) specifies the pattern of results that are desired and lets the language system determine the low-level details to generate them.

4th generation languages are often proprietary to one company. They typically take the most common operations in a particular domain (such as database access or statistical analysis) and support those directly within the language. Thus, a statement in SQL (an industry standard 4GL for accessing databases) may look like this: SELECT CUSTOMER WHERE ANNUAL_SALES > 10000 to create a table of all customers who have ordered more than $10,000 of goods this year.

Example 4th generation languages include FOCUS (the language used by SAS Institute's products), xBase, and PowerBuilder.

Under this classification Java is a traditional, block-structured 3rd generation language based on ANSI C, augmented with support for object-oriented programming. Java does not represent a dramatic breakthrough in new technology. It is made up of tried and tested solutions, improved in many small ways.

Some of the complexity of C++ is due to its origins in C. C has been a phenomenally successful programming language, but its biggest weakness has been its weak support for data types. Data types were a late addition to C, grafted on as an afterthought when the language was ported from the original PDP-7 implementation to the PDP-11. The rules for the interaction of data types in C are particularly obscure and poorly thought out. Some of the rules depend on the underlying hardware and so have different results for each implementation. This aspect of the C language makes a poor foundation for C++, but unfortunately it is also the main area of further development.

Feature combination makes C++ too complex

"If you think C++ is not overly complicated, just what is a *protected abstract virtual base pure virtual private destructor* and when was the last time you needed one?"

When software author and consultant, Tom Cargill, issued that challenge in the Fall 1990 issue of the *C++ Journal*, he was making a point about how C++ had evolved to become too complicated for mere mortals to program in. There was no one feature that could be held responsible for the difficulties of C++. The problem was mastering the elaborate, Byzantine rules governing the interaction of several features taken together.

Taking this complicated phrase step-by-step and comparing it to Java, the phrase breaks into two parts "a pure virtual private destructor" that is inherited from a "protected abstract virtual base." The first part is easy: Java doesn't have destructor methods (these are methods called automatically when an object's lifetime ends). Also, all methods are virtual (overrideable) by default, so the concept of "a pure virtual private destructor" doesn't exist in Java. The nearest thing would be an abstract method. The second part of the phrase "protected abstract virtual base" refers to a base class shared by multiply-inherited classes. Java does not support multiple inheritance, which because of its complexity and limited value is a controversial feature in C++. The most complicated phrase you could build out of Java keywords this way would be something like a "protected abstract method"—maybe still confusing to nonprogrammers, but just not in the same league as C++.

Because of the unrealized goal of backward compatibility with C, C++ kept all of C's rules for data types and added very many refinements of its own. The result is hard to teach, hard to learn, and hard to write a compiler for. C++ has been a bold experiment that taught us much about what was possible and what was practical, but the use of the language has crested at this point. The reason is Java. There are many reasons to start a new project in Java at this point, and very few to start a new development in C++.

What the designer of C++ said about Java

Bjarne Stroustrup, the designer of C++, has this to say about Java: "At a recent conference, a speaker asked for a show of hands and found that twice as many people claimed to hate C++ as had ever written even a single small C++ program. The only word for such behavior is bigotry."

Bigotry is a strong word to throw around as the reason why people don't like your programming language. I think a much more likely explanation for what happened at the conference is that all the people who *had* written C++ described their experiences to the person sitting next to them.

Stroustrup also said this: "Much of the relative simplicity of Java is—like for most new languages—partly an illusion and partly a function of its incompleteness. As time passes— assuming that it gets used in more application areas and environments—Java will grow significantly in size and complexity. It will double or triple in size and grow implementation-dependent extensions or libraries."

That quote is one opinion, and mostly mistaken. Because C++ ended up as overcomplicated, its designer perhaps understandably extrapolates the experience to all languages. The Java language has not grown significantly since it was born. The libraries have grown in number, but they are not implementation-dependent libraries that differ on each system. Everyone involved with Java understands the crucial significance of retaining platform portability, and considerable effort is being spent on compatibility suites and conformance testing.

C++ was a noble experiment that taught us many lessons about what doesn't work in a programming language. Stroustrup himself hinted at the shortcomings of C++ when he said "C makes it easy to shoot yourself in the foot. C++ makes it harder, but when you do it blows your whole leg off." The designer of Java paid close attention to the lessons of C++ and he still has both his feet.

Languages never die completely, and C++ will be with us for a long time, but the dynamics of the industry have already moved to Java. Only developers as a whole can decide to replace C++ entirely with Java, but the signs are that C++ usage has now reached its peak and that it is entering a period of use only for maintenance. One such indicator is the number of compiler and software tools companies that have switched their investment from C++ to Java, in some cases, totally.

Java performance

One of the design goals of C++, which was achieved, was to ensure that the language would run as fast as C, so a number of trade-offs against pure "object-oriented" features were made. In C++, no methods are virtual unless the programmer explicitly asks for it. This saves a couple of memory references on a method call.

Thus, in C++, only methods that use inheritance pay the cost of the extra lookup to find the right function at run time. In Java the design trade-off was along the lines of "make the compiler and language check for common bugs, even if this takes a little longer than not checking at all." All Java methods are virtual by default. Although that is not the highest performance apporach, it yields a simpler language. Java checks all array accesses at run-time to ensure that the index is within the bounds. C and C++ systems usually do not offer this level of checking, even as a compiler option that is off by default.

As a result, you have two ends of the spectrum, and some people at both ends are trying very hard to push towards the middle:

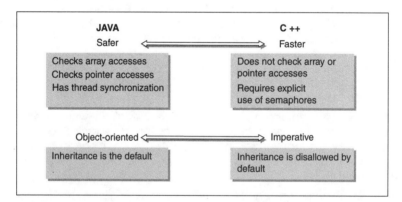

The C and C++ community is demanding memory management tools to help debug and remove memory leaks. The Java community is demanding Just-In-Time compilers to translate bytecode into machine language and execute it as quickly as possible.

In theory, it is possible to use C and C++ in safe ways and combine high performance with type safety. In practice, it has been proven many times that the only effective type safety rules are those enforced by the compiler.

The current state of the art of Java performance is:

- Performance only makes a difference on programs that are CPU bound. For programs whose execution time is dominated by GUI or network operations, Java is no faster or slower than other languages.
- The first release of Java was about an order of magnitude slower than optimized C on CPU-bound tasks.
- The first Just-In-Time compilers improved the situation from Java taking ten times as long to Java taking twice as long. People continue to work on Java performance, including advanced compilers that look at the characteristics of a program as it is run: which loops should be unrolled, which hot-spots should be translated to machine code..

Systems designers need to be aware of the performance aspects of Java, and balance longer execution times against the shorter software development times and the more reliable systems. Java is well positioned to benefit from the trend toward faster, cheaper hardware each year.

Some of the reasons to use C++ versus the reasons to use Java are listed in Table 8-1 and expanded on in the rest of this chapter.

Table 8-1 C++ Use versus Java Use

Reasons to continue existing development in C++

- Compatibility with existing code base
- No staff retraining

Reasons to start a new development project in C++

- Currently has better performance than Java (but Java compilers are improving and closing fast on C++)
- Currently has more mature software tools

Reasons to do new development in Java

- Software portability to virtually all computers
- Simpler language, leading to quicker development
- Standardized libraries for all mainstream computing
- Easy access to new paradigms of distributed computing
- Prevention of certain kinds of bugs by language rules
- Minimal staff retraining from C++
- More secure language

Object-Oriented Programming

"Structured Programming = slow, Modular = bloated,
Extensible = late, Reuseable = buggy,
Object-Oriented = Structured, Modular, Extensible and Reuseable"
Futurist Programming Notes *by Paul Haeberli and Bruce Karsh*

Pioneered in the 1960s with the language Simula 67, object programming came
back in vogue in the 1980s with C++, Object Pascal, Object COBOL, and others.
Just as "structured programming" was the dominant theme of the 1970s in the
software industry, object-oriented programming (OOP) is the paradigm of the late
1980s and 1990s. Structured programming boiled down to the simple rule of
"Make your program control structures match your data structures." Object-
oriented programming is similarly based on a few simple ideas and can be
viewed as a refinement of structured programming. OOP is not the be-all and
end-all of programming. It is a technique for organizing system design, and it is
proving useful in practice.

> **Note:** The following sections are full of technical details for those who want an
> understanding of the key elements of object-oriented programming. If you do
> not need to understand it at this level, you can just skip these sections and go to
> page 183.

Let's motivate an explanation of OOP basics by walking through an easy example
showing the changes between ordinary programming and programming in an
OOP language. Consider a program that processes data about rectangular shapes.
Perhaps it is the data for a fabric store or a lumber yard cutting shop. The central
data structure might be a record that stores dimensions like this in C:

```c
struct rectangle {
    int length;
    int width;
}
```

And there will probably be a few routines that operate on this data type: Routines
to create and initialize, to calculate the square area, to work out the perimeter (this
would be of interest if you had to sew a hem on it or paint it with sealant), and so
on. One of these routines might look like this in C:

```c
int calculate_perimeter(struct rectangle r) {
    int result;
    result = 2 * (r.length + r.width);
    return result;
}
```

The code defines a function called `calculate_perimeter` that has one parameter, called r of type `struct rectangle`. It adds the length and width of r, doubles the value, and returns that as the perimeter calculation.

This often works fine, but it is possible in C for a programmer to call the `calculate_perimeter` function with the wrong type of argument. In particular, instead of being invoked on a rectangle, it may accidentally be invoked like this:

```
struct circle { int radius; } my_circle;
int circumference = calculate_perimeter( my_circle );
```

That statement will `call calculate_perimeter()` on a nonrectangle argument and give a result that is nonsensical. To provide compatibility with early versions of C, the language stipulates that argument types are not checked for consistency with function definitions unless the function has already been seen when the call is compiled.

The First Tenet of OOP: Encapsulation

The first tenet of object-oriented programming is *encapsulation*. Encapsulation means bundling together a data structure with the functions that process it. Then, functions cannot be invoked on other data structures (like `circle` above), nor can the data be processed by other functions than the ones it is bundled with.

Encapsulation takes a big step towards data integrity. The actual way that a programmer expresses "these functions belong together with this data structure" is to make a *class* out of them. The term "class" is used in the sense of "category" or "type." A class represents a programmer-defined data type, just as a floating-point variable is a language-defined data type. A class in Java looks like this:

```
class rectangle {
    int length;
    int width;

    int calculate_perimeter() {
        return 2 * (length + width);
    }

    /* more functions can go here */
}
```

Once a class or data type has been defined, objects of that class can be declared. An object (as in "object-oriented programming") bears the same relationship to a class that a cookie bears to a cookie cutter. The class (cookie cutter) defines the shape and contents, the object (cookie) is a specific instance created by that template or mold. In a sense, the paradigm is more accurately called "class-oriented programming." An object in Java might be declared like this:

```
rectangle my_rectangle;
```

This creates a variable called `my_rectangle` that can hold an object. We might initialize it (give it an actual object to hold) like this:

```
my_rectangle = new rectangle();
```

The functions in a class are called *methods*. Method just means "function that belongs to a class." Every class gets an implicit method with the same name as the class. This is known as the constructor because when you call it, as in the code above, it creates, initializes, and returns a new object of that class for you. You can also define your own explicit constructors that take arguments, usually using them to initialize fields in the object you are creating. A constructor for rectangle might load values into the length and width fields like this (referring back to the class on page 175:

```
rectangle(int l, int w) {
    length = l;
    width = w;
}
```

This constructor would need to be placed inside the class. All methods and constructors live inside some class in Java. The constructor might be invoked like this:

```
my_rectangle = new rectangle(10,20);
```

You might also define another constructor with no arguments that initializes a rectangle to a default size:

```
rectangle() {
    length=10;
    width=20;
}
```

There are a number of keywords (`public`, `protected`, `private`) that can be applied to methods and data in a class to give different levels of visibility. By default, every field of a class will exist in each object of that class. However, there is also a keyword in Java (`static`) that, when applied to a field, says "There is only one of these for the whole class, and each object of this class shares and uses this one field." As the example hints, there are some simplifications to do with the way you access a data field and some built-in assumptions about the object whose data you are operating on. A method is invoked on an object like this:

```
int size_around = my_rectangle.calculate_perimeter();
```

These details are explained at greater length in any book on programming in Java, but briefly, all methods are invoked on objects. You cannot call a method without explicitly providing an object of the correct class. That object is passed into the method as an implicit parameter. When the method references and updates data fields of the class, it is actually referencing the fields of the specific object on which it was invoked.

The Second Tenet of OOP: Inheritance

So far, so good. Encapsulation gives us a good way to control the modifications to a data structure, but we'd also like a way to refine, extend, and vary that control. In real life, there are often special cases and refinements of rules. Inheritance gives us the ability to recognize these and fine-tune a class to create a new, more specialized class. Inheritance is about code reuse.

The dictionary tells us that inheritance is what you get from past generations, and in object-oriented programming, it is the same: Inheritance means adopting one class as your base and then modifying or adding to it to create a new class. But there's an important distinction between inheritance as used in the dictionary and inheritance in the OOP world: Normally, we talk about one individual (an object) inheriting characteristics or property from another. But in the OOP world, it isn't objects that inherit from other objects, but classes of objects that inherit from other classes. This distinction catches a lot of people, so it's worth pointing out.

Let's extend the `rectangle` class that we used above to create the specialization of a `square` class. What is different about a square compared to a rectangle is that the length and width fields are always equal. That means by the rules of geometry that the diagonal is a constant proportion (actually the square root of 2) of the length of one side. In Java and other object-oriented programming languages, we can define a class `square` that extends or inherits from the class `rectangle`. We also will provide an additional method that only applies to squares and that calculates the size of the diagonal.

```
class square extends rectangle {

    // has all the methods that rectangle has
    // plus the one below of its own.

    double diagonal() {
        return Math.sqrt(2.0) * length;
    }

    // this is a constructor
    square(int l) {
        length = l;
        width = l;
    }

}
```

This code says that the class square inherits (has) everything that rectangle has, namely, two int fields called length and width, and a method called calculate_perimeter. It also defines a new method of its own called diagonal that calculates the diagonal of a square. (The lines beginning with a // are comments; the compiler discards these.)

Note that we go from the general to the specialized and not the other way round. All squares are rectangles, but not all rectangles are squares. square is thus a specialization of rectangle and can be a subclass of rectangle, but it cannot work the other way round. The base class rectangle is termed the *parent class*, and the inheriting class square is termed the *child* or *subclass*. Inheritance goes only from the parent to the children. The diagonal method can be invoked only on a square; it cannot be invoked by a rectangle object.

We would declare a square object like this:

```
square my_box = new square(10);
```

It turns out that the ability to add new methods to specialize a base class is very useful. It provides a good way to structure a system, and it makes program maintenance easier by making it obvious where code changes must be done. If the code change relates to a square, it will be done in the square class. If it relates to a rectangle, it will be done in the rectangle class. Encapsulation already makes sure that data fields are accessed in a controlled way, using the defined functions.

Inheritance allows programs to build on existing classes and to specialize them to create new classes. These can in turn be specialized though further inheritance, and hierarchies of five or six related classes are not uncommon. Many people cited inheritance as the key feature that would lead to the Holy Grail of software: code reuse. In practice, the code reuse achievements of C++ have always fallen a long way short of the enthusiastic claims made for it. It takes a certain amount of processor power to support inheritance seamlessly. The designer of C++ felt that high performance was more important than ease of code reuse and was unwilling to pay the overhead. Events have shown that this is now the wrong design decision; simpler programming is more useful to more system implementors than gaining the last ounce of performance.

The Third Tenet of OOP: Polymorphism

The third tenet of object-oriented programming is *polymorphism*, a rather grandiose term which means "reusing the same name in a base class and a derived (inherited) class." We have already seen how inheritance allows new methods to be added to a class, creating a subclass. Polymorphism allows a subclass to provide a *different version* of a method with the *same name* that exists in the base class. Like inheritance, this is aimed at code reuse. It lets you take a routine that someone else wrote a while back, that you might not even have source code for, and say "my code acts exactly like that other code, except for these one or two routines."

As an example, the `rectangle` class contains a `calculate_perimeter` method, and we can provide a version of this method that is specialized for squares. Let us discard the previous example class of `square` and use the one below, along with the `rectangle` class, as our example.

```
class square extends rectangle {
    int calculate_perimeter() {
        return 4 * length;
    }

    double diagonal() {
        return Math.sqrt(2.0) * length;
    }

    /* more functions can go here */
}
```

As in the previous example, `square` adds a method called `diagonal()` that computes the diagonal. But it also provides a *polymorphic* (name-reusing) method called `calculate_perimeter()`. There is a method of that exact name in the parent class. The way you calculate a perimeter for a square can be slightly different than that for a rectangle: you can just multiply the length of any side by 4. For a rectangle, you must add the length and width, multiplying the total by 2. It happens that they result in the same answer for these two shapes, but there are plenty of more complex examples where something slightly different is needed. Let's assume we are optimizing for speed and wish to avoid the additional arithmetic operation of the original rectangle calculation. When we invoke `calculate_perimeter()` on a rectangle, we get the rectangle version.

```
rectangle shape1 = new rectangle();

// calls rectangle.calculate_perimeter()
int i = shape1.calculate_perimeter();
```

When we invoke `calculate_perimeter()` on a square, we get the square version even though the two routines have the same name.

```
square shape2 = new square():

// calls square.calculate_perimeter()
int j = shape2.calculate_perimeter();
```

The real cleverness comes in at run time. In all the examples that we have looked at so far, we always know what class we are dealing with. But that is not always the case. A variable of a parent class can be used to hold a parent object or any of its child classes. In other words, with

```
rectangle r;

if (some_condition)
    r = new square();
else
    r = new rectangle();
```

the variable r can hold a rectangle or a square and at compile time we don't know which. At run time when we invoke the `calculate_perimeter()` method, if it is currently an object of class rectangle, it will invoke the rectangle method of that name. If r is actually holding a square object, it will invoke the `calculate_perimeter()` method belonging to the square class. The selection of the most appropriate method for the actual type of the object is done automatically as part of the run-time system. The programmer does not have to worry about it.

The examples used here are all functions, with names that are strings of text. The polymorphism feature can (in theory) also be applied to arithmetic operators. Some languages—C++ is one example, Ada is another—allow a programmer to overload operators such as "*" (multiply), "/" (divide), and "+" (addition). In other words, in languages that allow operator overloading, an expression like

```
a = b * c;
```

might not be the multiplication that it appears to be. Depending on the type of the operands a, b, and c, which might be objects rather than integers, the expression might cause a programmer routine called "*" to be invoked. Languages that allow operator overloading make program maintenance much more difficult, because a programmer cannot make assumptions about what is happening in an expression. It is necessary to be sure about the types of all the operands and look for alternative definitions of the operators. At its best, operator overloading can have some value, but it comes at a heavy price. All code becomes harder to read, the language specification has an extra chapter of detailed rules, and compilers are larger and slower. Java allows programmers to overload only ordinary methods, not the built-in arithmetic operators of the language.

Polymorphism is a powerful OOP feature that allows objects to be responsible for their own behavior and to interpret polymorphic method calls in the way that makes the most sense for that object. A common example concerns a method called print(). If a method on this name is defined for all your classes of interest, then whatever object you have, you will be able to invoke print() on it and cause it to print itself out. This can be a useful debugging technique, and in fact Java features a method called toString(), which is defined in the built-in basic class called Object. If you can get a string representation of an object, it is very easy to print it or write it to a file.

Object is the parent of all other classes in Java, so all classes inherit toString() from Java. They get a basic implementation of toString(), but if they wish to override (specialize or customize) the definition, they can do so. Polymorphism ensures that their special version of toString() will be invoked for objects of that class at run time. There are several more theoretical refinements to OOP, and there are very many language-specific rules that cover the interaction between different features. However, the previous description covers all the essential elements of the topic.

Java had its origins in a Sun Microsystems research project that was trying to develop small computers for embedded multimedia applications. The software needed to be small, fast, and effective. The Sun engineers started out using C++, but quickly ran into a number of limitations and difficulties that convinced the project team a better language was needed. Since they were all world-class programmers, they went right ahead and designed and implemented it.

The C language was a natural starting point, although backward compatibility with C, C++, or anything else wasn't a requirement. The only real constraint was that the language had to be an improvement that proved itself in practical use.

It had to be simple (unnecessary complexity was a particularly unwelcome characteristic of C++), and it had to do the job. Java was the result. Designed by one man, Canadian computer scientist James Gosling, and implemented by a small team including James and a couple of others, Java incorporated ideas from a variety of languages such as Smalltalk, Eiffel, LISP, Objective C, and Cedar.

Simplicity in a programming language comes in two varieties: first, in leaving out unneeded features, and second, in making the supported features work in clear and intuitive ways. Java does a good (but not perfect) job in both areas. Java is definitely based on C, and Java statements and expressions will be immediately recognizable to C programmers. Table 8-2 lists the C/C++ features that were left out of Java.

Table 8-2 C/C++ Features Omitted from Java

C Features Omitted	C++ Features Omitted
pointer arithmetic	templates
goto statement	operator overloading
typedef	multiple inheritance
preprocessor	multiple ABIs
structures, unions, and enums	
stand-alone functions	
global variables	
automatic type conversion	
nonuniform data types	

Because of its partial backward compatibility with C, C++ permits programmers to program with equal ease in an object-oriented manner or without using OOP features. In other words, just because a system is implemented in C++ does not mean that it is an object-oriented system. C++ allows a programmer to "cheat" and build an ordinary imperative system. Java affords no such opportunity. By dispensing with structures, stand-alone functions, and global variables, Java requires that all programming be done in terms of classes and objects. The language cannot force the programmer to have the best possible design, but Java does force the program to implement the design by using OOP principles. It is not possible to break objects apart and allow other arbitrary methods to operate on their internal data. This is possible in C++ and leads to systems that are hard to debug and hard to maintain.

> C++ is lax enough to allow the programmer to use a mixture of old imperative style code and OOP. Java only allows the OOP style.

Another way of looking at this concept is to consider the features that were added to C to create Java, as listed in Table 8-3.

Table 8-3 Features Added to C to Create Java

• Classes and OOP support in general	• Automatic management of dynamic memory
• Uniform data types	
• Threads	• Exceptions
	• Java libraries for networking, windowing, etc.

We will examine each of these features in the remainder of this chapter and the next one.

Language Features: Uniform Data Types

Java's concept of uniform data types contributes greatly to simplicity and portability in the language. Different computer systems support different data types in their instruction sets. The first PCs used the Intel 8088 chip in which the natural size for an integer was 16 bits, and there was no floating-point hardware. Modern workstations support 64-bit integer arithmetic and all floating-point operations in hardware.

Because of the variety in what the underlying hardware might support, most language standards up to now let each compiler writer pick the best "natural" size for the data types like integer, short integer, and long integer. For many years, a common choice by compiler writers for the PC was to make integers 16 bits long, giving a range of –32768 to +32767. Most compiler writers for workstations and other more capable systems chose to make integers 32 bits long, with a range of –2,147,483,647 to +2,147,483,648. Some workstation compilers make integers and long integers the same size; others make integers 32 bits and long integers 64 bits.

Different choices for the same basic types complicates the porting of C code. When a C program is ported between a PC and a more capable system, the programmer needs to consider how each type is being used. Simply recompiling may well cause the size of a basic type to change, and that change has implications for data files and when type overflow will occur. It is not feasible to use an editor to globally change all occurrences of int to long because doing so changes the effect of type promotion in expressions and because different format specifiers are needed in print routines. The interchange of data files between different systems is unnecessarily complicated.

Java greatly simplifies this thorny area by requiring all implementations on all hardware to use consistent values for the basic data types. These values are shown in Table 8-4.

Table 8-4 Java Data Types

Java Type Name	Description
byte	8-bit two's complement signed number
short	16-bit two's complement signed number
int	32-bit two's complement signed number
long	64-bit two's complement signed number
float	32-bit IEEE standard 754 floating point
double	64-bit IEEE standard 754 floating point
char	16-bit Unicode character
reference type	32-bit pointer

These data types and sizes are uniform across all implementations of Java. All except char represent standard choices that any compiler writer would make nowadays on contemporary computer architectures. The choice of 16 bits for char, rather than 8 bits, is a little unusual. Requiring 16-bit characters provides support for alphabets used outside the United States and Western Europe. This will be further explained in Chapter 9 under Internationalization.

References (pointer types) are implicit in Java. You may have heard that "Java doesn't have pointers." That remark is an oversimplification. Java does have pointers (it calls them "references"). The critical difference is that programmers cannot do arithmetic on Java pointers or use pointers to access successive elements of an array.

All references are 32 bits long in Java, doing away with the awkward and error-prone "memory models" with pointers of different sizes common on the PC. In addition, all the Java library routines that return memory values return a 64-bit quantity, anticipating the day when 64-bit address spaces are the norm in computer systems.

The uniform data types help make Java programs "architecture neutral," meaning they behave in the same way no matter what hardware they are run on. If a value overflows in one execution environment, it will overflow on all. If an expression evaluates precisely on one system, it will evaluate precisely on all. In the past, different hardware vendors have optimized for absolute speed, even at the expense of code that would not run or would obtain different results on different systems. Java makes the trade-off in a different place: Consistent, accurate, reproducible results are more important than optimizing performance. It has taken a long time for the industry to realize this truth.

What Happens on Overflow?

What happens when an expression goes outside the representable values for its type depends on whether it is an integer or a floating-point quantity. In all cases, the result is well defined.

Java uses one of the choices for floating-point types defined by the IEEE Standard 754. Essentially all modern general purpose computer systems follow this standard, and those that don't will need to emulate it in software. The IEE 754 standard defines how numbers are stored in floating-point form and also defines a couple of nonnumeric values, namely "infinity" and "undefined result." The "undefined result" is called "NaN," meaning "not a number" in the IEEE standard.

When an expression is evaluated, one of four possible outcomes will occur:
1. The result fits within the type assigned to hold it. This is the most desirable outcome, and indeed is the usual case.
2. The result is too large to fit in the type assigned to hold it. This is called overflow.
3. The result is too small to be represented accurately by the type assigned to hold it. This is called underflow.
4. The expression does not have a mathematically well-defined result. The most common case is an attempt to divide by zero, either directly or by using the "%" remainder operator.

What is "floating point"?

Most readers will be familiar with integers, which map directly onto words in computer memory. The floating-point format is a way to use those words to represent non-integers—numbers that have fractional parts, such as 3.142 or –270.5.

The full details of how the numbers are stored is beyond the scope of this text, but the idea is to store each as two pieces: a raw number such as "3142," and a decimal indicator that says how many places from the left the decimal point should be written, such as "1 place." Assembling a number from the pieces "3142" and "1 place" gives a result of "3.142." It is called "floating point" because the decimal point "floats" or moves to accommodate the changing values as expressions are evaluated. It contrasts with the somewhat rarer fixed-point arithmetic in which a constant number of decimal places (such as 2 or 5) is always assumed.

Floating-point arithmetic is inherently less than perfectly accurate. For technical reasons to do with being represented in the binary system, the only numbers that can be represented perfectly are numbers that can be formed from adding integer powers of 2, such as 4.625, which is made up of $2^2 + 2^{-1} + 2^{-3}$. All other numbers are stored as a value that closely approximates the real value. Usually the approximation is good enough to do the job, and users don't notice. However, because it is an approximation, floating-point types should never be used where absolute precision is required. Floating-point variables should not be used as loop indexes; adding 0.1 ten times to a zero-ized floating-point variable will not give a final value of 1.0. The result will be very close to 1.0 but will not exactly equal it. It's usually better to compare two floating-point values for approximate equality by checking that the difference between them is small compared to the size of the numbers, rather than looking for exact equality.

Inexperienced programmers writing financial applications often use floating-point types to represent dollars and cents. This frequently results in mysterious rounding errors where the total of a column is slightly different from the exact arithmetic sum of all the values in it. A better approach where complete accuracy is needed is to hold all values as integers that represent currency amounts in cents. Instead of using a floating-point variable to store 7.75, use an integer or long integer to hold 775 cents.

The action that Java takes in the three problematic cases depends on whether you have a floating-point expression or an integer expression:

- floating-point expression:
  - overflow—the result is infinity.
  - underflow—the result is zero.
  - mathematically undefined result—the result is NaN.

- integer expression:
  - overflow— only the least significant digits are stored.
  - underflow—the result is set to zero.
  - mathematically undefined result—an arithmetic exception is raised.

Raising or "throwing" an exception means the program stops whatever it was doing that led to an error and branches to an error-handling routine. More details of an undefined integer expression throwing an arithmetic expression is given in the section *Language Features: Exceptions* on page 197. Floating-point expressions never raise exceptions in Java.

The key point is that, unlike almost all other languages, what happens in the presence of arithmetic error conditions is specified and is the same in all implementations. Programmers can rely on these properties to detect and recover from invalid expression results.

Language Features: Threads

Everyone is familiar with timesharing—the ability to run several programs at once on a computer by swapping between them and letting each run in turn for a very brief fraction of time. Multithreading extends this idea from having several different programs running in parallel to having several parts of the *same* program run in parallel. Each part of a program that can be running at the same time as other parts is known as a thread of control. Typically, when a multithreaded program gets its timesharing time slice, it will further share it among all of its different threads that are ready to run at that instant. On multiprocessor hardware, it is possible that several threads and/or several processes will truly be running in parallel. Figure 8–1 illustrates the difference between timesharing and multi-threading.

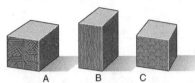

Several programs to run but a computer can run only one program at a given instant

Timesharing solution:

Slice each job up by giving it the computer for a fraction of a second. It will make some progress before it gives up the computer to the next in line. Each job runs for a brief timeslot, and they all share the computer, hence the name timesharing.

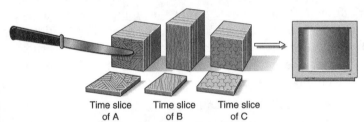

Time slice   Time slice   Time slice
   of A   of B   of C

Rather than simply scheduling the next job after the current job has finished, timesharing is used when jobs interact with a person online. Timesharing means a person doesn't have to wait for a computer.

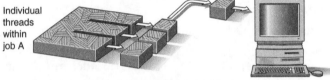

Individual
threads
within
job A

Multi-threading

Multi-threading is a similar idea to timesharing but applied to an individual job. A multi-threaded program divides up its time slices among several independent threads of control in it. Unlike timesharing, multi-threading doesn't usually provide better response time. It's a better way of organizing some programs and provides another tool for building systems.

Figure 8–1
Timesharing versus Multithreading

Threaded code is now universally recognized as a superior feature. At the beginning of the 1990s, no major operating system offered a threads library. By 1995 all volume operating systems, with one exception, provided a threads interface. The one exception is Microsoft's Windows 3.1 environment, which doesn't support threads because the underlying design doesn't allow for it.

One area where threads have proven to be useful is in user interfaces. A programmer can dedicate a thread to handling user input while other threads carry out lengthy calculations. Without threads, everything must be delayed while the computation takes place. With threads, the user interface can continue to respond and update the screen even while the calculations are being done.

By allowing a program to do more than one thing at a time, threads more closely match the real world and make some programs easier to write. Another common use of threads is at the server end of a client/server system. The simplistic way of writing a server is
1.   Listen for a client request.
2.   Serve the request (send the file, etc.).
3.   Go to step 1.

A problem occurs if step 2 is time consuming (say, it involves a database lookup and extraction). The server can serve only one client at a time. The first client there is dealt with, and all other requests back up behind it.

A better way to write the server is like this:
1.   Listen for a client request.
2.   Spawn a new thread to serve this request; thread runs.
3.   Go to step 1, while serving the client independently.

By pushing the service function into a different thread, the server is almost immediately free to accept a request from the next client, instead of being delayed by the amount of time it takes to fill the first request. Although the ultimate amount of work done is the same, the throughput of the system can be much greater when threads are used. Of course, you do need a computer system that is powerful enough to run several threads in parallel.

Multithreading within a program has a lot lower overhead than timesharing among different programs. Context swapping (saving the state of an entire process) is an expensive operation, but it is not needed when switching from one thread to another in the same process. All that needs to be saved when switching between threads in the same process are a few registers such as the program counter and stack pointer.

Like object-oriented programming, multithreading is an old idea that is now enjoying a resurgence in popularity. It is helped by new multiprocessor architectures: The more parallelism you can introduce into a program, the more you will benefit from having several CPUs ready to run code.

Multithreaded programs are not completely without cost. Organizing a program in this way invariably makes it a little more complex, a little harder to understand and debug. In particular, programmers have to be very careful to ensure that they never have two threads updating the same piece of data at the same time. Consider a variable representing "total records processed" and assume there are two threads that do the work and update the variable. As each thread completes the processing of a record, it will increment the variable. To do this, it will need to load the current value from memory into a register. Then, it will add 1 to the value in the register and store it back into memory. Each step is a separate instruction. The problem arises when the other thread wants to update the variable at the same time. You want things to happen in this sequence:
1. Load the variable from memory into a register.
2. Add 1 to the value in the register.
3. Store the register back into memory.

Because the threads are running independently, the sequence with two threads may actually be overlapped like this:

thread A   **thread B**
variable value starts as: 23
1. Load the variable (assume the
    value is currently 23) into a register.   1. Load the variable (value 23)
                                                       into a register.

2. Increment the register, moving
    23 to 24.   2. Increment the register, moving
                                                       23 to 24.

3. Store the register back in memory.

                                                   3. Store the register back in memory.
Interleaved execution of threads can scramble your data.

The final result is that the value in memory is only updated once to 24, instead of twice to 25. This situation is known as a "data race" or a "race condition" and can lead to catastrophic software failure. A data race can occur whenever data is updated by more than one thread without measures being taken to serialize the access. In this case, the data race results in one of the updates being lost. Instead of the variable being updated to 25, it has the value 24. A race condition can also mean that the data is left in an inconsistent state that depends on which thread was the last to finish accessing it.

How to Prevent Race Conditions

Software protocols alone are not enough to prevent race conditions. A little help is needed from the hardware. All general-purpose computer systems support some variant of a "test and set" instruction, which in a single cycle both reads the value of a memory location and sets it to a new value. It can then branch, based on the value that was previously there. Sometimes the instruction is called "swap," sometimes it is called "load and store," and sometimes it is called "compare and swap." They all do the same basic, indivisible test-and-set operation used as the basis of higher-level locking and synchronization operations.

The way we prevent data race conditions is to place "locks" around shared data structures. A thread must hold a lock before it can update the data, and only one thread can hold a given lock at a time. The lock thus "serializes" access to the data. It can cause a bottleneck and choke performance, so locks should only be used where necessary, and they should protect the minimum region of code necessary.

There is a variety of locks that can be built on the primitive test-and-set instructions. These are the most common kinds:

mutex lock   A "mutual exclusion" lock. It is the simplest kind of synchronization primitive. The first thread to call `lock` is granted the lock, and further requests cause the requesting thread to block. When the lock holder calls `unlock`, any blocked threads contend to acquire the lock. One of them will be successful, and the other threads continue to be blocked.

A mutex lock can be built directly out of the test-and-set instruction. A mutex lock is too low level (hence, error-prone) to be supported directly in Java.

reader/writer lock   A variant of the mutex that allows multiple simultaneous readers. As before, a writer requires unique exclusive access. The reader/writer lock is not supported directly in Java.

counting semaphor   A variant of a mutex lock that keeps a count of the number of threads that are queued up on it at a given instant. It is not supported directly in Java.

monitor   A region of code with a mutex lock associated with it. A thread must be holding the lock in order to execute the code. The group of statements protected by the monitor is known as a critical region.

Java supports a monitor directly with the `synchronized` keyword. `synchronized` can be applied to a block of statements, to an entire method, or to a class-level method.

condition variable   A more sophisticated locking scheme used when access to the shared resource is not enough. Typically, there will be an additional condition as well, e.g., you want to hold the lock, and there must be room in the buffer to store additional data. Or you want to hold the lock, and there must be some incoming data that needs to be processed.

A condition variable allows you to acquire the lock, test the condition, release the lock and be suspended if the condition is false, and later be woken up when the condition becomes true.

Condition variables are supported in Java by two methods, known as `wait()` and `notify()`, that are built into every object.

The kind of lock most frequently used in Java is called a *monitor*. A monitor protects a region of code and prevents more than one thread from executing the code at a time. Although we talk about *code* being protected by a monitor, the real problem is the data that the code accesses. If a piece of code does not access shared data, then none of these synchronization techniques are necessary. The whole point of mutual exclusion and locks is to prevent two threads from changing the same piece of data at the same time.

A monitor serializes access to the code (and thus, more importantly, to the data) by requiring each thread to hold the monitor lock before it can enter the code region. Only one thread at a time may hold the lock. All the low-level monitor operations are invisible to the Java programmer. The programmer specifies the region of code, and the run time system then takes care of allocating the monitor, maintaining its internal state, and queueing and releasing threads.

It is not just user code that needs to protect against multiple simultaneous access; library code needs to be protected against it, too. Java was designed with thread use in mind from the very start, but that is not true for many other language systems. The UNIX C run time library and other libraries have had to be modified to allow several functions or several invocations of the same function to be active at once. This has led to the following terminology:

MT-unsafe   The library or code has not been modified to make it safe to call into it from more than one routine at a time. MT just means "Multithreaded." Also known as thread-unsafe.

This is the standard state of any code that was not written with threads in mind or where performance is of sufficient concern that the overhead of MT-safety is considered unacceptable. In some environments, both MT-safe and MT-unsafe versions of a library are provided. Benchmark results are generally based on the MT-unsafe version, to show the fastest possible results that a user can obtain.

MT-safe   The library or code can be called from multiple routines at once. A cheap but very inefficient way to make a library MT-safe is to place a synchronization lock around the entire library so that although many threads can attempt to access it, no more than one thread at a time will be allowed access. This places a big bottleneck on performance. MT-safe code is also known as thread-safe.

MT-hot   An MT-hot library is one step beyond MT-safe. Not only can the code support multiple threads at once, but, where possible, global data has been eliminated, thus eliminating the possibility of data races. The library has been tuned to make the different routines operate independently and without relying on the state of other parts of the library. Code regions are protected by use of locks with fine granularity, perhaps down to just a few lines of code rather than the entire library. Ideally, you want all libraries to be MT-hot, as the Java run times are.

Figure 8–2 illustrates the multithreaded conditions.

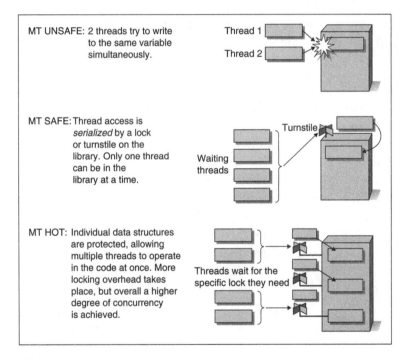

Figure 8–2
MT-unsafe, MT-safe, and MT-hot

One of the reasons Java was slow to appear on Windows 3.1 was the lack of a thread library. And one of the reasons a thread library was hard to implement was that the underlying Windows 3.1 run time library is thread-unsafe.

Thread programming is an important software paradigm for the future, and now that it is here, it is here to stay. Threaded software dovetails neatly with multiprocessor hardware, which is becoming increasingly common. Multiprocessor hardware offers the opportunity to literally run several processes simultaneously; threaded software splits up processes into pieces of finer granularity that are individually runnable. The two techniques are complementary.

The positive experience of multithreading the Solaris UNIX kernel convinced the Sun engineering community and its users that applications should be threaded too, leading Sun to support the POSIX effort to standardize a threads library. Unfortunately, the POSIX threads effort came a little too late to be adopted as the basis of Java threads. So Java threads are simpler, but not yet blessed by a standards community.

Language Features: Automatic Memory Management (Garbage Collection)

No program of any size is free of bugs when it is first written. The process of debugging is the art of removing enough of the obvious flaws that the software can be shipped to paying customers while debugging continues. The software industry is slowly beginning to acknowledge what seems like an obvious truth: The design of a programming language and its libraries can make a big difference in the amount of debugging a program needs and how quickly the debugging can be done. Some features like the original FORTRAN I/O library are just plain poorly designed. Some features like Pascal conformant arrays—support for arrays of different sizes as procedure parameters—are needlessly hard to understand. And some features like templates in C++ interact with many other features in the language to create something that is complicated and hard to learn.

Some programming language features are easy to understand but just plain error-prone. The COBOL "altered GOTO" falls into this category. The altered GOTO (which was eventually withdrawn from the language) allowed you to change at run time the destination of a branch! The code would still read GOTO mylabel, but at run time it would branch to somewhere else!

In C and C++, dynamic memory management is a highly error-prone feature. The languages provide a way to acquire at run time more memory from the operating system. This memory can be used to build up dynamic data structures, which can also be freed after use. One example of the use of dynamic memory management would be in sorting a file. The easiest kind of sort needs the entire contents of the file to be in memory, but you don't know how big the file will be in advance. Rather than allocate a huge array that might not be needed most of the time, it is better to read in the file record by record, allocating new memory to hold it as needed. There are many other algorithms that work better when they use dynamically allocated memory. In C, memory is allocated by the malloc() library call and returned to the available pool by the free() system call.

Making programming languages work the way programmers expect

When I was the chief developer on the Sun Pascal compiler, I repeatedly received new bug reports for the same one issue, complaining that the compiler gave an error message for something that was "obviously right." The details of the actual feature are quite technical and unimportant—it had to do with conformant arrays (parameters that allowed for arrays of varying size). In fact, the programmers were trying to do something that looked like it should be meaningful but which the language actually forbade.

Pascal originally had no support for passing different-sized arrays to a routine in different invocations. It was such an obvious gap in functionality that support was later added. Unfortunately, it was a little hard to retrofit within the existing language semantics, and the new feature made arrays as arguments behave differently and be subject to different rules than arrays in other cases. Programmers found the Pascal conformant array feature difficult to understand, to the point where they were convinced the compiler was buggy.

The point is that the language designers had paid grossly inadequate attention to the "human factors" of programming. Since programming language designers should be very knowledgeable in this area, they (and not the artless programmers) were at fault in specifying a feature that did not work the way most programmers expected it to. Once an important language, Pascal is now just a footnote to programming language history. Unintuitive or difficult-to-understand features will always form a barrier to the acceptance of a language, as C++ is now discovering.

Dynamic memory management is unrelated to the Intel x86 processor

Note that dynamic memory management is completely unrelated to the memory management models on the Intel x86 processor. Those so-called memory models (small, medium, compact, large) and the corresponding sizes of pointer variables (…near, …far, …huge) are all concerned with overcoming historical limitations on addressing in the Intel x86 CPU. They do not apply to other processors, and they are not a general issue in systems design.

The kind of memory management under discussion in this section is run-time support for allocating and freeing new areas of memory to hold data structures that change in size. This has always been a very error-prone part of software development. Simply stated, in large systems it is just too easy for programmers to make a mistake about whether a region of memory is in use or not.

The problem is that explicit memory management by programmers is complex and very error prone. It is practically impossible to tell from looking at the program code what sequence of memory management operations will take place at run time. It's all too easy to make two kinds of mistakes:

- Leaks—something isn't freed after use. That memory is never reclaimed by the program and cannot be reused. If a user program has a memory leak, it is bad. If an operating system has a memory leak, it is disastrous, because the memory cannot be retrieved until the system is rebooted. A scarce resource of physical memory has "leaked away."

- Premature freeing—memory is freed, but then later written to through the same or some other pointer. This leads to all kinds of errors, usually showing up as memory corruption. The memory corruption shows up at a time and place far distant from the original error, so this kind of bug is very hard to track down.

There's even a third kind of problem that's less common but hard to deal with when it happens: fragmentation of the heap due to constant allocation and deallocation of blocks of varying sizes. This is one of the problems Java programmers don't even have to know of, much less worry about.

The problem of error-prone memory management is so acute in C and C++ that some innovative companies have brought out software tools to diagnose and pinpoint the errors. One company, Pure Software, highlights in its product documentation an error that it found in the reference implementation of the X Window System. The error was shown in just a few lines of code, and it really emphasizes the point that even very good programmers succumb to memory management errors, even in code that is open to public inspection. As an aside, Pure Software has recognized that Java removes the need for their innovative troubleshooting software, and the company has successfully diversified into Java-based tools for performance analysis.

In a quite amazing simplification, Java takes the burden of memory management off the shoulders of programmers. The problems of dynamic memory management revolve around whether memory is in use and when to return it to the system. In Java, dynamic memory is allocated as before. But the programmer does not explicitly deallocate memory to return it to the run time system.

Instead, there is a low-priority thread, executing in the background of all Java programs, whose job is to help with memory management. This thread is known as the "garbage collector," and it periodically considers all memory, looks at what is reachable through the pointers that a program has, and reclaims everything else, sweeping it onto the free list for reuse.

All that a programmer need do is clear any reference to an object that is no longer being used. The garbage collector will only reclaim objects that nothing points to. So, if there is even one reference to an object, it will stay allocated and the old "reference after freeing" memory corruption bug cannot happen. When nothing points to an object, it becomes a candidate for automatic garbage collection, and the old "memory leak" bug cannot happen. If there is still a reference to an object, it will not be freed. If there are no references to an object, it will be freed automatically when the garbage collector next runs. Figure 8–3 illustrates automatic memory management.

Garbage collection doesn't happen immediately or at predictable intervals. The run-time library will balance the need for memory with the CPU demands of user threads that are running. It will not fire up the garbage collector until it needs to. The disadvantage is that your program will be subject to additional CPU load at unpredictable times. Even though threads (in theory) allow the garbage collector to run in parallel with your code, it is usually not possible in practice. The garbage collector needs to look at all memory in use by a program, and it cannot work if that memory is being changed as the garbage collector reviews it.

Current garbage collection implementations need to freeze user code (suspend all threads) while they run. Microsoft in its J++ product has a garbage collection algorithm that trades off the need for twice as much memory, in return for faster collection times. This is probably an acceptable trade-off for general-purpose computer systems.

The use of garbage collection at all makes user programs subject to sudden stops at random times. For this reason, it's not usually used in embedded or real-time systems. These kinds of systems have operational constraints that demand speedy response times. Java gives programmers the ability to schedule garbage collection explicitly or turn it off altogether. Some combination of behind-the-scenes garbage collection, no garbage collections, or garbage collection at predetermined points is sure to be a better solution than the bug-ridden manual deallocation of memory resources that C and C++ programs currently use.

Language Features: Exceptions

Exceptions (popularized with the C++ language) are a language feature aimed at simplifying error processing. They do not reduce the amount of error handling that a program must do, but they allow it to be collected in one place and provide an easy automatic way to divert the flow of control there when something goes wrong.

Programming systems are built up from libraries of routines that pass arguments and call each other. A perennial problem has been finding a consistent way to

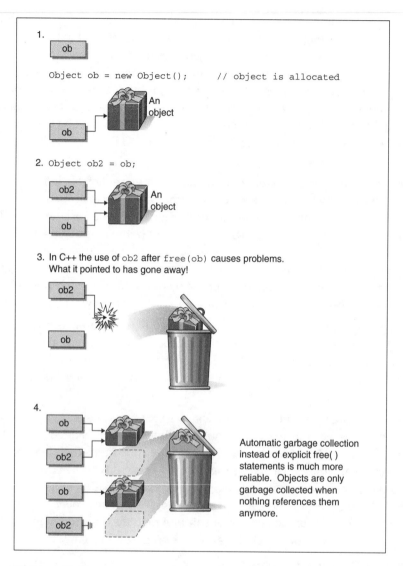

Figure 8-3
Automatic Memory Management

indicate back to the calling routine that a failure has occurred. For example, if a routine is passed a file name and is supposed to open the file, several things can go wrong:

- A file of that name might not be present.
- The file might be found, but the permission bits might be set to prevent the access.

- An I/O error might occur, e.g., the disk might be off line.

In the past, a routine had some mostly not very good choices for dealing with an unexpected error. It could try to indicate the failure by setting a global value or one of its arguments or a return value to some special result. Alternatively, it could take the drastic step of failing the entire program and branching to some central error routine that would print an error before ceasing execution. A third alternative was the one seen in MS-DOS: to try to involve the user in resolving the problem by issuing a message like "Abort, Retry, Fail?"

None of these choices worked really well. Programmers too frequently ignored return values, users generally had little luck with choosing anything other than Abort, and branching to an error routine precluded any attempt at recovering from an error.

Software exceptions are a new approach to solving these problems. The basic concept of exceptions is that when a program recognizes that something has gone wrong, it can force a transfer of control to an error-handler routine. Programmers can set up these error-handler routines wherever they like. In other words, programmers can choose the trade-off between having many specific error handlers or few, but more general, ones. This is perhaps best demonstrated by example.

We have a method that calculates an average, like this:

```
int average(int total, int number) {
    int av = total / number;
    return av;
}
```

Most of the time this method will work without problems. However, if the function is called with a zero value for the number parameter, it will cause a division by zero inside the function.

Recall that with integer arithmetic, any mathematically undefined result (such as division by zero) raises an arithmetic exception. What that means is that inside the `average` function, the expression evaluation ceases and exception processing takes over. The run-time system recognizes that an exceptional event has occurred and starts looking for an exception handler to process it. The system looks in ever-widening circles, like the ripples caused by a stone dropped in a pond.

First, the system looks for an exception handler in this method in the block surrounding the statement that raised the exception. Not finding one there, it widens the search to the statement that called the `average` method, and then any block that contains it, and then the place from which that function was called, and so on. If it gets right up to the top level of where it was called from (this will either be the main () routine or the run () routine of a thread) without finding an exception handler, then the program will halt with an error message being printed.

The more usual case is that the programmer will have put an exception handler in place to look for these events and handle them. In this case, an exception handler in the average method might look like:

```
int average(int total, int number) {
    try{
        int av = total / number;
        return av;
    } catch (ArithmeticException) {
        System.err.println("averaging over zero!");
        return 0;
    }
}
```

Alternatively, we might leave the average method the way it is and put an exception handler in the routine that called it:

```
int average(int total, int number) {
    int av = total / number;
    return av;
}


void some_other_routine() {
    try {

        int sum = readFromFile();
        int count = getFromSomewhereElse();

        int ave = average(sum, count);


    } catch (ArithmeticException) {
        ave=0;
    }

    . . .
```

The general form of an exception handler is a try ... catch ... block. Where the try part says "try executing these statements" and the catch part says "if any of these list of exceptions occur, I will handle them in here." The statements inside the blocks can be as simple or as detailed as desired. In the average example, if there is no exception handler, eventually the exception will propagate to the top level, stopping execution of the entire program with a message like:

```
java.lang.ArithmeticException: division by zero
        at myexample.main(myexample.java:13)
```

As with most of the other features of Java, there are a number of other subtleties that are not described at length here. For instance, exceptions come in two varieties: user-defined exceptions and predefined exceptions common to every Java system. Most of the predefined exceptions are *run-time* exceptions, meaning that the exception is raised by the Java run-time libraries, and you cannot do much after the fact to recover from it, except perhaps retry the operation with different operands or arguments.

In contrast, it makes sense to anticipate and handle user-defined exceptions. If the programmer defined the exception, he or she should also be clear about the recovery possibilities. An exception in Java is an object (like almost everything else). There are about 30 predefined exceptions, each of which has a class name that describes the nature of the error (see Table 8-5) and programmers can define their own exceptions as needed.

Table 8-5 Some Predefined Java Exceptions

```
ClassNotFoundException
IllegalAccessException
ArithmeticException
ArrayIndexOutOfBoundsException
NullPointerException
FileNotFoundException
```

For every statement in your program, every declaration you make, every method you invoke, and every expression you evaluate, the run-time system checks for any of these predefined error conditions. Here's an example program fragment that will trigger the ArrayIndexOutOfBoundsException.

```
char name [] = new char[5];
int i=10;
if ( name[i] == 'K' ) ...
```

The reference to name[i] is a reference to name[10], but as declared, the name array has elements from 0 to 4 only. Unlike an array in C or C++, an array in Java can never be referenced outside its bounds. The Java program will throw an exception before the invalid memory access takes place. There is a certain cost to checking that all array indexes are within range, but experience has proven repeatedly that programmers need this kind of help. It's a good trade-off.

Programmers can define their own exceptions to represent some error conditions that could arise. Exceptions look just like any other object definition. Let's assume that we support and sell a Java library that checks its callers with a password protocol, then provides access to a database. We want to keep tight control over the database, so on each potential access we demand that the user send over his identity again. As long as the identity matches those on our approved list, we allow the access; otherwise, we throw a security exception. At its simplest, the exception could be defined like this:

```
class SecurityException extends Exception { }
```

This says that the `SecurityException` class is a subclass of (inherits everything from) the `Exception` class. Here's an example of how one would use this user-defined exception. At various times, users of the library would call a write routine:

```
synchronized void writeData(int data[], String id)
      throws SecurityException {
   if ( found_on_OK_list(id) == false )
      throw new SecurityException();
   // otherwise go on to update the database
```

In the event that the `id` is not on the OK_list, a security exception will be thrown, and since there is no local handler, the exception propagates back to the point where `writeData()` was called. For this to work properly, the operation of updating the database must be inaccessible to user code except through this gateway function.

You will probably not be surprised to learn that this technique is exactly how the access restrictions on an applet are enforced. All attempts to use the run-time library facilities to open a file, read environment data, etc., are routed by the browser Java run-time library to a `SecurityManager` class. If the access is permitted, the checking routine simply returns normally. If the access is not permitted, the checking routine instantiates (creates an object variable) a security exception and throws it. In the calling routine, the requested access then does not occur.

Methods need to announce the list of exceptions that they may throw. The list appears after their arguments. This listing allows routines that call the method to be well informed about the possible exceptions that may come back instead of a normal return. It gives the calling programmer a chance to write a handler for those exceptions if appropriate.

Exceptions don't reduce the amount of error processing that a program must do, but they collect it in one place and give the programmer great flexibility about where that place can be. The programmer does not clutter up the main logic with lots of auxiliary tests for every possible thing that can go wrong. Exceptions are superior to return values because they cannot be ignored. When an exception is raised, the flow of control is changed whether the programmer has prepared for it or not. If the programmer has prepared for it, the exception will be handled at an appropriate place. If the programmer has not prepared for it, the program will stop running before any further errors occur. Overall exceptions provide an improved way for error handling and structuring a system for reliability.

Case Study 5: USPS Use of Java

Neither rain nor sleet nor dark of night will delay this Java project

Now that we have looked at the characteristics of object-oriented programming and some of the other features of Java, here is a case study of an organization that is programming in Java. The organization is the United States Postal Service (USPS), which is run as an independent corporation and is the fourth largest company in America.

The largest part of the Postal Service's work is business mail. To make things run more smoothly, the postal service has about one dozen paper forms that businesses have to complete when they order particular mail services. For example, one of the forms is PS 3602-R, which is used to submit a bulk mailing. The PS 3602-R is full of boxes that have to be checked, filled out, added up, correlated, and it looks alarmingly like an income tax return. Delays sometimes occur when users leave the form incomplete or fill it out inconsistently.

Accordingly, the USPS has written some Java software that automates the completion of the form. Users provide the basic information once, and the Java program calculates the dependent information (so many items to mail at such-and-such a rate, etc.). The program carries the data forward and automatically generates totals. The Java program then generates a facsimile of the official PS 3602-R form, which the user can print out and take to the post office along with the mail. Alternatively, the form can be submitted directly over the Internet. Figure 8–4 illustrates both sides of the form.

The Java program is not especially complicated, but it does automate a process that was error prone and previously done by hand. The USPS displayed commendable insight in choosing a small, easily understood project to use as their test

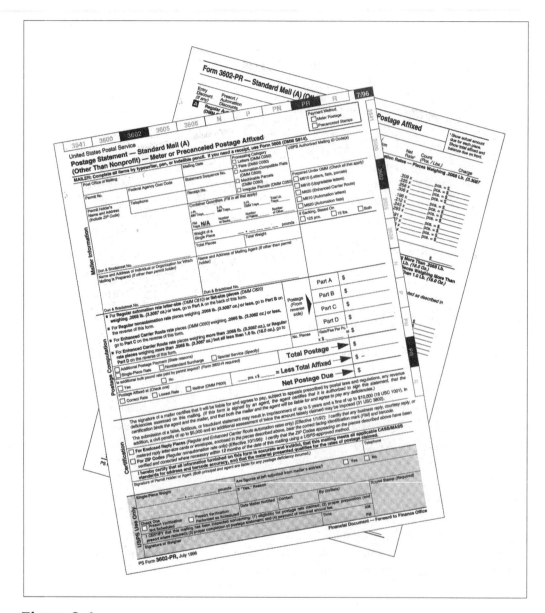

Figure 8–4
USPS 3602-R Form
(reprinted by permission of the United States Postal Service)

bed for evaluating Java. Their successful results highlight the importance of a
phased approach to new technology. By concentrating on a single, simple applica-

tion, the programmers at the USPS were able to learn the new features of Java without having to worry about application complexities at the same time. This contributed significantly to the project's success. The USPS home page is at http://www.usps.gov. The software itself is at http://www.usps.gov/formmgmt/webforms.

The Java forms software was launched in December 1996 and can be manually downloaded for free and installed on computers at businesses. Note that the "obvious" system design of using an applet to serve the form and calculate the entries was not used, because it places a load on USPS servers. By making users download and install the software on their computers, the USPS supports one download per *user* rather than one per *program use*.

The system offers two benefits: Businesses will never run out of the official forms, and the post office gets a greater assurance that each form is completed correctly. The goal of the USPS is eventually to support an on-line interface with customers for the submission of all administrative documents like these. In the meantime, Java allows the USPS to use today's technology to take the first steps to that goal.

Summary

- Java is a modern object-oriented language. It blends successful features from many existing programming languages, always emphasizing simple ideas that have been proven by successful, practical use.

- Object-oriented programming has three fundamental ideas at heart:
    - Encapsulation—bundling a data type with the code that operates on it, to form a class.
    - Inheritance—the ability to define a new data type that is a refinement of an existing class, with some additional or different operations.
    - Polymorphism—a fancy word for "name reuse" or "name sharing." The same name can be given to methods in a class and its subclasses. The right method will be called, based on the actual type of an object at run time.

- An object is just a variable that belongs to some class and, hence, contains a set of data fields and has a number of functions you can apply to it. This is the only data it contains, and these are the only functions you can invoke on it.

- The Java language supports:
    - Uniform data types—the same on all computers
    - Threads—more than one thing happening at once
    - Exceptions—better error handling and recovery
    - Automatic control of memory deallocation—memory corruption and memory leak bugs can no longer happen

CHAPTER
9

- Core Libraries

- Standard Extension Libraries

- APIs for Specific Hardware or Applications

- Beans, Media, and Swing

- Internationalization

- Related Initiatives

- Some Final Words on Productivity

- Summary

Java Libraries

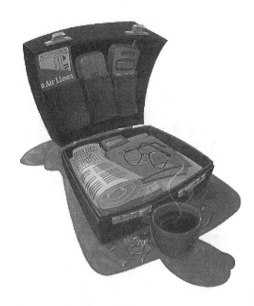

The Java Libraries—The Process and the Purpose

This chapter provides an overview of the utility classes and libraries that accompany Java. There are two distinct ways to support a feature in a programming language. It can be made part of the language itself, as was done for formatted I/O in COBOL. Or it can be put in a library and made part of the language API, as was done for formatted I/O in C. Java uses the second approach.

Putting functionality into libraries keeps the language small and clean. It also makes the language easier to learn, by compartmentalizing or encapsulating all the features for specific application areas. For example, until a programmer is ready to tackle Java database access, that library can safely be ignored. This compartmentalization makes Java especially suitable as a teaching language at schools and colleges for teaching computer science principles. New libraries can be introduced when the corresponding topic is reached in the syllabus.

Java has an extensive collection of libraries. Sun Microsystems has added more and more APIs since Java was launched in 1996. New APIs are important in two ways: They expand Java to new applications areas, like database, telephony, and speech processing. Second, they bring Java computing to ever-smaller devices (like set-top boxes, smart cards, and other embedded applications). Every additional API makes the overall system larger, and that imposes an ultimate limit on the total number of APIs.

In its first release, Java came with a few dozen basic classes that implemented common data structures and operations. The successive releases and their contents are listed in Table 9-1.

Table 9-1 Java Releases from Sun Microsystems

Jan 23 1996	JDK 1.0 FCS. Did not include the HotJava browser that had been available in earlier alpha releases. The now-historic first FCS release of Java for Solaris, Windows 95/NT.
	JDK 1.0.2 came out in May 1996. This was an update with security bug fixes, and support for the Mac and Solaris on x86.
Feb 18 1997	JDK 1.1 FCS. The first feature release after 1.0. Introduced better GUI event handling, printing, Java database access from an applet, internationalization, and some performance improvements.
Dec 1998 (est.)	JDK 1.2 FCS. This release introduces GUI support equal or superior to native libraries, finer control over security, and many other API improvements. It includes a Just-In-Time compiler.

Many ISVs have commented that 12 months between releases is too long, but six months would be too frequent for a feature release. Sun has addressed this with quarterly dot-dot maintenance releases which contain bugfixes, but no feature changes.

New feature releases cause upheaval. First, the release comes out in Beta form and the brave try it. There may be several beta releases, and a couple of months after the final one, it comes out in FCS form, and more people start to use it. It is almost always a mistake to ship a product around features that are still only available in beta.

Some development environment products are built on top of Sun's JDK, and they need some time to "buy back" Sun's new release after it FCS's. No matter when Sun ships a new release of the JDK, it doesn't get into general use until it is incorporated into new browsers and operating systems. Old browsers cannot (generally) run new Java programs. So, if you use the new libraries before they get into browsers, people might not be able to run your programs, but if you use the old libraries, everyone can. That acts as a drag on the adoption of new APIs. The Java Plug-In resolves this problem, if users are willing to download it.

In addition there is the problem of release-to-release incompatibility, which hinders adoption of a new release. Sun tries to keep incompatibilities to a minimum, but some changes are inevitable as the system is improved. As Java grew in popularity, it grew in size, too, as JavaSoft and interested partners co-designed and supported more libraries. Several of these libraries were released unbundled over the summer of 1996 and then moved into the JDK for the 1.1 release. Sun has stated that this will be its policy for the future, too: To beta-test new libraries unbundled and then bundle them into the next feature release. (A feature release is a so-called "dot" release, such as 1.0 or 1.1—there is one dot in the name.)

The Java libraries can be divided into three broad categories:

1. Core libraries bundled with the JDK. These are the class libraries that every JDK must support.

2. Standard extensions to the JDK. These are the class libraries that are optional. However, if the feature is supported, it must be supported with this API. An optional addition will generally be distributed with the JDK if available.

3. APIs for specific hardware or application areas. These are not necessarily intended to be distributed with the JDK. Rather, the API provides a way to do something in Java. Examples: the Java Electronic Commerce Framework, the Java Embedded System API.

Subset implementations are not allowed. If an API is in the core set, all JDKs must have it. If an API is in the extension set, an implementation can choose whether to include all of it or omit all of it. There are so many additional libraries and packages announced for Java at this point that this aspect alone makes a topic for a pretty thick book. What we'll do here to cover the topic is provide an overview of the classes in these three categories.

1. The Core Libraries

The APIs that are a central part of JDK 1.2, are:
- Java Language and Utilities classes
- File Input/Output, including localization support
- Graphical User Interface, including applet support. The biggest API family in this area is the "Java Foundation Classes" (JFC), and the biggest part of that is the Swing package that provides platform-neutral GUI support. Swing is described later in this chapter.
- Network communications. Java supports common operations in the TCP/IP protocol. The support is not exhaustive but provides a compromise between simplicity and function. Unlike most other languages, opening a socket connection to a remote machine looks just like opening a file. You read and write the socket just by doing file I/O. Other (non-TCP/IP) protocols such as SNA or AppleTalk are not supported at all. Users on non-TCP/IP networks are sometimes surprised to learn that they must install TCP/IP in order to get any Java networking. They will have to switch to TCP/IP eventually if they want to talk to the entire rest of the world, so this doesn't seem too large a cost.

- Database connectivity support. Support for connecting Java to SQL databases.
- CORBA integration, including IDL support. CORBA is an industry standard for object-oriented programs to communicate and share data in a client/server manner. IDL is the language-independent way to describe the CORBA API.
- Security. The Java Security APIs form a framework to let developers put security-related features in their applets and applications. The features include cryptography with digital signatures, encryption, and authentication. Respectively, these allow you to say who you are, secretly, and have other people believe it.
- JavaBeans (software components)
- Java Media–2D graphics and audio

These are known as the "core APIs." They must be part of every regular Java implementation. Programmers can rely on the presence of these libraries.

2. The Standard Extension Libraries

In addition, there are optional APIs, not a core part of the Java Development Kit version 1.2, but useable with it, and available for download from JavaSoft. There are half a dozen of these API families. They include such libraries as:

- **Java Media**—3D, video, telephony, audio processing, and speech. Some of the Java Media libraries are in the core API, and some of them are standard extensions. The Java Media libraries that make heavy demands on the hardware (like video streaming) or require special peripherals (like the telephony library) are optional standard extensions.

- **Java Mail.** This API provides a platform-independent and protocol-independent framework to build Java-based mail and messaging applications. It provides Java implementations of IMAP and SMTP services.

- **InfoBus.** The InfoBus API lets Java Bean components or applets dynamically exchange data. It specifies a small number of interfaces and the protocols to use them. Cooperating Beans can pass large amounts of data to each other using InfoBus. The name comes from the notion of a software equivalent of the hardware data bus.

- **Java Communications** (serial and parallel port) API. This API and implementation contains support for Java control of/access to RS232 serial ports and IEEE 1284 parallel ports.

- **Java Help.** The JavaHelp software is a platform-independent, extensible help system that lets developers and writers put on-line help into applets, applications, operating systems, and devices. Authors can also use the JavaHelp software to deliver on-line documentation for the web and corporate intranets.

- **Java Enterprise APIs.** The Enterprise APIs are for building large-scale software applications that can run an entire organization. There are half a dozen APIs in this family, including a Naming and Directory Interface, Enterprise Java Beans (software components running on a server), Java Transaction Service, and Java Messaging. The Naming and Directory Interface API offers a standard way for applications to look up information about files, directories, users or other on-line data. The NDI was jointly agreed upon between Sun, Hewlett-Packard, IBM, Netscape Communications Corp., and Novell, Inc. JNDI provides access to industry-standard directory services, such as LDAP, NDS, NIS, and DNS. Java programs don't need to know which of these different protocols are running; they can ask for and receive naming information in a platform-independent manner.

These APIs are known as the "standard extensions."

Each API family generally contains several related APIs, and each API (termed a *package* in Java) may be composed of several classes, so there is a hierarchy. Figure 9–1 illustrates the hierarchy.

Most of the APIs above are complete now, a few are still in draft form as a specification, and one or two are still under development. Sun developed the APIs, using an open process that is unprecedented in the industry. The API proposals are drafted with the participation of industry leaders in each area. The Java 2D Graphics API was developed jointly by Sun Microsystems, Taligent (IBM subsidiary), Adobe Systems Inc, and other participants. The JavaBeans specification was jointly developed by Sun Microsystems, Apple Computer, Inprise (Borland), Baan Company, Corel, IBM Corporation, Informix, Oracle, Lotus, Netscape, Oracle, Symantec, Novell Inc., and other companies too.

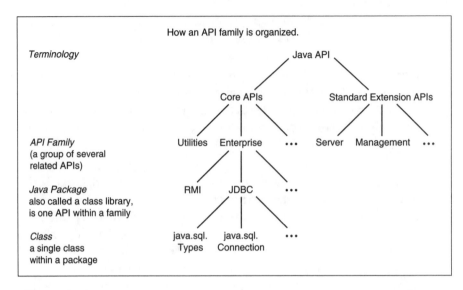

Figure 9–1
Composition of an API Family

The results of these collaborative efforts are published on the web for public comment and review before the specifications are finalized. The API initiative is clearly aimed at moving Java to become a complete software solution, open to all, and scalable from the smallest embedded chip in an automobile to the largest computer in a corporate data center.

3. The APIs for Specific Hardware or Applications

The APIs that are intended for specific hardware or applications are:

- **Personal Java.** This is the API for Java-capable mobile computers, such as Personal Digital Assistants like the Palm Pilot. Such devices are often quite memory limited, so the Personal Java specification is a subset of the full Java API. Personal Java runs in 1.59Mb RAM and 3.2Kb ROM. Personal Java programs are upward compatible with full Java implementations.

    There is also a Personal WebAccess browser, written in Java, that runs on Personal Java, and provides an interface to the web. Sony, Motorola, TCI, and 30 other leading companies have licensed Personal Java.

– **Embedded Java**. The Embedded API is aimed at supporting Java code on very resource-constrained embedded microcomputers, such as those used to control cell phones, pagers, network routers, process control hardware, and instrumentation. Embedded Java allows manufacturers to get the Java advantages of ease of development, code reuse, built-in security, and some code portability for these traditionally hard-to-program devices. Embedded Java is configurable, and lets vendors omit support for features that are not needed, like file I/O on a cell phone. Embedded Java is a subset of Personal Java, and so upward compatible with both that and the full Java API.

Lucent Technologies, WindRiver Systems, Microtec, Acorn, Chorus and several other embedded software companies have signed up as resellers of Embedded Java systems.

– **Java Card**. The Java Card API describes how Java technology can run on smart cards, and other devices with limited memory. The Java Card API allows applications for one Java Card-enabled smart card platform, to run on any other Java Card-enabled platform.

The Java Card Application Environment (JCAE) has been licensed on an OEM basis to smart card manufacturers representing more than 90 percent of the worldwide smart card manufacturing capacity. This market segment really appreciates the advantages of programming in Java!

Smart cards are not yet widely used outside Europe and Asia, but that will surely change as more applications become available. In 1998 almost 1 billion smart cards will be produced and issued. For comparison, there are about the same number of credit cards in existence worldwide. Smart cards are used to operate coinless public phones, authorize access to restricted premises or systems, store updateable information securely, and store and dispense monetary value. A chip card can easily hold and power an 8-bit microprocessor, 16Kb of ROM and 0.5Kb of ROM.

– **Java Electronic Commerce Framework**. This framework is a family of APIs and JavaBeans that supports speedy development of e-commerce systems. It includes the Java Wallet classes.

– **Jini**. Jini technology enables spontaneous networking of a wide variety of hardware and software—anything that can be connected. Jini puts a JVM and a small amount of Java code into arbitrary devices on the network. By following a few simple conventions, devices and services can register themselves with a central federation. Anyone needing, e.g. a printer service, can ask that central federation what's available, and what capabilities it offers.

Jini is a brilliant idea that needed Java technology to come to life. The following companies have signed up to partner with Sun on Jini: Aplix, Axis, Canon, Computer Associates, Datek, Encanto, Epson, Ericsson, FedEx, Mitsubishi, Network Objects, Norwest Mortgage, Novell, ODI, Oki, Quantum, Salomon Brothers, Seagate, Siemens,Toshiba.

– **Other miscellaneous Java products** and APIs. A full list of these can be found at `http://java.sun.com/products/`

It's a little bit arbitrary whether an API is listed in this category (APIs for Specific Hardware or Applications) or in the previous one (Standard Extension APIs). The Sun web page is not clear on the distinction, possibly because of the very quick growth in the number of APIs. The list given above uses the classification shown on the Sun web site.

Three Important Libraries

This section gives a little more detail on three of the Java libraries. We outline what JavaBeans are, describe the Java Media Framework, and finish up by explaining the significance of the Swing API.

Two of these APIs (Beans and Swing) are core libraries, present on all systems. The third API, the Media Framework, has the simple parts as core, and the more complicated parts are standard extensions. We'll start with JMF.

The Java Media Framework APIs

The core part of the Java Media API family includes support for:

- 2D graphics—The 2D graphics API in the Media family is based on the Adobe Bravo document-imaging system. It provides an abstract imaging model that extends the 1.0.2 AWT package with scalable fonts, line art, images, color, transforms, and compositing.

The standard extension part of the Java Media API family includes support for:

- 3D graphics—Java 3D provides an interactive imaging model for behavior and control of 3D objects. Objects can be viewed in light or shade, rotated to be viewed from different angles, and seen as solid or wire frames. The library was developed with help from Silicon Graphics, Inc. (SGI), and is a subset of SGI's Cosmo software. The Java 3D API provides a higher-level API than other 3D libraries like Direct 3D, OpenGL, or XGL. Unlike OpenGL, Java 3D contains extended rendering modes, including an immediate mode, a retained mode, and a compiled-retained rendering mode.

Java 3D for Solaris and Windows NT is implemented by calling into the OpenGL API to actually do the rendering. This allowed the speedy implementation of the API with reasonable performance, but the implementation only runs on systems that support OpenGL. It does not run on Macs, or Solaris on x86 for instance. There is no technical reason why the API cannot be implemented on systems without OpenGL, it just takes a little more time and money.

- Advanced Imaging—This API is being jointly developed by Sun Microsystems, Autometric, Inc., Eastman Kodak, Inc., and Siemens Corporate Research, Inc. The API will offer a set of core image-processing capabilities, such as image tiling, regions of interest, and deferred execution. It will also support a set of image-processing operators, including many common point, area, and frequency domain operators.

- Media Framework (standard extension)—Intel and Silicon Graphics worked with Sun on the development of this media framework API for playing audio, video, and (eventually) MIDI. The framework lets users synchronize and play full audio and video streaming. Audio/video input are not in the first release. The supported video formats include AVI, MPEG-1, MPEG-2, Quicktime, and Vivo H.263.

- Java Sound—The Java Sound API supports high quality 32-channel audio rendering, and MIDI (Musical Instrument Data Interface) control of a sound synthesis engine. Java Sound provides reliable, high-quality sound on all Java Platforms.

  Java Sound supports the following audio file formats: AIFF, AU and WAV. It also supports the following MIDI-based song file formats: TYPE 0 MIDI, TYPE 1 MIDI and RMF. The Java Sound engine can render 8- or 16-bit audio data, in mono or stereo, with sample rates from 8KHz to 48KHz. These rates might be found in streaming audio or any of the supported file formats.

- Java Speech—this API lets Java programs include speech technology in their user interfaces. The API defines a cross-platform API to support command and control recognizers, dictation systems and speech synthesizers.

  The Java Speech API was developed by Sun Microsystems, Inc. working with leading speech technology companies: Apple Computer Inc., AT&T, Dragon Systems, Inc., IBM Corporation, Novell, Inc., Philips Speech Processing, and Texas Instruments Incorporated.

- Java Telephony (JTAPI)—Lucent Technologies (the new name for Bell Labs) took part in designing the telephony API, along with Dialogic, IBM, Intel, Nortel, Novell, Siemens, and Sun Microsystems. The telephony API integrates telephones with computers. It provides basic functionality for a full range of telephone services, including simple phone calls, teleconferencing, call transfer, caller ID, and DTMF (dual-tone multi-frequency) decode/encode. Java applications will be able to interact with the phone system to place calls, automatically identify incoming calls, and interface with voice mail systems—all in a standard way.

  ISVs and companies that build communications cards have expressed great interest in JavaTel. It is compelling because of the recent interest in TCP/IP as a network control interface. People are also experimenting with using Internet to carry voice traffic. JavaTel will handle call control both for the desktop and for enterprisewide telephony. It is a layer over other computer-telephony integration middleware such as Microsoft's TAPI, Novell and Lucent's TSAPI, and Sun's SunXTL.

JavaBeans API

The JavaBeans API is a component-object model, just as Microsoft's ActiveX (DNA, Network OLE, OLE) is a software-component model. The Beans API was first shipped as part of JDK 1.1. The JavaBeans family defines a portable, platform-neutral set of APIs for software components to talk to each other.

Software components are fragments of programs—smaller than a complete application, but larger than a single method. The component framework provides a way to organize and invoke these components. What makes this useful is that you can do it dynamically, with two components that have never seen each other before. If I have one Bean that knows how to save mail, and another Bean that knows how to encrypt a data stream, I can plug them together and save all my mail in encrypted files. There is usually some kind of visual editor that helps you to plug software components together by dragging and dropping icons.

Software components are largely unknown on UNIX at present. JavaBean components are able to plug into existing component architectures such as Microsoft's OLE/COM/ActiveX architecture. Unlike ActiveX, Beans run on all systems that support Java, not just on Windows 95 and NT.

We will examine JavaBeans in much greater detail in Chapter 12, after we have covered the necessary background on software components. If you hunger for Beans now, you can read that chapter out of sequence.

The Java Swing API

From the earliest public releases, Java came with support for cross-platform windowing. The windowing support came in a package known as the Abstract Window Toolkit (AWT). The AWT implementation relies on and uses the underlying native window system (MS-Windows on PCs, X-Windows on UNIX). Figure 9–2 illustrates the AWT concept.

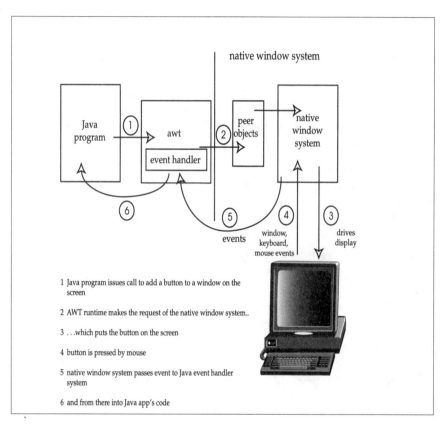

Figure 9–2
Java AWT Native Window System

A Java program makes calls to the JDK Java run time. These calls are the same on every computer. The Java run time then makes calls to the underlying window system, which is different on each type of computer (Mac, Windows 98). So the

Java application code is portable even though it does things that are different in different window systems.

The AWT use of the native window system is a clever scheme, but it has a flaw: window systems have subtle differences, and these differences undermine true program portability. To give a trivial example, a "File" menu appears on the right end of a menu bar on Windows, and on the left under Motif's window system. Too often, Java applications that used AWT had a different appearance on different computers, or even worse, a different or buggy behavior.

The Swing library changes that! Swing is a very full set of GUI components (scroll bar, button, menus, checkbox and the like written in Java. At the lowest level, Swing uses a drawing surface (e.g., a canvas, window, or whatever the window system calls it) from the native window to render these components. But Swing makes practically no use of native window system semantics. The only semantics for the Swing scrollbar, checkbox, menu, are those that Java gives it. And since the components are written in Java, they work the same way on every platform.

Better yet, the appearence (or "look and feel") of the Swing components is pluggable. Under the AWT, your GUI programs always looked like a Windows application when running on a Windows computer, like Motif when running on UNIX, and like a Mac program when running on a Mac. This was because it was based on the native components on each platform. With Swing, that look and feel is drawn by Java code, and the user can change it at run time. That is to say, the user can choose to have a consistent Java look and feel to an application regardless of the platform it is executed on, or he can choose to make it look like a native application on every computer, e.g., like a Mac application on a Mac computer, and change his mind about it each time it runs.

The pluggable look and feel may sound like a small thing, but small things make a huge difference in user interfaces. Here's an example of what a pluggable look and feel means in practice. The illustration shows a "tabbed pane" as it appears in

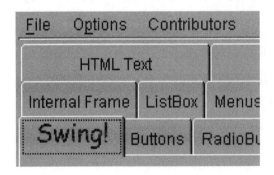

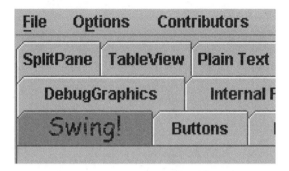

Windows, this depiction shows the same tabbed pane using the Java look and feel. A user can choose to have an application display either way. The slight difference in style will appear for all components: scrollbars, buttons, menus, etc. Here is how a tabbed pane looks on the Mac

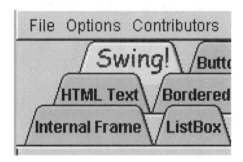

Programmers can even design their own "look and feel," implement their own components, and make that one of the run time choices for users. Due to license restrictions imposed by Microsoft and Apple, the look and feel of these platforms cannot be used on different platforms.

The Java Foundation class also has an accessibility API, designed to help people who need to read larger sized print, or cannot type on a keyboard. Often these are people with physical disabilities, and the accessibility API lets programmers create systems that can adjust to meet their needs.

Swing has moved Java up from having a barely adequate GUI, right up to having equal or better support for GUI operations than competing native window systems. With Swing, it is now easier to write a Java application that runs well on Windows, Solaris, HP-UX, and the Mac, than it is to write a Win32 application

that runs well on just Windows 95 and Windows NT. The following code is an
example of that.

A Windows program to draw an oval at an angle (slanted)

```
// Win32 version of program that draws an ellipse
rotated 30 degrees

#include <windows.h>
#include <math.h>

void paint(HDC hDC)
{
    double theta = 30 * 3.141592 / 180.0;
    XFORM xform;
    xform.eM11 = (float)cos(theta);
    xform.eM12 = (float)sin(theta);
    xform.eM21 = (float)-sin(theta);
    xform.eM22 = (float)cos(theta);
    xform.eDx = 0;
    xform.eDy = 0;

    SetGraphicsMode(hDC, GM_ADVANCED);
    ModifyWorldTransform(hDC, &xform,
MWT_LEFTMULTIPLY);
    Ellipse(hDC, 80, 40, 230, 115);
    ModifyWorldTransform(hDC, &xform,
MWT_IDENTITY);
    SetGraphicsMode(hDC, GM_COMPATIBLE);
}

long FAR PASCAL
WndProc(HWND hWnd, UINT message, WPARAM
wParam,
                    LPARAM lParam)
{
  switch ( message )
  {
  case WM_PAINT:
    {
      PAINTSTRUCT ps;
      HDC hDC = BeginPaint(hWnd,&ps);
      paint(hDC);
      EndPaint(hWnd, &ps);
      return 0;
    }
  case WM_DESTROY:
    PostQuitMessage(0);
    return 0;
  }
  return
DefWindowProc(hWnd,message,wParam,lParam);
}
```

```
int PASCAL WinMain (HINSTANCE hInstance,
HINSTANCE hPrevInstance,
             LPSTR lpszCmdLine, int
nCmdShow)
{
    static char szAppName[] = "Ellipse";

    WNDCLASS wc;
    wc.style       = CS_HREDRAW |
CS_VREDRAW;
    wc.lpfnWndProc  = WndProc;
    wc.cbClsExtra   = 0;
    wc.cbWndExtra   = 0;
    wc.hInstance    = hInstance;
    wc.hIcon        =
LoadIcon(NULL,IDI_APPLICATION);
    wc.hCursor      = LoadCursor(NULL,
IDC_ARROW);
    wc.hbrBackground =
(HBRUSH)GetStockObject(WHITE_BRUSH);
    wc.lpszMenuName  = NULL;
    wc.lpszClassName = szAppName;
    RegisterClass(&wc);

    HWND hWnd = CreateWindow(szAppName,
"Ellipse Test",
        WS_OVERLAPPEDWINDOW,
CW_USEDEFAULT, CW_USEDEFAULT,
        500, 500, NULL, NULL, hInstance, NULL);

    ShowWindow(hWnd, nCmdShow);
    UpdateWindow(hWnd);

    MSG msg;
    while (TRUE)
    {
        if (PeekMessage(&msg, NULL, 0, 0,
PM_REMOVE))
        {
            if (msg.message == WM_QUIT)
                break;

            HACCEL hAccel = NULL;
            if (!TranslateAccelerator(hWnd, hAccel,
&msg))
            {
                TranslateMessage(&msg);
                DispatchMessage(&msg);
            }
        }
    }
    return msg.wParam;
}
```

This program is written in the Win32 API. The Windows 95 version of that API
does not support drawing figures at an angle. This Win32 program runs on NT
but will not run on Windows 95/8.

Now compare this with the equivalent Java program on the next page.

A Java Program to Draw an Oval at an Angle

```java
// Java version of program that draws an ellipse rotated 30 degrees.

import java.awt.*;
import java.awt.geom.*;
import java.awt.event.*;

public class Rotate extends Canvas {
    public void paint(Graphics g) {
        Graphics2D g2 = (Graphics2D) g;
        g2.setRenderingHint(RenderingHints.KEY_ANTIALIASING,
                RenderingHints.VALUE_ANTIALIAS_ON);

        AffineTransform at = new AffineTransform();
        at.rotate((30*java.lang.Math.PI)/180);
        g2.transform(at);
        g2.draw(new Ellipse2D.Float(80, 40, 150, 75));
        g2.setTransform(new AffineTransform());
    }
    public static void main(String s[]) {
        WindowListener l = new WindowAdapter() {
            public void windowClosing(WindowEvent e) {System.exit(0);}
            public void windowClosed(WindowEvent e) {System.exit(0);}
        };
        Frame f = new Frame("Rotate");
        f.addWindowListener(l);
        f.add("Center", new Rotate());
        f.pack();
        f.setSize(new Dimension(400,300));
        f.show();
    }
}
```

The Java version does the same thing as the preceeding NT program, and it runs fine on Windows 95 as well as Windows NT. Not only that, the Java version automatically does anti-aliasing too, and is shorter and simpler! Anti-aliasing is a sophisticated graphics technique to make lines appear smoother. Not only can you run on more Windows platforms if you use Java than if you use the Win32 API, but you also get more functionality!

The output from the Java program is shown below.

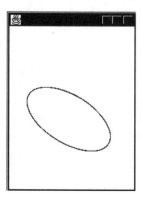

Internationalization

Internationalization is the way we support software that can be used in many different countries. Different countries have different languages, currency, different formats for numbers and dates, and different sorting conventions for their alphabets. Internationalization (often abbreviated to i18n because there are 18 letters between the "i" and the "n") is the framework that allows us to write the software once and make it independent of all these variations.

Localization (often abbreviated to L10n) goes hand in glove with i18n. It is the process of customizing the software for one specific locale or region of the world. The biggest part of internationalizing software is replacing hardcoded assumptions with calls to library routines and designing user interfaces that deal with layout changes arising from different language requirements (English vs. German vs. Japanese). Apart from changes in currency specifiers, date formats, and number punctuation, the programmer must extract all the message strings into a separate file. Different versions of that message file can then be substituted in different locales. Figure 9–3 illustrates i18n and L10n techniques.

When a software company wants to trade globally, its costs are lowered substantially if it uses internationalized software. With i18n, the company merely needs to provide a new localization for each country. Without i18n, it is faced with porting the entire program for each locale. Most i18n schemes require one locale to be set for an entire computer system or at best a process. Java supports a different locale for each individual object. You might use more than one locale in a program that does currency conversion.

I18n is a comparative newcomer to the software scene. I18n is part of the 1989 ANSI C Standard, but support in C is clumsy in the extreme. The character type is 1 byte long in C by definition, which unfortunately doesn't match the modern reality of non-European human languages. That means that C requires special 16-bit-wide versions of all the string routines, and at least two versions of the software (Asian and non-Asian) are needed.

Java bit the bullet from the start by defining characters as 16-bit Unicode characters, a choice that is unique among programming languages. Unicode is a code set like ASCII, but because it allows 65,536 different characters rather than the 128 of 7-bit ASCII, Unicode supports essentially all characters of all languages of the world. Seven-bit ASCII is a subset of Unicode. There was early dissent among the Java design team over making a character a 2-byte quantity because doing so doubles the amount of storage needed and slows everything down. But it is now seen to be the wiser course, and it means that Java can represent all the characters in the world and treat them all consistently. (One wishes that the various OS designers had been similarly forward looking in moving from 8-bit ASCII to 16-bit Unicode

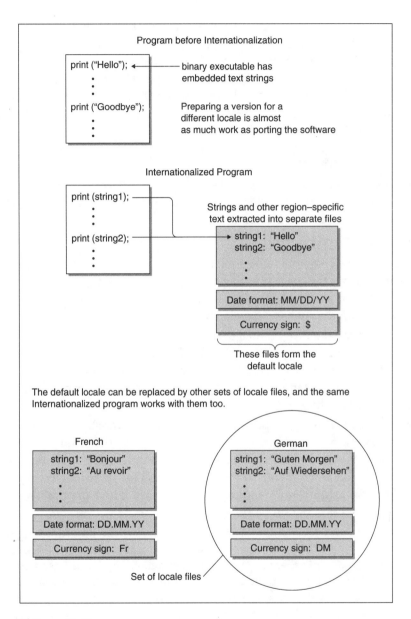

Figure 9-3
Internationalization and Localization

when the opportunity presented itself. In the UNIX world, one such opportunity was the transition to SVr4 UNIX; another was the transition to 64-bit address spaces.) Microsoft's NT operating system has 16-bit Unicode support.

Although 16-bit characters were in Java from the start, full i18n support didn't come until the JDK 1.1 release introduced the necessary APIs for adapting text, currency, numbers, dates, to local formats. The heterogeneous nature of Java, and its "download to anywhere" model gave i18n a special importance, but i18n still relies on underlying support from the browser or OS. If the execution environment cannot input or output Chinese characters, then neither can Java, though it can manipulate them internally.

Related Initiatives

Sun Microsystems has recognized at the highest levels within the company that Java is a significant new technology that should be nurtured and sustained. Several initiatives have been announced.

Programmer Certification

In September 1996, Sun announced the certification process for Java programmers. This matches the corresponding certification process for Microsoft Windows programmers. Two levels of capabilities are recognized by Sun Java Certification: programmer and developer.

- Sun Certified Java Programmer—This level tests for overall Java knowledge as well as programming concepts and applet development skills. An independently administered examination must be passed to achieve the Sun Certified Java Programmer status. Training courses are available from Sun and other companies to help people prepare for the test.

- Sun Certified Java Developer—Candidates must have passed the Java Programmer exam prior to taking this exam. The Sun Certified Java Developer level tests the candidate's ability to perform complex programming through an application assignment, followed by a test on the knowledge required to perform the assignment. Candidates are provided with a program specification and a set of program modules.

  To become Sun Certified, candidates must complete the programming necessary to develop a fully running, functional application. In addition, candidates must pass an independently administered exam that is based on the work undertaken to complete the programming application. Upon successful completion of the examination, the individual candidates may use the designation "Sun Certified Java Developer."

100% Pure Java

The 100% Pure Java initiative was launched in December 1996 to build industry momentum behind the guarantee of wholly compatible Java. Sun felt it important to form an industrywide coalition to champion platform portability.

The thrust of the 100% Pure Java effort is an exacting test suite that checks program compatibility. This test suite provides certification and branding for applications that pass. A similar test suite checks JVM implementations for compatibility. It currently contains thousands of tests and takes all night to run on Sun's fastest desktop system. A similar process was put in place 15 years earlier for Ada compiler validation.

The 100% Pure Java brand is a kind of quality seal of approval that assures ISVs and customers alike that the software will run on all platforms. It's like a stronger version of the "Windows compliant" brand. The branding effort has a special "100% Pure Java" logo (see Figure 9–4)

Figure 9–4
100% Pure Java Logo

The announcement of the 100% Pure Java effort was made at Internet World exhibition and included support from IBM, Apple Computer, Inc., Oracle Corporation, and Netscape Communications Corporation. It is critically important to all these companies and to the computer industry as a whole that Microsoft fail in its bid to fragment Java and undermine program portability. The computer industry has the chance to respond and show that it understands and values the keystone of Java: the ability to write programs once and have them run anywhere, regardless of the underlying operating system or microprocessor. Over 300 software products and systems were awarded the 100% Pure Java brand in the first few months of the initiative.

The Java Lobby

Java Developer Rick Ross, founder of software house Activated Intelligence, formed the Java Lobby in 1997. The Java Lobby is a grassroots organization of developers dedicated to furthering platform-neutral software. Membership is free. The Java Lobby was joined by more than 20,000 people in its first year, and has been very successful at voicing the concerns and wishes of ordinary developers. In summer 1998, the Java Lobby embarked on its most difficult crusade: an initiative to persuade PC vendors to bundle a standard Java VM and browser plug-in with their PCs. The software is available for free from a couple of sources, and technically it is quick and easy to install.

The problem for PC vendors is that bundling standard Java would annoy Microsoft greatly, and PC vendors are dependent on Microsoft for their operating system. Most companies are afraid to defy Microsoft's wishes. In July 1998 Unigram reported claims from a former employee of PC vendor Acer. The ex-Acer product manager said that Acer persistently yielded to pressure from Microsoft Corporation to use its products at the expense of competitors. Acer is said to have cancelled a software licensing deal with Corel Corporation, when Microsoft told Acer company bosses it would displease them.

Before PC vendors will bundle standard Java, they will need to be convinced of "pull" from the market. They will need to overcome their fear of Microsoft with a greater fear that they will lose business to a competitor. The first one will be hard to convince, but then the floodgates will open. The Java Lobby has a web site at `http://www.javalobby.org`.

Java in Operating Systems

When Java applets are run, there is no issue with software installation. The browser contains a JVM, and the executable applet is downloaded from the web page being browsed. However, when a user wants to run a stand-alone Java application, the JVM must first have been installed on that system. This requirement is a barrier to portability.

The way to meet the requirement is to have the JVM bundled as a standard part of the operating system, just as other common software tools, such as a simple calculator, a text editor, and mail program, are bundled. That's exactly what has happened. As early as April 1996, all the leading computer companies committed to embed Java directly in their operating systems. When this embedding is done right, Java programs can be run directly without the need to specify the Java interpreter on each invocation. Instead of typing the command—

```
java myprogram
```

—the user can just type

```
myprogram
```

—and the system will recognize that the program is a Java class file and send it to the JVM, just as it currently recognizes that batch files (shell scripts in UNIX) are executed in a different manner from binary executables. This makes Java programs as convenient to run as any other programs on the system. The vendors and the operating systems that bundle Java are shown in Table 9-2.

Table 9-2 Operating Systems Which Have a Java Virtual Machine

OS Vendor	Product
Windows	
• Microsoft Corporation	Windows 95, Windows 98, NT
Macintosh	
• Apple Computer, Inc.	MacOS
OS/2	
• International Business Machines	OS/2
UNIX	
• Hewlett Packard Corp.	HP-UX
• Hitachi, Ltd.	Hitachi OS
• International Business Machines	AIX
• Silicon Graphics, Inc.	Irix
• Sun Microsystems, Inc.	Solaris
• The Santa Cruz Operation, Inc. (SCO)	UNIXWare
• Tandem Computers (Compaq)	Non-Stop Kernel
• Digital Equipment Corp (Compaq)	Digital Unix
• Linux Community	Linux
• Santa Cruz Operation	UNIXware
Network OS	
• Novell, Inc.	NetWare 4.0
• Sun Microsystems	JavaOS
VMS	
• Digital Equipment Corp (Compaq)	VMS
Other OS	
• QNX	QNX
• Wind River Systems	VxWorks
• Be, Inc.	BeOS
• Acorn	RiscOS
• Amiga	AmigaOS
• StrongARM	RiscOS
Mainframe OS	
• International Business Machines	MVS (OS/390)
• International Business Machines	OS/400 Version V3R6

Bundling creates an important new distribution channel for Java, as well as offering a new capability for the operating system. Developers will have easy access to the Java Virtual Machine. They'll be able to write software, using the full range of APIs described earlier. They will be assured that their software will work not just on the development system, but on all the systems on which Java is installed. Users are spared the bother of downloading the JDK in order to run portable software.

Microsoft is perhaps a surprising addition to the list of licensees, as it has most to lose from portable desktop software. Microsoft's approach is to fragment and extend the Java API with a series of proprietary software lock-ins. Microsoft diverged from standard Java early, and with each new release J++ gets further away. The language has some unnecessary new keywords, and it lacks important libraries like JNI, Beans, Swing, RMI, and Java 2D. A federal judge issued an injunction forbidding Microsoft from claiming that J++ is compatible with Java.

So why did Sun license Java to Microsoft? Because Microsoft added credibility to Java at an early stage. Before Microsoft became a Java licensee, deals were pitched to other OS vendors and debated at great length one by one. After Microsoft announced its intention to license Java, the remaining OS vendors fell over themselves in their eagerness to become Java licensees.

Now that Java is a standard feature of all these operating systems, application developers can feel confident in writing to it, and users can expect to use it. Being bundled with essentially all operating systems is a powerful new distribution channel for Java. If you use standard Java on a PC at work, consider asking the PC vendor to preinstall it.

Some Final Words on Productivity

The wide range of library functions provided with Java undoubtedly has a positive effect on programmer productivity. Each programmer can build on the core APIs and doesn't have to keep reinventing the wheel. What does that contribute in measurable terms? Programmer productivity is notoriously hard to measure. There are no universally accepted metrics, so some people judge by what is easy to measure (lines of code per day). An automotive repair garage typically has a manual for each type of vehicle, showing the standard labor times to carry out each repair. For any given make and model of car, it tells the standard time to replace the clutch, to fit a new brake cylinder, and so on. There is no such manual of standard times for programming tasks.

A second difficulty is that many tasks in software are next to impossible to estimate in advance. When I get a bug report about a defect in a massive and highly complex system like the Solaris operating system kernel, the aspect that takes my software team the longest time is usually understanding exactly the nature of the fault, why it happens, and when. Often the code to repair it is just a few lines long to take care of some obscure special case, but on really hard bugs, it can take weeks to locate and diagnose that failure.

However, by far the biggest part of the problem is that individual programmers vary so much in their productivity. When I have some software that needs to be written, if I assign the task to one programmer on my team, it will be completed in a week. A different programmer will be able to do it in a day. If I assign the task to a third programmer, he may never be able to get the job done.

That's why I am skeptical about the software metrics that have been proposed so far. They completely omit the critical issue of programmer ability, and they oversimplify the difficulty of measuring the creative design process in favor of measuring things that are easier to measure. We won't even consider the problem that when people know their productivity is rated on something like lines of code, they can easily inflate it artificially. Managers who use software metrics tacitly assume that measures of the output (lines of code, number of variables, and the like) bear some kind of direct productivity relationship to the process that created them. But I dispute that assumption. You can't tell by reading *Catch-22* that it took Joseph Heller 20 years to write it. And even if you know that, how do you relate his slow productivity as a writer to the quality of the work?

About all that software engineering managers can do is fall back on experience. We try to classify tasks as similar to ones that we have seen before, and we know how long it took last time. Then we fold in our knowledge of individual team member capabilities and come up with an overall estimate that can be passing-fair accurate.

So, having written the world's longest disclaimer on programmer productivity, let me add a few words about empirical experience. Many programmers report that they are more productive when writing in Java than in other comparable languages. They claim that they can write more working code faster and that the code has fewer bugs which are easier to find than in, say, C++. I have heard claims ranging from 25 percent more productive than in C++, all the way up to five times more productive (Mike Lehman, Cereus Design Corp.), which is quite possible on some tasks.

Sometimes, when evaluating Java, a manager will ask "How much do you claim it will speed up development time?" The answer is "what methodologies do you currently use to measure software productivity?" If an organization is not currently keeping track of software productivity, how would anyone know if there was an improvement or not? Because the field of software productivity is not well-defined, it boils down to anecdotal evidence, and reports from programmers on their personal experiences. My personal experience programming in Java, in C, and in C++ is that there is significantly less scope for creating bugs in Java and those that are created are caught at run time at the point of failure (e.g., bad array indexes cause an immediate exception). This makes programming both faster and a more pleasant experience.

Case Study 6: How Java Affects Programmer Productivity

Programmer productivity is hard to measure against standard benchmarks, but changes in productivity are easier to see.

One experienced programmer, Jim Frost of Boston, Massachusetts, has programmed a variety of software systems over the past 10 years: first in C, then later in C++, and most recently in Java.

"In C," explains Jim, "it was relatively easy to achieve high performance, but the libraries offered only very basic functionality. If you needed a hash table or some other data structure, you had to write and debug your own.

"C++ offered little improvement in the early days, but as it matured, many class libraries became available to supply those features. Unfortunately, C++ was also considerably more complex than C in many ways. Productivity gains realized through larger basic building blocks and easier reuse were often lost in managing the greater complexity of the language itself." As a result, Jim often chose to avoid new C++ features to keep down the code complexity.

One area in which C++ offered little improvement was in heap management, a large thorn in the side of its predecessor as well. Jim says, "Heap management in C and C++ is a huge problem—large enough that entire commercial products like Purify, CodeCenter, and Bounds Checker have been built primarily to detect them. Unfortunately these tools are only as effective as the testing practices of the development organization, so many failures still make it into released code."

Jim first came into contact with Java in 1995 while he was working on the creation of a GUI front end for an Internet service provider. He says, "I took one look at the language and decided that it solves virtually all of the problems I'd run into using

C++." The most obvious problem that Java solved was heap management; garbage collection and run-time error checking eliminated any chance of heap corruption and made management of complex data structures much simpler. But the benefits didn't stop there.

"A lot of the complexity and ambiguity present in C++ is simply not there. Many people complain about the lack of features like operator overloading, but my experience has been that those features are almost universally abused; I can live without them."

Jim also points to problems caused by C++'s incremental development. "One serious problem in C++ is that the language did not have exception handling built in from the start, so it is an optional element. This makes it easy for a programmer to fail to handle exceptions, so reliability isn't as good as it could be. Furthermore, failing to handle an exception can cause the omission of heap cleanup operations in intermediate frames, so you often see memory leaks."

In Java the list of thrown exceptions is part of the method signature; it must be handled explicitly. This tends to lead to fine-grained error handling in the first code creation pass, and that means that applications are generally more robust right from the start. And since heap management is handled automatically, simply passing on exceptions causes no resource loss.

Improvements are not found only in the language itself, however, but also in typical implementations. Since Java compilers read superclass information from compiled representations rather than the C++ technique of using the source, compilation is often much faster. Furthermore, the Java technique of packaging only class-local information in the compiled representations makes subclasses far less dependent on superclass implementations, minimizing the number of classes you may have to recompile. Lastly, Java virtual machines perform program linkage at run time—eliminating an entire step in the compile-to-debug cycle compared to C++. Says Jim, "My edit/compile/debug cycles in C++ tended to take a minimum of five minutes, even with precompiled header files and incremental linkers. In Java they rarely take more than a few seconds. That allows me to make much smaller changes and test them more frequently than was practical in C++."

The overall result? Not only is Java code generally more reliable, but productivity is often improved significantly. "My productivity using Java is approximately 300 percent greater than it was using C++ on average, and defects are much rarer and easier to correct," says Jim. "I was very much surprised, as I thought I was doing quite well with C++."

Not everyone will see such benefits, however: "Java's productivity benefits differ significantly depending on what you're doing. I'm only about 50 percent more productive when building GUI-intensive code without a construction tool." In other areas, however, productivity enhancements with Java have been "literally amazing," according to Jim. "In one recent case I needed to write identical client/server communications code in both C++ and Java. The Java code represented about two thousand lines of code and was finished in a day. Only one bug has ever been reported against it, and it was fixed in less than ten minutes. My initial estimates for the C++ implementation were three days, using my typical three-to-one C++-to-Java productivity ratio. This turned out to be very optimistic; it required fifteen days to complete the initial implementation, and three more days were dedicated to tracking down subtle bugs in heap and thread management. The code was nearly three times the size of the Java implementation, despite nearly identical class library support at the outset."

Can other programmers expect to repeat the experience that Jim Frost had? "Certainly," said Jim. "We've found that we can bring competent C++ programmers up to speed in Java in a matter of days, and they achieve a high degree of fluency in a matter of a week or two. Moreover, we've found that many programmers don't want to go back to using C++."

A number of features in Java eliminate the opportunity for bugs that bedevil developers in other languages. These Java features definitely increase productivity and reduce the cost of software development—it is just really hard to quantify. The productivity gains of using Java should be considered as one immediate benefit that you get for the cost of retraining your staff.

Summary

- Java comes with a very rich set of standard libraries that cover all important areas of computing, including windowing, networking, and enterprise database access.
- The Swing Java library bundled with JDK 1.2 (and available unbundled for JDK 1.1) provides a toolkit at least as good as any other modern toolkit, and in some respects far better. Java GUI programs can change their look and feel to suit the preferences of individual users.
- Microsoft's best shot at containing Java lies in undermining its portability. The rest of the computer industry's best shot at containing Microsoft lies in supporting Java and Java portability.
- Sun is backing Java by several key means:
  - Building industry support for Java portability
  - Programmer, language, and application certification
  - Creating Java versions of the various Microsoft Windows support initiatives and channels
- Considerable empirical evidence suggests that programmer productivity is increased by Java's simplicity, its memory management, and its libraries.

CHAPTER 10

- What Is Client/Server?

- Scaling Up: Intranets and Extranets

- One-, Two-, and Three-Tier Systems

- Case Study 7: Multitiered System across the Internet

- Summary

Client/Server and the Intranet

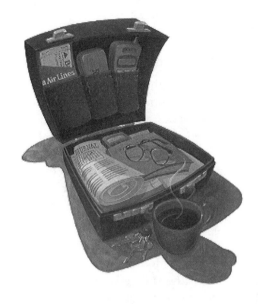

What Is Client/Server?

The term *client/server* describes a broad range of computing techniques, some of which have existed for decades in one form or another, although not always under that name. In general terms, a *client* is something that uses a service or a resource, and a *server* is something that supplies the service or resource to the client. Attorneys have clients. Physicians have clients. In this context, attorneys function as legal advice "servers," and physicians serve as health maintenance "servers." Their clients need legal advice or medical help. In general, the service provider (server) is not dedicated to a single client but rather shares its resources among many clients at their request.

In a computing context, a client is a computer in need of some computer-related service or resource, and a server is a computer that provides it. There are generally many clients connected to a server. A typical service is access to a file system or a database. The most common present-day example of a client/server system is a corporate SQL database on a mainframe (the server) connected to many PCs (the clients). The PC sends the mainframe requests to extract or update data. The mainframe responds to the requests by sending over the data. The PC formats and displays the data for the user. On UNIX workstations, it is very common to have a "home directory server" that stores the personal disk space for many users and serves it up to them, using the Network File System (NFS). Instead of individual users each having a small disk, a larger central disk farm is attached to a server. It is cheaper per byte and much easier to back up and administer.

How Is Client/Server Different from Timesharing?

How does the client/server setup differ from the older timesharing model of hundreds of dumb IBM 3270 (or DEC VT100, or similar) terminals attached to the same mainframe? The IBM 3270 terminal was the mainstay of on-line mainframe systems from the late 1970s on. It grew to be a capable output device with some ability for simple data validation (e.g., you can program a forms-like interface on a 3270 and specify "this field can only accept numbers"). When data had been entered in all fields on the screen, the terminal transmitted the whole screenful as one event to the host to be processed. The 3270 was only ever an I/O device and had no generalized processing power.

When the I/O terminal has essentially no processing power of its own, the client/server terminology is not applied, even though the server CPU would be useless without some output peripheral. When the terminal has some role to play in the processing, suddenly a client/server relationship emerges. The critical distinction is that under the client/server model, both ends of the connection have processing power. Why does this make a difference? There are three principal reasons.

- First, the distributed processing shares the load, making it possible for one server to handle many more requests than if it had to do all the work. Users see better overall response times, and expensive centralized mainframe cycles are traded off for cheap local PC cycles.

- Second, intelligent clients—PCs and workstations—have far better graphical user interfaces than terminals with no local processing power. It's possible to display 2D and 3D graphs, animate them, and generally visualize data.

- Third, extracts from the mainframe data can be incorporated into local spreadsheets, word processed documents, and analysis programs. The technique is termed "screen scraping" because data is peeled off a display and rolled into a program for number crunching. This flexibility was impossible under the old timesharing model.

Figure 10–1 illustrates some examples of typical client/servers. Figure 10–2 illustrates a common system configuration that is not a client/server example.

Why Client/Server?

Client/server computing has become popular because it fills a real business need. That need was for a growth in specialization coupled with a reduction in resources and a shortening of reaction time. Faced with increasing local and global competition and ever-higher service expectations from their customers, companies must continually find ways to become more market driven and to do so with less investment. One way to do that is to flatten the company hierarchy and

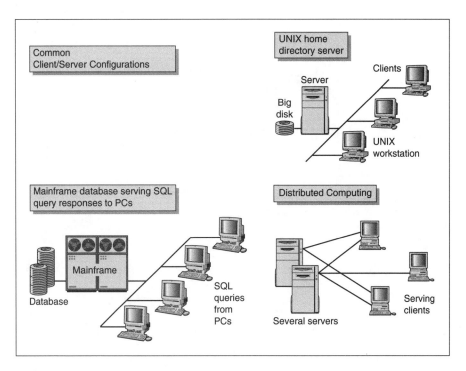

Figure 10–1
Common Examples of Client/Server

give more decision-making power to a wider range of people. In order to make these decisions, people need increased MIS support, but under the influence of the resource cutbacks, that support also had to be pushed out into regions while accessing central databases. Client/server computing is the only way to connect all these dots.

With client/server, the specialization in the staffing and marketing strategies can be mirrored in the MIS architecture, although at the loss of some control and at the risk of higher costs in hardware, software, networking, and administration. Nevertheless, the increased flexibility and reduced reaction time has proven its worth, and client/server has been the enterprise computing paradigm of the past decade.

The client/server model is a range of solutions in between the two extremes of totally centralized computing and totally decentralized (just PCs) computing. The two end points are shown in Figure 10–3.

Client/server offers the chance to occupy other positions between these ranges. Client/server computing has become the enterprise computing paradigm of

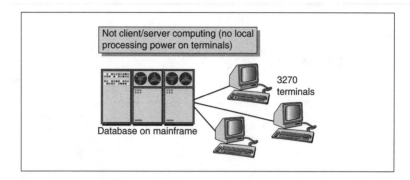

Figure 10–2
A Common Non-Client/Server Configuration

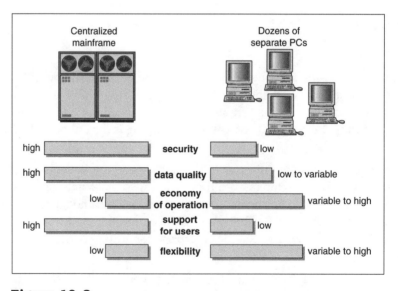

Figure 10–3
The Extremes of Centralized and Decentralized Computing

the 90s. For nearly the first three decades of its existence, enterprise computing was dominated by the mainframe-with-attached-terminals configuration. Although such configurations are still around (in the airline industry, for example), their growth has slowed considerably, if not stopped altogether, in favor of client/server models.

Advantages and Disadvantages of Client/Server

Client/server offers these advantages:

- Specialized front/back ends—The mainframe can do what it is good at: warehousing large amounts of data under tight central control. The desktop computer can do what it is good at: visually displaying and processing small extracted amounts of data according to individual preferences.

- Centralized administration, security, backups—These expensive but essential functions work best when they are under central control. The client/server model ensures that data is appropriately safeguarded.

- Distributed processing—Client/server allows the PC easy access to centralized corporate data on several different servers. Users get used to working that way and seem to like it. Once you put a PC on a desktop, it's very hard to dislodge it.

- Capacity—Because the client/server model splits the work across the client and the server, a given server can handle more clients, deferring costly upgrades of mainframe hardware.

- Scalability—It's easier to add capacity to a client/server environment than to a mainframe. If the mainframe is inadequate for the load, you generally have to replace it with a bigger, faster, higher-capacity mainframe at an extreme cost in money and time. Augmenting a client/server environment is easier and generally a lot cheaper.

- Algorithm benefit in splitting system design—The software design is usually simplified by separation into multiple components. On the other hand, you now have multiple components to test and get working together.

- Geographical separation—Client systems ease telecommuting by providing a virtual presence at the central site, as well as independent local processing. Large companies can be spread over the world and yet still have branch offices on line.

Client/server has these drawbacks:

- Teleprocessing and networking cost—Extra communications hardware is needed to connect freestanding PCs to a mainframe. The cheapest connection is a dedicated line to one central processor, but the most useful connection is a generalized network allowing the client to talk to any other system on the net, including other clients.

- Client administration can be costly—The next chapter describes the hidden costs of PCs. These costs can be significant in terms of "person hours consumed." When an employee is restoring a data file from backup, or even worse, trying to reconstruct lost data that was not backed up, there is an opportunity cost of more productive work that is delayed or left undone.

- Extra software needed—Both ends of the client/server connection need communications software. Users need to learn how to use this software and troubleshoot simple problems.

The key feature of the client/server model that contributes to its popularity is its adaptability. But to get that adaptability, there are financial and control costs that have to be paid. The enormous and rapid growth in the use of client/server computing by organizations of all sizes is evidence that these costs are not perceived as a fatal drawback to client/server by the MIS community.

Here's the bottom line. If you have massive amounts of data over which you need to exercise lots of control, put it into a big, centralized site. If you have no need for taking regional or local data into account (after all, the flight schedules for an airline are the same whether you are looking at them from Poland or Poughkeepsie), then you can save capital by hooking up dumb terminals to the central mainframe. On the other hand, if your organization is small enough or focused enough to stick to a very small number of specialized PC-based applications, then you may find all your computing needs can be satisfied solely by deploying PCs. Most organizations will be somewhere in between these two end points. This means that some flavor of client/server computing may be the right architecture for you.

Newer paradigms have always replaced older ones in computing. On-line systems replaced many batch-processing applications. Client/server systems are frequently an improvement over elementary on-line systems (see Figure 10–4), and now Java computing is becoming the latest in the sequence.

No one technique is perfect for all circumstances. There are values for each of the critical parameters that could well tip the decision in any of the three directions: centralized systems, PC-based systems, or client/server systems. Furthermore, the "rightness" of the decision could change drastically over a span of five or ten years because of changing circumstances in product, market, or infrastructure.

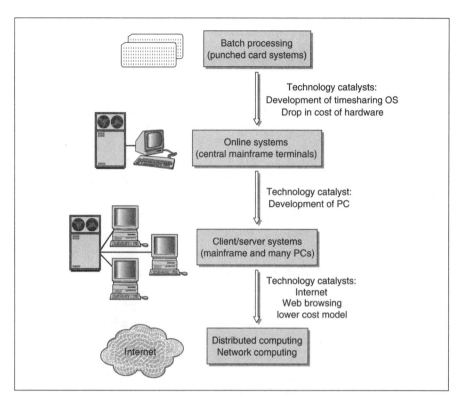

Figure 10–4
Technology Catalysts

The critical advantage of Java is that it works smoothly with all of these paradigms. Java runs on the client, on the server, and as any application middleware or glue connecting them. Companies that have standardized on Windows find themselves implementing in three different languages: Visual Basic on the client, T/SQL on the corporate database, and C++ to connect the two. They also must master the complexities of COM, DCOM, and/or COM+ to tie the pieces together.

Scaling Up: Intranets and Extranets

The earliest printed reference to the term "intranet" is in the April 24, 1995, edition of Digital News & Review in a story entitled "Intranets Fuel Growth of Internet Access Tools," by Stephen Lawton. Although the technique had not yet been named, it was already in widespread use, as Lawton pointed out when he wrote, "In many cases, intranets have grown on the corporate side of the firewall in ways that emulate the public, capital 'I' Internet, and have assumed an almost anarchistic approach. Because of the relatively low cost and readily available Web server software, almost anyone who can write in HyperText Markup Language (HTML) can set up a Web server, analysts agree."

We've already talked about the amazing growth of the worldwide Internet in an earlier chapter. By now you either already know or have correctly guessed that an "intranet" is the name for a computer network like the Internet, except that it is dedicated to communication within a single organization rather than across the whole world. An *intranet* is an internet (collection of networks) that exists inside something, such as inside a company or an educational institution. In this case, "inside" can mean either physically, as within a building, or logically, as within a protected private network between distant sites.

The private network might actually share bandwidth with the Internet e.g., e-mail to faraway branch offices may be routed on the Internet for final delivery. This then becomes an *extranet*. An extranet is the use of the Internet to communicate with partners, suppliers, and customers. Overall, the intranet is a private facility inside an organization, and the extranet extends access to the same software and data across the Internet to geographically-remote sites. A typical use here is allowing customers to directly view certain price/delivery information and place orders. No expensive special reprogramming is needed to turn an internal intranet application into an external Internet one. All that is required is to make the appropriate URL visible through the company firewall. (You need to review whether this is appropriate from a security perspective). The case study at the end of this chapter gives one such real-life example. The term "extranet" only appeared in 1997. Again, companies were using the technique before it had a name. Things happen fast on the Internet.

Extranets and intranets let organizations use the data formatting, searching, retrieval, presentation, and context switching that are so characteristic of the World Wide Web. Java is right in the middle of this revolution, as the only software technology that allows secure execution across the web. It provides safe, consistent services for both an extranet or an intranet. And it includes the GUI, networking, and database services that the applications demand.

Once someone in a company provides intranet infrastructure, users quickly catch on to web publishing. The infrastructure might be put in place by the MIS department, but it is so cheap and easy that it may even be done by technically alert users themselves if the MIS department falls too far behind the times. Although a few vendors still offer proprietary network protocols, they are trying to move as fast as possible to the TCP/IP alternatives. UNIX workstation vendors have been built on TCP/IP for a couple of decades, so all the key Internet tools were developed on and for UNIX originally.

The term "intranet" was first used in early 1995, though the technology had been established and matured over the previous two decades. The diagram below shows an intranet.

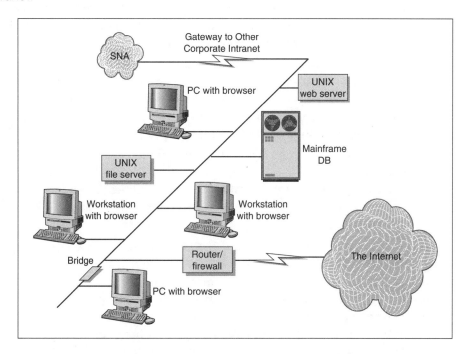

Intranets are made up of five key building blocks:

- browsers (the client interface)
- server software
- the TCP/IP network that connects clients and servers
- platforms (server and client operating systems)
- firewalls (to keep the site secure from outside penetration)

When a computer supports TCP/IP, it can be connected to any other piece of hardware that also supports TCP/IP, with vendor incompatibilities reduced to a thing of the past. An intranet can thus be built incrementally at low cost, connecting existing hardware. It costs about $300 per seat to glue clients and servers together in an intranet. At some point, a critical mass of information producers and consumers is reached, and completion of the intranet becomes a priority. This critical mass of users means that an intranet, like any LAN or WAN (Local- or Wide-Area Network), is probably not cost effective for SOHO (Small Office, Home Office) users.

Companies usually start web publishing with "brochureware" applications. They may be mundane, but they are undeniably cost effective in distributing information. There are three principal side benefits:

- The information is distributed in paperless form. Many previous systems relied on hard-copy memos being hand carried to in trays. Paperless distribution is faster, more private, and more reliable.

- The distribution model changes from "push" to "pull." Although apparently trivial, this is actually a significant change. Instead of the information provider being responsible for making sure all users are issued current copies when something changes, the user now browses a web site and automatically gets the latest, freshest copy of the information.

- Because it is easy to publish and share information, users tend to do this. Each individual department in a company will likely create its own web site, naming the people in the team, what their responsibilities are, and the best ways to schedule work in that department. Overall communication and awareness in the organization is raised.

Because of the World Wide Web, many kinds of research that were largely ignored because of the effort involved can now be undertaken in seconds by the relatively unskilled. In today's global business climate, important decisions may sometimes need to be made in minutes, and rapid availability of data may be the only institutional advantage at hand. Somewhere in your company there are probably pockets of useful electronic resources to which access either does not exist or is too restricted. These pockets may well be an important source of knowledge with potential to give you an edge over your competitors. An intranet can make these pockets available around the enterprise more easily than could any other previous combination of hardware and software technology available to you—and for a moderate outlay (assuming you've already begun deploying client/server). Does that sound useful?

Your new company intranet may not actually supply your employees with business data substantially different from what they have been used to in the past. But because of tools such as browsers, web servers, HTML, VRML, Java, and so on, now being made available for networks designed like the Internet, accessing and researching this data will be orders of magnitude more easy (and less costly to implement) than could have been possible over any other previous form of internal company network. Maintaining the support structure that makes this intranet possible will also be easier, given these same tools. You really ought to consider what an intranet could do for your enterprise.

Once the early adopters in a company have successfully installed the brochure-ware applications, it is a natural next step to go on to more ambitious projects. The pioneers then use their intranets to send more mission-critical information around the company and finally use the company intranet to distribute executable content to the desks of key decision makers. At this point the intranet has moved from "interesting new technology" to "core business asset." Table 10-1 summarizes reasons why MIS departments worldwide are adopting intranets as their company internal network.

Table 10-1 Why Intranets Have Become the Way to Build a WAN/LAN

- Intranets are simple to create and configure.
- Intranets offer a standard way to publish information using a server and web browser.
- Only a minimum investment is required for starting.
- An intranet runs on your existing servers.
- It can be started piecemeal.
- It runs with minimal risk.
- It solves real communications problems.
- Intranets provide a flexible foundation for "future-proof" software applications, including Java-based software.
- Intranets are based on proven established open technology.

The one sentence summary of intranets is that they are the most cost-effective way to tie together clients to arbitrary servers.

In late 1996, Forrester Research carried out a poll of 50 major American information technology sites. The results were telling. Just under one-fifth of the companies (16 percent) had already installed a TCP/IP intranet. Bear in mind that the term didn't even exist 20 months earlier. By the end of 1997, fully two-thirds of these major computer users had the installation of a corporate intranet already planned or under consideration. Many, perhaps most, of these companies had corporate networks in the past. What is novel here is the speed of transition to open networking using web-based techniques. Figure 10–5 illustrates this growth.

Market watcher Zona Research predicted that intranet server revenues will be $7.8 billion worldwide by 1998. This makes the intranet business almost four times the size of the $1.8 billion Internet server market. By the year 2001, says European market research group Input, intranet-related products and services will account for 20 percent of the entire IT product and services market.

These spectacular growth figures indicate how intranets have moved from obscure UNIX technology to local web presence and then to strategic business asset. Software vendors have been quick to get on board. Lotus is building web

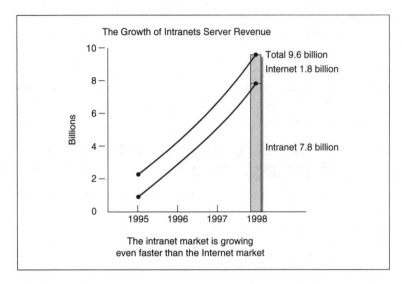

Figure 10–5
The Growth of Intranets

access into Lotus Notes, allowing users to browse the Notes database. SAP has similar plans for its R/3 business software. Systems integrators such as EDS and Andersen Consulting are now offering custom-built intranet services.

Intranet Security

As we've mentioned, passing company data over an enterprise intranet is more secure than passing it over the Internet. The most secure intranets are those that do not interact either logically or physically with the Internet. They are also the most expensive. Moreover, such a configuration takes away opportunities for the customer and the employees to interact. The next most secure arrangement is to limit access between the Internet and your intranet to a very few gateways. These gateways must be served by firewalls.

A *firewall* is a computer (or computer built into some network hardware) that screens each and every bit of data being sent through it in either direction. The data is not scanned for content, but rather for its form and type. The mechanism to perform this screening is called a *filter*. The firewall software would have no way of knowing your database layouts and fields, so it cannot filter based on whether the data being transferred is, say, the CEO's salary history. Rather, the filters determine what kind of network transaction is taking place and can decide either to allow or to prevent the transaction from passing through.

What makes up an intranet?

An intranet is a private network, inside a single organization, that uses the same technologies as the Internet, and so provides the same kind of connectivity and can be managed with the same tools.

An intranet will use these protocols:

Service	Open Internet Protocols	non-Open Alternative
Network communication and switching	TCP/IP	IPX (Novell)
Network administration	SNMP	CMIP (OSI)
Web browsing	HTTP	Lotus Notes
Text formatting & processing	HTML, DHTML, XML	MS Word
File system sharing	NFS, WebNFS	CIFS, DFS
Remote login	telnet and rlogin	—
E-mail service	SMTP, IMAP4 , POP3	PROFS, SNAD (IBM)
Object services and communication	IIOP (CORBA), Java RMI	COM (Microsoft) DSOM (IBM)
Downloadable executable	Java applet	Microsoft OLE or ActiveX

Java Security

A firewall filter can be set up that permits an e-mail transaction to pass, but not a request for a file transfer. Likewise, network control and internal routing messages can be blocked, but web page accesses (the http protocol) can proceed. The ongoing battle between network security and the ingenuity of crackers lies in the sophistication of filters versus the cleverness of making one kind of transaction look and act like another.

One important consideration worthy of mention here is that, from the outset, Java was designed to make it possible to bring executable code into an intranet (past the firewall) without exposing the intranet client to a security risk. While not, of course, guaranteeing that every applet ever fetched will be a secure one, it reduces to an acceptably low level the possibility of system penetration by a malicious outsider. No other form of automatically distributing executables over a network offers this feature.

There has been some ill-informed reporting on the topic, such as Beth Davis's story in Information Week, June 30, 1998 which made the mistaken claim that "Fortune 1000 companies agree that Java applets and ActiveX controls threaten to violate and destroy their networks." The part about ActiveX was accurate; the part about Java applets was guilt by association.

No technology implementation can guarantee absolute security, but the Java security architecture is the most secure model available to date for "network-mobile" code. In contrast, ActiveX technology which is the backbone of Microsoft DNA has given rise to several well-documented cases of system penetration across the Internet. It is a wise security precaution to block ActiveX packets at the firewall. There is no security-related reason to block Java applet packets.

In August 1998 a very high profile security bug was discovered in some popular PC mail products such as Microsoft Outlook and Outlook Express distributed with Internet Explorer, Windows 98, Windows 97, and Office 97. The bug was serious enough for the U.S. Department of Energy Computer Incident Advisory Capability (CIAC) to release a bulletin warning of it.

The e-mail programs did not properly handle the MIME name tags used to identify attached files. An invalid name tag could cause a buffer overflow condition which could be exploited to run any code. Thus the bug allowed an e-mail message to contain arbitrary malicious code which would be executed simply by reading the mail. The code could do anything, from plant a virus, to reformat the hard disk. Some Windows newsreaders and Netscape e-mail services were also vulnerable.

The buffer overflow vulnerability is, by now, a well-known weakness of C and C++. It was the weakness exploited by the Morris Internet worm in November 1988, and here it is turning up again a decade later. If the Microsoft e-mail programs had been written in Java, this potentially catastrophic bug could not occur. The buffer overflow vulnerability occurs when a program fails to check that a string will fit within the allotted memory space. Modern programming languages, including Java, do this check automatically, and the malicious programmer is not able to get around it. In java, if the data is too large for the buffer, an exception is thrown, preventing the stack from being overwritten or data corrupted. There is a certain performance cost to checking that every array access is within bounds, but incidents like this serious mailer bug show that the cost is a wise investment in a world of Internet computing. Older programming languages simply lack the security features built into Java.

One-, Two-, and Three-Tier Systems

The onslaught of the Internet and subsequently of the intranet concept has modified the client/server view somewhat by introducing the concept of software "tiers." In a one-tier system, one program on the host computer does everything. This is just the old "mainframe and 3270 terminals" model. The mainframe stores the database and also the programs that access it. A user sits in front of one of the directly connected terminals, logs in, and runs the extract/update/report software directly on the mainframe.

Introducing more than a single tier (client/server) is a way of imposing some organization and management on what otherwise might be a chaotic situation. It's also a good way of improving the distribution of your data processing resources. Figure 10–6 illustrates a one-tier system.

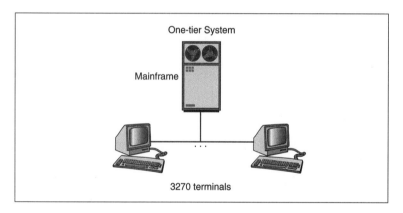

Figure 10–6
One-Tier System

The two-tier topology is representative of the classical client/server model. One tier is the server and one tier is the client. The classic client/server topology has a major drawback. Namely, the client-side software is replicated on every client. In a real estate broker's office with twenty sales people, keeping that client-side software up to date with maintenance releases and enhancements is not an overwhelming task. Doing that same task for a Fortune 1000 corporation, with thousands of client systems, is an expensive and more demanding effort. Multiply the number of client systems by the number of applications being maintained and you begin to get an idea of why maintenance and administration is so costly. Figure 10–7 illustrates a classic two-tier system.

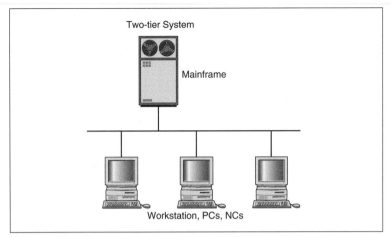

Figure 10-7
Two-Tier System

In a three-tier client/server model, the first tier is typically a large mainframe working as a database server, and the next two tiers divide up the client tier between them. The third tier is solely a GUI. It simply displays screens to the user, captures the input, and passes it to the middle tier. The middle tier in a three-tier system has all the "application logic." The middle tier knows how to talk SQL to the database server. It understands and implements the company's accounting rules, such as "Customers over 120 days in arrears with balances over $100 are delinquent." The middle tier is both a client (of the top tier) and a server (of the bottom tier). Figure 10–8 illustrates a three-tier system.

The middle tier is separated out for several reasons:

- It frees clients from dependencies on the exact implementation of the corporate database. This allows the database vendor to be changed (from Sybase to Oracle, say) without affecting client software at all. The database could in reality be several physical databases, each contributing a portion of the data. A three-tier system allows client/server to be easily deployed, using existing systems and infrastructure.

- It allows the "business logic" to be concentrated in one place. If the company's procedures change, for example, so customers over 90 days in arrears are now regarded as in default, the software change is solely restricted to this layer. There are many fewer servers in the middle layer than there are clients, so updating software is much cheaper. The middle tier is independent of the client GUIs.

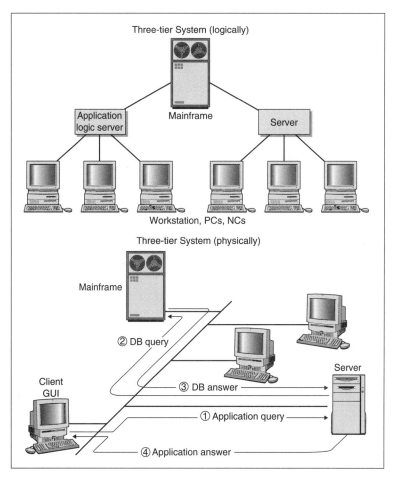

Figure 10–8
Three-Tier System

- It lets a system be implemented more efficiently. If the middle tier can batch teleprocessing requests from many clients to the database, it can greatly improve overall system throughput. In a two-tier system, if the client needs to calculate the total of some field, it will have to ask the database to transmit every record to it—a request that potentially places a very heavy load on the server and network.

- Scalability. The top and middle layers need not be a single system, but could be implemented by multiple servers for logistic, security, or performance reasons. The multiple sources will be hidden from the GUI layer.

You may also hear the term *middleware*. The strict definition of middleware is "anything that connects an application program to its data or adjacent tiers." The software in the middle tier often has middleware. Other people prefer to call it the "second tier" to avoid the inevitable confusion when people think that middleware is identical with the middle tier. The Java Database Connectivity library is middleware. The CORBA object communication system described in Chapter 12 is middleware. Some people use the term fat client to mean a client in a two-tier system, and thin client to mean a client in a three-tier system (i.e., a client that solely handles the GUI).

What is middleware?

Middleware is an increasingly common term, and it covers a multitude of things. The strict definition of middleware is any software that connects your program to its data or connects any two layers in a multitier system.

Middleware is typically communications and transport software, concerned with marshalling bits and moving them over the network. It might be as complex as a teleprocessing monitor or as simple as an http daemon.

Some examples of middleware are:

OS Communications middleware: OSF's Distributed Computing Environment (DCE), Novell's Netware, UNIX's named pipes, Banyan Vines LAN Manager and LAN Server.

Database-specific middleware: ODBC (Open DataBase Connectivity), JDBC (Java DataBase Connectivity).

Transaction Processing middleware: IBM's Customer Information Control System (CICS), Tuxedo's ATMI and /WS, The Open Group's TxRPC and XATMI. IBM has written new interfaces to CICS to ensure that Java programs can be well integrated.

Remote Object Communication middleware: Object Management Group's CORBA, Java's RMI. Microsoft's DCOM.

Groupware-specific middleware: Lotus Notes calls, UNIX's Simple Mail Transport Protocol (SMTP), MAPI.

Middleware encompasses all the software pieces that you need to connect the client to the server and pass meaningful data between them. It supports the *interactions* between the client and the server. Middleware has often been invisible, particularly when it just consists of network infrastructure, but it is gradually going to become a lot more important. In fact, the World Wide Web is middleware on a global scale. Middleware used to be just about telecommunication. Now it is about resource access. In the future, it will comprise a value-added layer with special purpose processing.

Note that with true client/server processing, we are talking about partitioning the system design, and this partitioning is independent of what computer systems are used to execute it. A three-tiered system could even have all three of its tiers executing on a single computer. The office of a real estate broker won't see any bene-fit from partitioning its application into a three-tier system, but a Fortune 1000 company certainly could. And what kind of software do you suppose best fits into the role of being supplied from a server to a client "as needed"? Why, Java-powered software, of course! As we shall see in Chapter 12, Java is rapidly matur-ing in its ability to serve at any tier of a client/server architecture, including any necessary peer-to-peer accesses (between server peers) that might be required.

The real benefit of a multitier system is in partitioning a software system so that the most cost-effective hardware is used at each level. In addition, it is easy to retrofit a multitier system onto an existing on-line system. Doing so lets users enjoy the benefit of modern GUIs and data analysis tools, while retaining the existing investment in large corporate databases.

Case Study 7: Multitiered System across the Internet

Network-based client/server computing offers cheap, timely access to informa-tion that other computing paradigms cannot provide at almost any price, as the following case study illustrates. The application is a three-tier system that oper-ates across both a corporate intranet and the Internet. It can also be thought of as an extranet system because the users come in across the Internet.

Federal Express is a highly successful overnight parcel delivery service. The idea occurred to a young business student at Yale University: Instead of routing par-cels from all points to all points, fly everything into a large central site, sort it, then fly everything back out the same night for final delivery by truck. This plan went against the established wisdom of decentralized sorting offices, and the professor gave the student only a C grade, commenting "an idea must be feasible to merit a higher grade." The student, Frederick Smith, went on to graduate, to found Fed-eral Express based on his central depot idea, and to grow it into a company with a $10 billion annual turnover. Federal Express service is more expensive than deliv-ery by mail, but much faster and more reliable.

Federal Express has always been aggressive in its pursuit of technology. Its busi-ness depends on the timely management of information, and it continually seeks new data processing techniques that can reduce costs or improve communication. Federal Express' web-based tracking system is among the most impressive of these. Each FedEx address label contains a unique bar code. The sending cus-tomer retains a copy of the label and bar code. At each stage in parcel processing, the barcode is read by automatic scanners and the tracking database is updated. This system lets FedEx offer a parcel tracking service. Customers can phone

FedEx, read off the bar code on their copy of the label, and a FedEx clerk will confirm the latest known location of the parcel, allowing accurate predictions of delivery time.

FedEx extended this simple but effective system to allow customers to query parcel location from a web browser. FedEx publishes a URL that is readable from anywhere on the Internet (and anywhere on a company's intranet if it is connected to the outside world). The URL contains an HTML form that is filled out by the customer with the barcode information. When the form is submitted by a customer browser, a CGI script runs to extract the information from the parcel location database and send it back to the customer's browser. Figure 10–9 illustrates the process.

Customers can track their own parcels at any time, without the inconvenience of waiting for a FedEx shipping clerk. FedEx offers a new service to customers and saves on labor costs at the same time. The self-service tracking system has proved very popular with customers and has reportedly decreased FedEx's labor costs by $2 million, while improving service to the customer.

An extranet forms the middleware connecting the client tier and middle tier in this three-tier system. The tiers are shown in Figure 10–10.

A few years ago, it was not possible to build a system like this because there was no commonly agreed-on standard for routing data between computer networks in different companies. An intranet is the common industry standard that solves this problem, among others. An intranet carries the computer industry "dial-tone" that allows hardware from numerous different vendors to communicate.

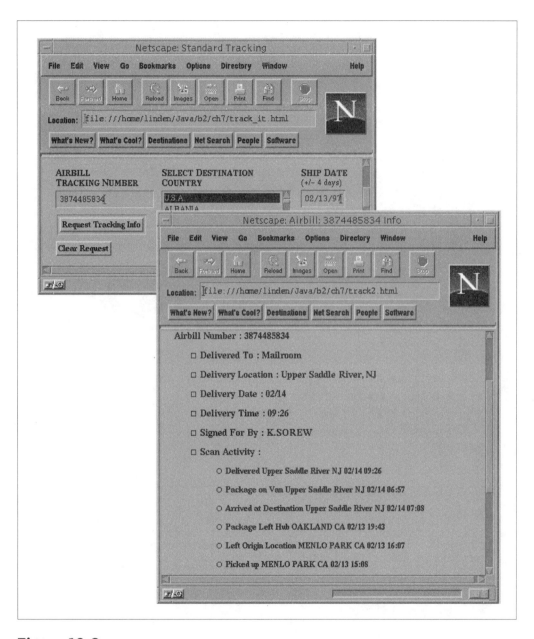

Figure 10-9
Tracking FedEx Packages Using the Web

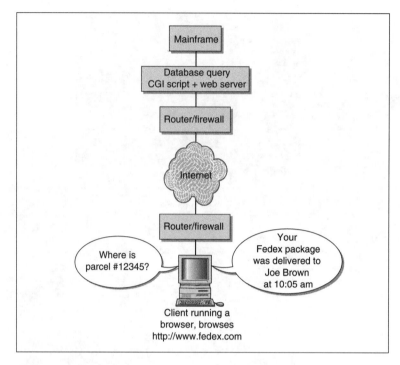

Figure 10–10
Multi-Tiered System Used by Federal Express

Summary

- The centralized computing model consists of a mainframe and its attached dumb terminals. It is still the model of choice where a high degree of control over MIS resources is needed and local processing needs are minimal.

- A server is a host that has resources available for distribution to others upon proper request. A client is a host that requires a resource or service not immediately available to it. A typical client must have some processing capability of its own.

- Client/server computing is a computing model that distributes resources among many client hosts and some fewer number of server hosts. Its strength lies in its ability to adapt to a large variety of business climates and structures, and to permit rapid structural changes to occur. It has two principal drawbacks: more difficult system administration, which leads to a somewhat higher price tag, and somewhat reduced security over a centralized model.

- An intranet is a private internal network of client/server systems implemented using tools and techniques designed for the Internet. An intranet is the TCP/IP network glue allowing clients to connect to any server. A web browser is the software. Intranets are redefining distributed processing and dramatically lowering costs compared with older forms of client/server. Because of its simplicity and immediate benefits, browser-based computing is in an explosive phase of growth.

- Java runs on the client, on the server, and in any layer connecting the two. You can now easily build information systems that otherwise need a mish-mash of different technologies and tools. The appeal of accessibility to data is so great that the most ubiquitous piece of software today is the Java-enabled web browser.

- Client/server computing can be classified according to the number of layers, or tiers. A one-tiered client/server has both client terminals and server on the same host. A two-tiered client/server is the more common case, in which a separate server host serves multiple clients. A three-tiered client/server adds another layer of server(s), generally a middle layer that operates as a software server.

- Three-tiered systems running on an intranet and using Java in the middle layer, with network computers running Java applets in the client layer, offer cheap, robust, secure distributed computing. You can now build information systems that formerly could not be built at all.

CHAPTER
11

- The Hidden Costs of PCs

- The Iceberg Model

- What Is a Thin Client?

- Network Computers

- Summary

Network Computers

The Hidden Costs of PCs

At first, people thought that client/server computing would be cheaper than time-sharing. The argument was that although PCs cost twice as much to buy as dumb terminals, the ability to do local processing would save expensive mainframe cycles and defer costly upgrades. Although there was some merit to that belief, it also overlooked the hidden costs of PCs.

The cost of operating a PC is more than just the purchase price. One must also factor in the cost of the software, system administration, installation and rein-stallation, the consumables, annual upgrades, and maintenance. By far the biggest hidden cost is that of system administration and support. It's easy for computer professionals (like the readers of this book) to overlook the fact that the majority of PC users do not want to do their own system administration. Any time they are forced to spend learning how, as well as actually doing it, is unproductive overhead.

Several computer industry research groups have studied the TCO (total cost of ownership) to keep a single PC running over a five-year life. They have arrived at a range of figures, but the common theme is that the PC environment is barely under control. Because administration is done on individual desktops, end users are commonly diverted from their productive responsibilities by it. End-user time spent on non-job-related PC activities accounts for half of the cost of PC owner-ship according to one Gartner Group study. Some authorities, such as Alan

Cooper in his GUI book "About Face," actually suggest discarding a PC after 2 years, simply because typical upgrades, installs and system changes will have made it too hard to continue to manage! Reducing the purchase price of a PC, as in the furious PC price war of 1997/8, does nothing to address the biggest cost: maintaining and adminstering the system.

The Iceberg Model

Even if you have a home PC and (because you don't pay yourself) you put your cost of labor as zero, the hours you spend tracking down missing DLL files are not productive hours. The time spent reinstalling Windows 95 because of a corrupted registry is time that cannot be spent on something more fruitful. Part of the problem is Microsoft's policy of shipping OS bug fixes as part of applications.

When you install Microsoft applications you often also get new system libraries. The new libraries may contain bug fixes, or they may be needed so the application can work, or both. Some applications deliver overlapping subsets of libraries, but at different revision levels. Since library versioning is not used in Windows, the arrangement of system libraries that you end up with depends on the order in which you install applications. It leads to mysterious system failures, because there are far too many combinations to test properly. Microsoft has inadvertently increased the cost of Windows administration because it blurs the line between applications and operating system.

If PC's have hidden costs, why are they used so much? Why aren't we all still using dumb terminals connected to a big IBM mainframe? Because PCs also offer great applications, at low prices. PCs put computing power where it is most needed: on the desktops of individual users. What is needed is a way to gain the the productive aspects of a PC while more tightly controlling the costs..

A good analogy for understanding PC costs is the so-called "iceberg model" shown in Figure 11–1. Popular folklore holds that the bulk of an iceberg lies unseen, beneath the surface, and indeed that's what sunk the Titanic. Only a tiny part of the iceberg was visible, so the lookouts on duty could not see it until it was too late. So it is with PC costs. A manager signs a purchase authorization for $1000 for a PC, but the true costs are many times higher and are incurred over the life of the system in keeping it running, modifying it, upgrading it to match the applications introduced elsewhere in the department and so on.

When the PC installation is a small concern with just three or four PCs, administration is simple: get the desired applications working, and then *do not touch anything*. Some organizations try to cope with configuration problems by putting all PCs in a standard form: 32 Mb memory, 400-Mb disk, Windows 3.11 plus Lotus 123 and half a dozen other applications. The problem with standard configura-

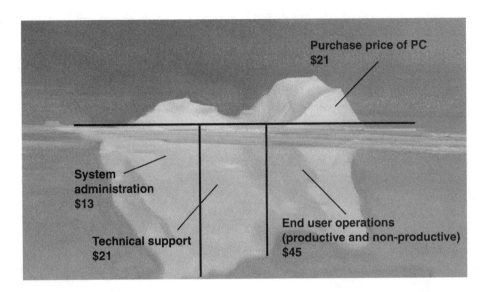

Figure 11-1
The Lesson of the Titanic — Where Each $100 of PC Costs is Spent

End-user operations—All use of the system for running programs. It includes productive time spent feeding data into programs, processing it, and reviewing the output. It also includes unproductive use of the system—experimenting with software, learning new techniques, writing business letters, modifying fonts and other system parameters, playing games, sending and reading business-related e-mail, browsing the web for fun, and so on (45%).

Technical support—The time spent solving technical questions, tracking down missing or moved DLLs, troubleshooting registry problems, and answering user problems. It includes the time cost of both the user and the technical support team (21%).

Capital cost—This covers the purchase and upgrade costs of the hardware and software over the life of the system. It includes replacement of hardware components, such as keyboards and diskettes, that wear out. It also includes reasonable upgrades for peripherals, such as 9.6K modems and double-speed CD-ROM drives, that become outmoded (21%).

Administrative—The administrative cost is the value of the time spent installing the system, adding software, updating software, configuring hardware upgrades, inventorying the system and its peripherals, backing up data files, and related administrative tasks (13%).

tions is that "one size fits all—badly." You are either paying for features you don't need or you're forced to use applications other than the ones you would have chosen. The large numbers involved magnify the problem. The main benefit of standardized configurations is that PCs become plug-in components. When a PC fails in some way, you just roll it out and roll in an identical but working one. For applications like financial trading where each minute of downtime has a real cost, standardized configuration clients have been a practical solution.

When the user is an organization with thousands of PCs, each with subtly different hardware, OS revision, and applications software, the cost of administration becomes much greater. A system administrator (or worse, each individual user) must:

- Decide which software to buy, then buy it

- Install and configure the software

- Confirm that it is compatible with all the other hardware and software on the system

- Learn how to use the software

- Perform regular data backups

- Keep the software up to date with new versions, while retaining data compatibility with old versions in case a fallback is needed

- Update and upgrade hardware as needed

- Maintain connections to corporate servers and nets

- Adhere to all organizational data and security policies

If a user has to do this in addition to his or her regular job of, say, accountant or designer, it's easy to see why PC costs are so high. If there is a dedicated PC support organization, then (unless the systems and work are very uniform) companies need one administrator for as few as every 25 PCs. Keeping a general-purpose PC running in a business environment costs real money.

Other PC Costs: Security, Reliability

There are two other costs associated with Windows desktops, namely security and reliability. Windows was designed as a single-user system, and never made any provision for security features. There is no login password, and if you have access to the system, you have access to all its resources, for good or bad. Viruses propagate too easily under Windows, leading to problems of data corruption and system integrity. This can be an expensive problem. It's now common for MIS directors to install virus scanners in batch files on the PC to check for viruses as part of each reboot. It is also common for MIS directors to physically remove the floppy disk drive from new PCs before issuing them. The costs of dealing with viruses on floppies is higher than the cost of not using floppies. Removing standard hardware is not an adequate long-term solution to the PC's data security problems. Windows NT offers adequate support for security, but is not configured for security as it comes out of the box.

A second pervasive problem with Windows 3.1, Window 95, and Window 98 is its general lack of robustness. There seem to be two kinds of desktop users: those who stick to the well trodden paths of a small number of widely-used applications, and a second group who use the system more extensively. The first group is using word processors and spreadsheets on small files, and hardly ever encounters any system hangs. Everything usually works fine. They not only never see any problems, their personal experience leads them to believe that nobody else does either. They typically never have long-running processes, and they shut the system off each night.

The second group of people are the power users: they have large amounts of data kept in big files. They want to run a compiler from one window, an editor from another, and a debugger from a third window. They make extensive use of scripting, and expect to leave the system running for long periods of time, so it can build software and accept mail while they are not there. This group of people is well used to the sudden failures, hangs, and panics of Windows. Many of them sooner or later move to Linux, or Solaris to get their work done.

Early in 1998 I bought a state of the art Sony multimedia Windows 95 PC because I wanted to be able to edit videotape footage. The system comes with all the editing software, but I soon discovered drastic limitations. Video signals take up megabytes of file storage for just a few seconds worth of footage. It's easy to assemble a clip bigger than the PC filesystem limit of 2Gb. If you do that, the application just crashes. It does not give you an error message or warning, or the chance to save your work up to the 2Gb limit; it just crashes. Windows has no separation between the OS and applications, and the failing application takes down the whole OS. You have to power cycle, reboot, run the scandisk utility, and start the whole editing process all over again. The data file you were working on is lost, along with perhaps several hours of work. If you're unlucky, you also have to reinstall the OS.

It's all too easy to hang Windows in numerous other applications. An interrupt that comes in at the wrong time, a browser that does something at an inopportune moment, a buggy application or system utility, a modem or network request that Windows wasn't prepared for, can all lead to "the blue screen of death." In con-

One system administrator in a large state university in the northwest described his experience with Windows 95 this way.

"I work in a labratory containing, among other things, 58 networked Win95 machines. We offer a self-service walk-up service to graduate students and academics. They bring their data on floppy disks and use statistical programs on the lab PCs to analyze it.

Over a couple of years we have gradually reached the realization that spending an extra 45 minutes on a Friday night to completely reinstall every PC in the lab is essential to our continued reliable operation. In a single week of use our users have changed, deleted and reconfigured enough registry information that it is simpler to start all over again, than to try and go through and fix every new problem individually. Every Friday night, before going home, we wipe the hard drives and reload the OS and all applications. We have developed our own program to copy a raw disk that makes this drastic task fairly simple.

Furthermore, on average between 3 and 4 of the lab systems crash without warning or reason every day (we keep a running log, and the actual average over the last two months is 3.7 crashes per day). This is a site where we know what we are doing, and we maintain the software and the hardware well. We are actively evaluating the Linux OS as an alternative to Windows. that will be more stable, and allow us to better administer our systems without weekly reinstallation."

trast, Unix workstations typically run for hundreds of days without rebooting. The most frequent cause of a reboot in the Unix world is a power failure in the building.

The sad truth is that the stability problems of Windows don't matter to many users. Virtually all PC users not only accept but expect and tolerate reboots, reinstalls, conflicts, and crashes as a fact of life. Software professionals with a background in UNIX or mainframe computing consider that type of behavior completely unacceptable. Ironically, most of the rest of the world considers it standard behavior. More demanding users find alternatives to Windows. Cisco Systems used to run its network printing services on 50 NT servers, supporting 1800 printers. Cisco reportedly concluded that NT was not reliable enough for the task and replaced all the NT software with Linux. The Linux software running on the same hardware has been perfectly satisfactory.

How Microsoft Has Addressed Fat Client PC Costs

There is nothing Microsoft can do about the security and reliability problems of Windows, except migrate the user base to NT while trying to improve NT's track record. And that is the plan. No more releases of Windows are planned. Windows 98 is the end of the line.

Windows NT crash leaves navy cruiser USS Yorkdown disabled at sea

Windows NT failed in a high profile way in September 1997, disabling the USS Yorktown to the point where it had to be towed into port. The paper Government Computer News quoted a civlian engineer from the Atlantic Fleet Support Center in Norfolk, saying "Using Windows NT on a warship is similar to hoping that luck will be in our favor."

The Aegis missile cruiser USS Yorktown was part of the navy's "Smart Ship" program designed to reduce personnel and costs. While on maneuvers off the coast of Cape Charles, VA, the Yorktown lost all propulsion. The failure was apparently the result of a simple division by zero in an application. The application failed, and took down the NT operating system, which brought the network down with it. With so many systems off line at once, the ship was dead in the water for nearly three hours and had to be towed back to port. A previous loss of propulsion had occurred in May 1997, also due to the software.

Despite the setbacks, the navy awarded a large contract to Litton to continue with ship automation. The problem is not that an application failed. The problem is that a bad application was able to hang Windows NT, and thence the network. Many observers were surprised that the navy used a consumer product like NT, instead of a fault-tolerant or enterprise-ready operating system in mission-critical applications.

Further information:

1. Government Computer News, 20 Apr 1998

2. RISKS newsletter, volume 19, issue 88

3. US Naval Institute Proceedings, April 1998

4. Wired News, 16 July 1998.

Microsoft has sought to address the spiraling costs of managing a PC user base in three ways. **"Zero Administration for Windows"** (ZAW) is an initiative that has the goal of eventually allowing central (server-based) control of desktops. The main first product is the Zero Administration Kit for NT 4.0 and Windows 95. It's a set of policy templates and scripts that centralize a few simple client things on a server. More of ZAW is promised for NT 5.0, but industry analysts like Gartner group are openly questioning how much of it will actually be delivered.

The second approach involved Microsoft working with the PC vendors to develop a minimal PC specification known as **"NetPC."** The specification was released in March 1997, and immediately sank without trace, a casualty of the 1997 PC price war. As well as having a price under $1000, NetPC was also supposed to allow remote adminstration from servers. The price was easy to hit; the software was a lot harder, and it never happened. Entry level PCs (including monitor) were available for $750 in spring 1998, and $500 by fall, leading to a lean year for, and much belt-tightening by, all PC vendors

The third approach at cutting TCO on PCs is the **WinTerm** initiative. It is often termed "multiuser NT" because standard NT can only support a single logged-in interactive user profile. WinTerm—Windows-based Terminals—is really a new name for a dumb terminal client attached to a central server.

Citrix Systems developed the WinFrame software and WinTerm hardware product that changes Windows NT Server 3.51 into a multiuser system. Microsoft liked this technology, and pretty much forced Citrix to partner with them and port it to NT Server 4.0 under the name Terminal Server. Citrix had two choices: cooperate with Microsoft in bundling WinFrame into NT, or go out of business as Microsoft developed its own version. Citrix still offers WinFrame on NT 3.51, and also the MetaFrame server. MetaFrame provides support for all non-Windows clients (UNIXs, Java, OS/2) and additional transport protocols (notably ICA). It allows these clients to display the results of server-based NT applications.

The NT server runs Terminal Server and the applications, while WinTerm has just enough hardware to display the results. WinTerm offers the same advantages and disadvantages of the old timesharing mainframe approach. It is advertised as a thin client or client/server solution. But, because all the processing is done on the server, it is really neither. WinTerm puts all the work on the server, and drags down network traffic, as every mouse click and key press must be sent to the server for processing. The WinTerm is a dumb client whose processing is limited to displaying results locally.

WinTerm terminals have a monitor, keyboard, network interface, possibly a serial port, but no local disk storage. Since the processing is all done on the server, the server hardware and operating system must scale well if your goals include flexibility or future growth. Inability to scale well is the biggest current limitation of NT, of course. WinTerm, like WindowsCE, is a reaction product hastily launched to fend off network computers. The technology underpinning isn't there to sustain it, and it will eventually be backwatered or dropped by Microsoft. WinTerm is already priced to discourage its use. To run the client end of WinTerm (a dumb terminal, remember). Microsoft insists that you also buy an NT workstation license.

The "Zero Administration for Windows" is a statement of direction by Microsoft, and an acknowledgement of the high cost of PC administration. When ZAW is delivered in NT 5.0 or NT 6.0, it will use the NT server to hold user contexts (such as registry information) for each local client. Microsoft promises that it will be possible to install a new OS onto the client from the server, and to prevent the client from changing its own configuration through a process known as "lock-

How is a WinTerm different from a network computer?

A WinTerm is an unusual special-purpose client computer of a form that was first popularized in the UNIX world in the early 1990s, under the name "X terminal." X terminals are the UNIX equivalent of Windows WinTerms.

A WinTerm is a bit-mapped graphics screen and a local processor dedicated to receiving Windows graphics commands and drawing the corresponding images on the screen. So, it is a clever terminal, but it is still only a terminal because it has no ability to run any software of its own. The purpose of a WinTerm is to provide PC-quality graphics at NC prices. You still need a server to run the real software and tell the WinTerm what to render.

A WinTerm has no general-purpose, local-processing capability. If you were to execute a Java applet in a browser and display it on a WinTerm, the applet would actually be executing using CPU cycles on the server. Therefore, a WinTerm is not a network computer or a thin client.

---

down." The first piece of ZAW is available with NT 4.0. It lets system administrators query the configuration of client machines, and install applications and patches.

ZAW may eventually address the big weakness of PCs, but its current incarnation misses the point. As long as desktop systems must be installed and administered individually, it makes little difference whether this is done at the client or at the server. "Zero Administration" is quite an overstatement. Administration will never get down to zero. It will always be needed for client systems. Administering systems one by one from a server is hardly much of an improvement over doing it one by one on each client. Microsoft is planning some much needed improvements but still will not meet the thin client model.

Some observers, such as journalist Nicholas Petreley, think that Microsoft will not be able to deliver on its ZAW promises. Petreley points out that NT was only ever designed to be a single-user desktop operating system—a reimplementation of Windows to get it to a maintainable code base. To stretch NT into keeping separate client-user contexts, while sharing application libraries is a bigger task than most people realize. But the problem doesn't stop there.

Petreley points out that the Microsoft applications also assume a single-user viewpoint. He gives the example of the "Fast Find" utility in Office. That utility builds a searchable index file on every fixed drive in your system. It makes it easier to look through Office documents for some particular string. Fast Find runs fine when there is only one user on a system. But on a multiuser server, 50 independent users could be running Fast Find at once. Worse still, all of them would be competing to update the same index files on each drive. Fast Find is a CPU hog. A single instance of it can swamp 90 percent of a system. Fifty copies of it running at

once will surely crash an NT server. According to Citrix (experts in NT client/server systems), the only answer is to disable Fast Find for all users. There are dozens and dozens of single user/multiple user issues like this that must be solved for ZAW to work.

Gartner's results that (because of indirect labor costs) PCs were much more expensive than generally realized were also found by Forrester Research, Inc. In a February 1993 report, Forrester compared the total system cost of an AS/400 minicomputer and terminals to a client/server configuration of 140 PCs and 5 servers on a LAN. The total cost for a custom hardware and software system was roughly the same (about $2 million) under both alternatives. The client/server configuration was a faster and hence cheaper development platform, but the AS/400 was slightly cheaper overall. [reference: "Client/Server's Price Tag," the Computing Strategy Report, Forrester Research, Inc., Vol 10, No 4, Feb. 1993.]

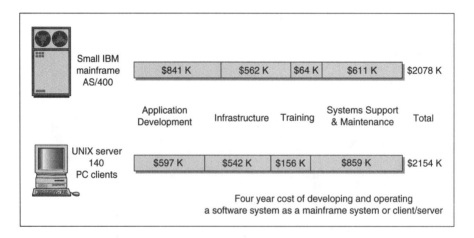

PCs are more expensive than generally realized. One study showed that a PC client/server mid-sized configuration was actually about the same cost as a minicomputer configuration. The client/server system was more flexible and led to faster development, but client administration kept the overall costs high.

What is needed is a combination of the *local* processing at the client and *centralized* system administration and data management at the server. Voila! Thin clients and Java computing. By and large, the fewer resources of its own that the client has, the thinner it is said to be. A newer, perhaps more descriptive, name for a thin client is "network computer." Because of the rapid acceptance of Java by the client/

server computing community, several makers of "network computer" hardware have announced plans to build Java execution capability directly into their product, using "Java chips."

Definition: Thin client

A thin client is another term for a network computer. A thin client has *local processing* ability (like a PC) but does not have permanent *local state* (unlike a PC). A thin client needs to download its software, user profile information, and data from a server and upload back to the server any new data files it produces.

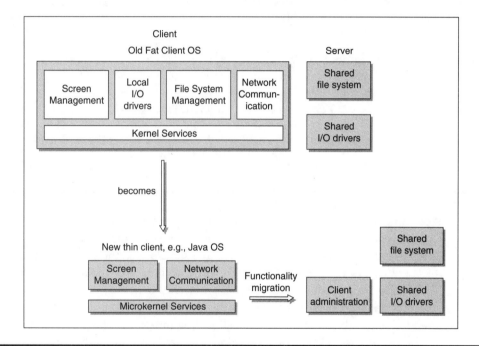

What Is a Thin Client?

The thinness or thickness of a client really has to do with finding the balance between the amount of work the server will do (server side) versus the amount of work the client will do (client side) in any given transaction. There are trade-offs to be made between the hardware and the software at both ends and what use is to be made of them.

A thin client is thin because it has no "fattening" local state. As in life, there are degrees of thinness; a thin client may have a local disk, but this is only used as a cache and temporary store, not for saving data permanently. Because it can do extensive local processing, it is "thin" (frugal) with its use of server CPU cycles and network bandwidth. The basic strategy of the thin client is to move the resources that need the most administration to a central site. This centralization modifies the problem of many separate PCs into maintaining one central server. This is a well-understood problem with standard solutions like shared file systems and centralized applications. It reduces the cost of administration enough to make the thin client worthwhile.

Thin clients exist because they provide a better balance between cost and functionality on the client side. A regular desktop workstation would make a better system for software development, but a thin client will often be a better (cheaper) system for application deployment. Since all programs and data are kept on the server, there is zero system administration on the client. Because of this, a thin client like the Sun Microsystems JavaStation, priced at under $1,000, is estimated to cost around $2,500 a year to run and maintain, compared with up to $12,000 for a traditional network-based PC.

Microsoft is searching hard for ways to reduce the PCs total cost of ownership (TCO). Users may stick with PCs if the TCO can be brought within $1,000 or $2,000 of NCs, but it's hard to see how that can be done in the current framework of fat client operating systems. System administration costs may be brought down by 25 percent by rigorously applying "best practices," but it's hard to see how they can be reduced by 80 percent of current levels.

Web servers have a provision, known as the Common Gateway Interface (CGI), that allows access to server-side computing resources from HTML pages passed down to a client. This gets the job done but also results in the server doing some of the client's work in addition to its own. The Java language makes it easy to move this workload out to the client, assuming that the client is "thick enough" to accommodate it (i.e., more than just a display terminal). A network computer is intended to be "thick enough" while still being much less costly to administer than a fully equipped PC or workstation. The goal still is that the server provides the data and the client provides the crunch, but that crunch could be a lot less expensive than even the thinnest personal computer now on the market.

Java computing—a term coined by Sun Microsystems—is a refinement of client/server computing. It centers around the use of intelligent clients that have a much lower ongoing cost than traditional PCs. Java computing does not demand that the investment in existing systems be discarded; rather, it involves retaining software and hardware compatibility while migrating to lower-cost platforms. Java computing lets companies change gradually to open, architecture-neutral systems that are object based and built on networks.

Why add disk to a thin client? Marimba!

We just made the point that a thin client does not have permanent local disk storage, because otherwise that disk storage takes effort to administer and you get back to the costs of the fat client.

Actually, there is one opportunity to use a local disk on a thin client without destroying the model: you can use the disk to cache (keep a local copy of) commonly accessed applets. You can refine this model so the cache copy is updated automatically and periodically from the server. An applet loaded from local cache starts running much more quickly than one sucked over the net from a server.

The Marimba company (a spinoff from Sun Microsystems by some of the original Java team) is building a business partly on this concept. Marimba provides software that runs on a thin client and periodically looks at

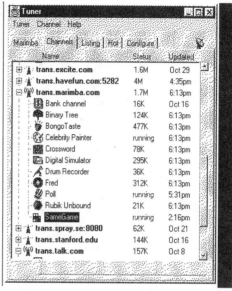

the server to see if something has changed. If it has changed, the Marimba software downloads just the changes necessary to update the cached client copy. That way, the latest version of the server software is always available on the client, with automated client-side administration. Because an applet doesn't have to be downloaded each time it is started, it can be much larger than if the user had to wait for it to come over the wire. Because the applet is available on local disk, it starts up almost instantly with no download time.

The model is straightforward, and Marimba has given it marketing names to help fix it in people's minds. The idea is to compare client updating to radio broadcasts. Marimba's Castanet™ software works by providing "channels" on a server, through which the Transmitter server sends down updates, which can be any kind of Java application, to clients running Tuner software. The Tuner software listens to the channels in the background so the channels can be updated without interrupting the other applications.

A thin client can do all the things that a PC can do, except work in stand-alone mode, but it does not have permanent local storage. When you power off a thin client, nothing is saved locally. The thin client may have a disk, but this disk is only used to hold temporary results or a cache while a program is running. A thin client downloads everything it needs (programs to run and data to run them on) from the server, as it needs it. Because a thin client does not have permanent local storage, it does not require any local administration. Individual administration is

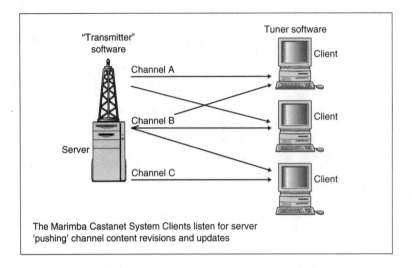

The Marimba Castanet System Clients listen for server 'pushing' channel content revisions and updates

Marimba (http://www.marimba.com) also has other products, including some innovative window components in a toolkit known as Bongo. The same marketing person (Kim Polese) who thought up the name "Java" also conceived the name "Bongo." A company called Trilogy has developed a component library, using Bongo, Marimba's visual tool.

The Marimba Castanet software is similar to the Pointcast advertising software, which can display news and information on your screensaver, but Marimba offers general-purpose content downloading. Apple plans to bundle the Castanet client software with the new Java run time that it is embedding in the Mac OS. Corel plans to use Castanet to deliver self-updating productivity applications.

what drives up the PC cost of ownership. You install applications software on the server, not the client. You install the client operating system on the server, where it will be downloaded to the client. Alternatively, you may put some or all of the client OS in flash PROM where it can easily be updated from the server. Flash PROM is a new kind of programmable read-only memory; although it is normally unwritable, its contents can be changed by a special sequence of instructions.

As an aside, all current Sun desktop workstations are fitted with flash PROM, but the possibility of rewriting it in the field has been disabled by setting a hardware jumper connection on the motherboard. This is a temporary measure while Sun engineers figure out how best to allow field updates to PROM chips by software without also making it possible for student programmers to crash a system into a state from which it cannot reboot.

Network Computers

We have set the scene by describing how the client/server protocol has proven effective. We have also described some of the problems associated with using PCs as clients. PCs are surprisingly expensive to purchase and administer, and they provide more capabilities than are needed in many client/server applications. This is where the network computer comes in. For a large number of client/server applications, a thin client is all that's needed. This realization is the key break-through behind network computers. If you don't *need* a thick client, don't *pay* for a thick client.

Bill Gates, chairman of Microsoft, spent most of 1996 disparaging the network computer concept before stating to shareholders at Microsoft's annual meeting that thin clients and their backers presented "perhaps the largest challenge that we have faced in a long, long time." He was wrong as proved in 1997; Java and Java computing is the largest challenge Microsoft has ever faced, larger even than the antimonopoly actions brought against Microsoft by the United States government.

In October 1996, Microsoft brought the Windows CE product to market, labeling it network based. Hewlett-Packard, Compaq Computer, and Dell Computer are among the hardware vendors for the new device. Windows CE came out of the NT source base and misses the essential element for a thin client: zero system administration on the client. It is a repackaging of the Microsoft "At Work" and Winpad operating systems that the market has convincingly rejected twice before.

In January 1998, when cable company TCI looked for an operating system for its future set-top boxes (a classic network computer) it choose Windows CE. In a clear signal to Microsoft, TCI specified standard Personal Java to run on top of CE. If there's any anti competitive funny business from Redmond, TCI can swap out Windows CE and swap in any of half a dozen other embedded OS's without changing the applications at all. But smaller customers cannot do that; Microsoft imposes a CE license condition of using its Java VM, rather than a standard one. The world's top three mobile phone manufacturers, Nokia, Motorola, and Ericsson announced in spring 1998 that they would not use Windows CE , but would instead work together to move forward with Java applications on top of their own OS. Cell phones can be viewed as a special kind of network computer.

Some computer manufacturers are very slow to understand that people don't want small computers of increased complexity. They want reduced complexity in current products. The runaway success of the Palm Pilot PDA testifies to this dramatically. With over a million units sold in 1997, the Palm has shipped more than ten times as many PDAs as its nearest CE rival (Hewlett-Packard). PDA users are rejecting something that looks like Windows, but doesn't have binary compatibility with it, requires them to buy all new applications, and suffers from the traditional Windows problems of over-feature-itis, code bloat, being hard to program, and has a screen/keyboard too small for Windows applications.

Industry papers like *PC Magazine* repeatedly print user surveys with results showing 80 percent of the users of products such as MS Word and Excel are only using 20 percent of the features. Too many specialized features just push up the training costs, the memory costs, and the disk requirements. Customers are turning away from old-style large integrated applications, rethinking their upgrade direction and starting to embrace thin applications to go with thin clients. In the past, features sold applications. In the future, too many elaborate features will sink an application.

A network computer costs less to run than a PC because it pushes up to the server the parts that are expensive to administer. On the server, that administration can be done once, and the results shared by all the clients. What you have left on the client is a lot more than a dumb terminal. A network computer has sufficient processing power for executing programs locally, using data sent over to it.

This concept was pioneered in the 1980s in the UNIX world under the name "diskless client," and it didn't take the world by storm then. What's different now? It's partly the changing market. At that time, UNIX workstations were still strongly tied to the technical computing market (the so-called "pipe stress fracture and crystallography modeling" crowd). It's partly the increased overhead of PC usage. At that time, a UNIX workstation was still an expensive purchase compared with a low-end PC, even if the workstation was zero system administration at the client. And, it's partly the approach. The diskless client had the same heavy operating system and relatively small memory, which meant huge demands on network bandwidth. As processors got faster, the demand on the network outstripped its capacity. So, the original UNIX diskless clients that paged their virtual memory across the network to the server weren't a good match for the technology limitations of the time. Today's model changes the diskless client to do locally the things that are cheap locally, and to do centrally the things that can cheaply be shared centrally.

With the increase in capabilities of modern PCs, their system administration costs have also risen sharply, narrowing the gap between PCs and workstations, for bad as well as good. Anyone who claims that Windows 95 has easy system administration has clearly never tried to install it on a system with nonstandard peripherals like SCSI disks. SCSI disks offer higher performance than the current IDE standard, so this is not an unreasonable hardware configuration. Finally, the great big Internet explosion hadn't yet happened when UNIX diskless clients first appeared in the 1980s, so the intranet "glue" to bind clients to servers wasn't used outside the UNIX workstation world.

Where Are the Network Computers?

The Network computing concept was launched by Sun Microsystems announcing its JavaStation 1. By the start of 1997 there were half a dozen competing NCs, led by products from Sun Microsystems and IBM. However, NC's were slow to take off. The software was plainly not ready. A few of the early reference sites, like Federal Express and 1-800-FLOWERS eventually switched their NC plans to other solutions. Initial network computer sales were disappointing. What happened?

The answer is an old familiar story in the computer industry. The NC hardware vendors, including Sun Microsystems underestimated the complexity of building a new software infrastructure. The promise was more than the software people could possibly deliver in the time alloted. Sun's Network Computers were built around a Java OS, and could only run Java software. But two years ago there were few Java applications. Because hardware vendors failed to execute on the software side of the NC, the entire concept has been delayed. Today, you have a choice of several office-compatible Java applications, and NC's are poised to try again.

What happened with NC software is similar to what is currently happening with Windows NT, summarized in Table 11-1. Microsoft's NT was launched in 1993 and sold as an enterprise operating system. Five years, four major releases, and a dozen or so service pack bug fix releases later, NT is still a "work in progress," mostly used for file and print servers. Sites that actually do enterprise critical computing, even high-profile Microsoft-owned sites like Hotmail and WebTV, run on Solaris or other enterprise-ready operating systems, not NT.

[The figures and dates in Table 11-1 are from IDC Corp.] Of course, NT is a general-purpose operating system, and is quite a bit more complicated than the OS for NC's. That OS, with smaller goals, will quickly stabilize and mature. Sun engineers are working hard to improve JavaOS, it's OS for NC's.

In September 1997, Sun bought French software house Chorus Systems. Their main product was the real-time Chorus OS executive. Sun plans to leverage the Chorus microkernel to improve JavaOS. A few months later, Sun pooled resources with IBM, and JavaOS is now a joint project of these industry giants. The first release of the joint product for the JavaStation will be in the early part of 1999.

The real appeal of network computers isn't in cheap hardware, but in vastly reduced administrative costs. Most of the PC industry missed this point when it embarked on a panic price-cutting reaction to the launch of the NC.

Table 11-1 Versions of Microsoft Windows NT

Version	date	Installed base	Comments
NT announced	1991	0	Under development since 1989, NT was originally slated to have an OS/2 interface and API's. After the Nov 1990 break with IBM, and the sucess of Win 3.0, NT changed to adopt a Win32 API.
NT 3.1	mid 1993	0	First release was not called v1.0, but used the same version number as then current version of Windows.
NT 3.5, 3.51	fall 1994	0.5M	Introduced OLE (components) and OpenGL (3D graphics). 3.51 was a quick bugfix release. It had about 5M lines of code.
NT 4.0	late 1996	3.2M	Most used as a file and print server, it is driving Novell Netware from the market. Has Win95 look and feel. Supports DCOM, Terminal Server, and some web tools. The window manager moved into the kernel to improve performance, at the cost of giving up on the original microkernel concept. Source base is reported to be 15M lines of code. Microsoft is spending $1bn/year on NT, funded from its Windows products.
NT 5.0	early 2000 (est)	41M (est)	Originally announced for mid-1998, and has been subject to repeated slips. Will support disk quotas, Active Directory, Kerberos authentication, Advanced Power Management. Source base is expected to be 35M lines of code.
NT 6.0	Fall 2001 (est)	65M (est)	Will contain the Win64 API and run on Intel's Merced chip in 64-bit mode This is the version that Microsoft intends as the "single desktop OS" replacement for Windows 98.

The most widely felt effect of the NC today is the fact that you can buy a PC for $500. The urge to cut prices led to a happy reinvigoration of x86 clone manufacturers Cyrix and AMD. PC vendors reduced their prices to be more competitive with NC prices, overlooking the fact that the real saving is in reduced system administration at the client. And that cannot currently be met by PCs, although there are promises of things to come in NT 5.0.

Table 11-2 lists some of the spreadsheets, word processors, and bridging software that is available today in Java for Network Computers.

Table 11-2 Java Application Software

Company	Product	URL
Lotus	e-suite	`http://esuite.lotus.com`
IBM	San Francisco	`http://www.ibm.com`
Star Division	Star Office	`http://www.stardivision.com`
Digital Harbor	Wav	`http://www.digitalharbor.com`
Corel	JBridge	`http://www.corel.com/jbridge/index.htm`
Applix	Applix Anywhere	`http://www.applix.com/anywhere/index.htm`
Visual Components Inc.	Excel compatible Java spreadsheet	`http://www.f1j.com`

Where Can a Network Computer Be Used?

The NC doesn't necessarily compete head on with the personal computer; under the NC Reference Profile, the personal computer with a web browser *is* an NC. The right way to think about NCs is that they drive the cost/performance curve to a new place. NCs combine the cost of a dumb terminal with the performance of a PC. There are at least five immediate niches for the network computer:

- **Webtops**—This is the niche we have dwelled on at length: as a low-cost thin client replacement for the desktop PC. This is also known as "webtop computing."

  A Java-enabled computing environment means shifting the emphasis from desktop to webtop computing. A webtop is your office computer workspace redefined for a Java environment. Your desktop environment looks like a browser, exists on a web server (not a specific local system), and is accessed by a password-protected URL.

  You retain the same control and customization of your personal workspace; you just access it differently. You run the same kinds of programs and productivity applications, but you do not have to install and configure them yourself.

  Java applets will supply data to the webtop from the network. The webtop hardware is inexpensive compared with current PCs and is a cheap, single field-replaceable unit in the event of hardware failure.

- **Single-Function Applications**—wherever a fat client is currently installed to run just a single application, it is a good candidate for swapping out in favor of an NC. A good way to identify these opportunities is to think "people with a keyboard and a uniform": car rental staff, hotel front desk employees, ticket

Ubiquitous computing

Webtop computing is an enabler for ubiquitous computing—an old idea that has previously been very difficult to implement.

Consider this: all your desktop environment and state (mail file, calendar, etc.) come from a server. Your local system is a thin client and just provides CPU cycles. The server downloads your state when you call for it, so the actual client you use does not matter at all! This is a goal for Microsoft ZAW in the NT 5.0 timeframe too, but some commentators say it will not be possible in NT.

You can go over to anyone's network computer, log in and it will be exactly like your own desktop. The system you use might be in an office down the hall or in a hotel room while you are travelling on business or in the Timbuktu branch office. When you are accessing your data across the Internet, the appropriate security infrastructure is needed. You will be able to visit client sites and demo software back in the home office or print out manuals, etc. This location-independent computing is called ubiquitous computing (from the Latin word for "everywhere").

Already, many people post resumés on Web sites and refer interested individuals to those. Now, imagine refining the concept with further layers of transparency and ubiquity. Anytime, anywhere, you can access your data—only you don't have to get it, it comes to you.

But wait, it gets better still. Imagine you have a large job that you want to run. You start to execute it on your ISP's server. The server notices the size of the job and looks around for the least-loaded of the other systems on its local net. These systems all have JVMs built in, so they can all run your program equally well (especially since the ubiquitous computing means they can all see your data). The job runs, and later that evening, you check on the progress from home during the commercials in your favorite TV program. You don't even have to get up from your armchair—the set-top box dials to your ISP and displays the results on the screen. The ability to ship jobs around the network to faster systems is termed "ubiquitous processing." It's a small step for a computer, and a giant leap for mankind.

offices, mechanics in a service department, police and security officer despatchers, nurses with patient records, airline front counter staff, lending library records (OK, librarians are not usually in uniform, but you get the idea).

- **Kiosks**—Dedicated kiosk-style applications. A kiosk is a public-access, limited-function device dedicated to dispensing specialized information (route maps, artistic performance times, food menus) on demand. The world's first network computer was the prototype of the JavaStation (a SPARCstation 5-based system) that Sun debuted at the Summer Olympics in Atlanta in Summer 1996 for this kind of application.

One scenario that has the telcos rather engaged is telephony across the Internet. Though they currently want ISPs to pay more of the toll, telephone companies have made billions of dollars out of carrying Internet traffic along with voice phone traffic. Now, Java has a telephony API, an Internet phone support (being called an "interphone") is a plug-in for Netscape Navigator 3.0 and Microsoft Explorer 3.0. An interphone allows end-to-end voice communication—a little slower and lower quality than a phone line, but essentially unmetered, so at zero cost to you. NCs will be able to compete directly with pay phones, at least until the telcos appeal to the FCC to regulate (prevent) this traffic.

The reason telcos are offering deals like "15 cents a minute, anytime anywhere in the United States, forever" (AT&T promotion, December 1996) is that they know perfectly well that phone rates are only going to drop from here as low-cost Internet connections become common. When only people in the computer industry have network computers, the usage will be low. When members of the general public have NCs installed in their house as a set-top box, along with cable TV, then usage will take off like a rocket. All those people who bought stock in the hitherto notoriously unprofitable Internet service providers, set-top box manufacturers, and cable TV operators will at last see a return on their investment.

- **Set-tops**—Low-end, home-consumer use (in-home kiosk). This is the set-top sector. Sony, Magnavox, and others launched the first set-top web browsers into the home market at the end of 1996.

These products all offer the same thing: a simple box of electronics that uses your phone line to call out to an ISP and plugs into your TV to display what it finds. WebTV's set-top box holds a 112 MHz RISC processor from MIPS Computers, Inc., combined with a 33.6-Kbps modem, 4 Mb of flash PROM, and a slot for a smart card (for purchasing) or possibly a printer. The set-top box comes with a keyboard and is essentially a *very* simple browser, intended to cater to the nontechnical domestic consumer. Another way to think of the set-top is as a protocol converter: it converts ASCII HTML into NTSC, PAL, or other television signal. The set-top also allows users to send and receive e-mail. Products start around $300.

A set-top box also contains some basic encryption software to enable online purchasing, and for this reason, it is classified as a munition by the United States government and cannot be exported without a license. The government is not expected to grant such a license, so American versions of these products cannot yet be sold in Japan or Europe as planned.

Set-top or WebTV (as it is also called) doesn't offer anything new to someone who already has a home PC and an ISP account. However, it brings down the cost of ownership and provides trivially simple access to a range of on-line services for those who have not bought a PC. Ironically falling PC prices are killing WebTV. A $300 WebTV is an immediate impulse buy, especially because when the TV is being used to surf the web, it is not tuned in to the advertising and entertainment drivel served up by American TV companies.

Let me just point out to anyone who hasn't realized it yet: The TV industry doesn't regard the function of advertising as paying for the TV programs. The TV industry regards the purpose of TV programs as keeping you in your seat long enough to be exposed to their recommended daily dose of advertising. The "product," to the TV industry, is your eyeballs, which are sold to advertisers. The NC provides cheap, convenient, and fast (33-Kb modem) access to a wide variety of services, like airline reservations, grocery shopping, and on-line banking. People who don't need a PC may find a set-top NC indispensable. Smart commercial services will extend the range of products that they offer over the Internet.

- **Appliances**—The very low end, below even set-top systems, is dedicated-purpose appliance computing. Network computing opens the door to these, and Java turns the key. The Diba Company (a spinoff from Oracle, later bought by Sun) is already demonstrating several special-purpose intelligent appliances, including a phone assistant and a chef's helper. This last sits under a countertop and holds a database of recipes and techniques. It sounds pretty special-purpose, and that's exactly the point! We now have the capability to build this kind of intelligence into devices cheaply enough that we can dedicate them to a single kind of use. Single-purpose systems can be much simpler to operate than general-purpose systems. Finally, below even appliances, there are smart cards—ICs on a card—for financial and security applications.

Some fat clients should stay fat clients

Most of the big advantages of swapping a PC for a network computer accrue to the MIS department. The former PC user has to learn something new but gets less obvious benefits like data backup, less downtime, and simpler applications. Because most of the benefits are felt elsewhere in the organization, PC users are likely to resist moving to network computers.

Organizations can encourage the migration to NCs by being open about the cost savings and by quantifying their commitment to user benefits like less downtime and better data restoration from archives. Organizations should take the opportunity to standardize on lightweight, downloadable programs. If a user needs applications that are not available on an NC or makes intensive use of the local computer (e.g., the user is a software developer or chip designer), then that user should keep a dedicated fat client or workstation. NCs will not replace all PCs—just the ones that can work equally well as thin clients.

What Java Brings to NCs

What Java brings to the table is that it is the first choice of language for client/server systems and especially for running on thin clients. It brings the same qualities that it brings to the Internet, namely, portability over all hardware, a proper security model, low cost, and rich libraries.

ISVs who rewrite their applications in Java can sell into a target market of 317 million desktops. This is about *twice as large* as the previous volume desktop API. And once your software is written in Java, you get that larger market without changing or specializing a line of code from the volume platform version. Better yet, Java actually offers a richer API set than some of the underlying systems support directly.

There is a class of systems even leaner than thin clients. These are the embedded systems, microcontrollers and processors dedicated to a single task. Sun is designing and licensing chips to serve this market segment. The chips, known as "Java Chips" have a JVM built in and can run bytecode as their native instruction format.

The Changing Role of ISPs

Internet service providers will prosper in this new era of network computing. They will no longer be mere gateways to the Internet. Under the new model of "renting software," a network computer user might rent application programs along with disk space on a server. For $40 per month, a user might be able to download and run the latest spreadsheet, word processor, tax management, or even games software.

Many software companies will gladly embrace pay-per-use software because it will let them maximize their return on investment by concentrating on improving features chosen by the majority of users. It also may give them a continuing revenue stream, assuming they get some of the rental fees. Instead of making money only when they ship a new version, software vendors can make money while the application remains in use, which gives them more reason to fix bugs and improve performance without making wholesale modifications.

As well as providing disk space and applications software, ISPs will be able to add value with features like a secure storage area for your data and end-to-end encryption when you access it. The ISP will take care of backups and restoration from archives (most ISPs totally ignore this service at present). Other centralized administration services such as an uninteruptible power supply will help to distinguish one ISP from another and provide "value-added" opportunities.

JavaChips, picoJava, and microJava

In October 1996, Sun Microsystems unveiled details of its JavaChip product. The core of the product is a picoJava I microprocessor that is essentially the JVM implemented in silicon. The picoJava uses bytecodes as its instruction set. It offers two main benefits: speed, up to five times faster than an x86 processor running just-in-time compiled code; and small footprint, allowing the chip to be built into smart phones, PDAs, and other devices where size is a constraint.

A number of electronics companies, including Mitsubishi, Northern Telecomm, NEC, and Samsung, have licensed picoJava. The picoJava architecture consists of a RISC-style pipeline with a Java bytecode instruction set. Designers can configure the picoJava I core with or without a floating-point unit and up to 16 Kbytes each of instruction and data cache. The picoJava I core is also designed to be implemented in a variety of CMOS processes, allowing licensees to configure for application-optimized power, performance, and price (probably significantly under $25 in some configurations). The architecture is based on a four-stage pipeline and executes the most frequently used instructions in one to two cycles. An internal hardware cache is provided for the first 64 stack entries, and these are spilled and filled in the background as needed.

The picoJava I directly executes the Java Virtual Machine instruction set. As a result, Java software applications (or other languages written to the JVM specification) are directly executed by picoJava I. The applications use less memory and run faster because no runtime software interpreter is needed.

The picoJava I core will be at the heart of a broad range of applications, including smart phones that connect to the World Wide Web, network computers, PDAs, and set-top boxes. Sun's strategy is to build a broad market through licensing and partnerships. The cumulative strength in marketing, product development, and distribution provides the formula for success.

Industry analysts estimate that the overall microprocessor and microcontroller market will grow to exceed $60 billion by the year 1999. Today, the average home has around 10 microcontrollers (these are in the VCR, stereo system, microwave oven, TV, garage door opener). By 1999, the average home will contain many more microcontrollers. Devices like picoJava greatly expand the market by making it cheap to embed controller logic and easy-to-write reliable software.

The picoJava I core is the first milestone in a series of JavaChip processors under development by Sun Microelectronics. The picoJava I core will be at the heart of the future microJava processor line, which combines the picoJava CPU with ASIC (application-specific logic) chips, I/O, and memory. The microJava products add the hardware "glue" to let products interact with users directly, rather than just control an embedded device.

Summary

- A thin client has no local system administration needs, whereas a thick or fat client may have a great deal. A network computer is essentially a thin client. A current-day PC is an example of a thick client. The Windows CE product launched in fall 1996 is a thick client; it reduces the hardware package but not the system administration needs.

- The single most expensive part of PC computing in an office environment is the hidden cost of system administration. It dwarfs the original purchase price.

- The promise of Network Computers is that they offer fundamentally the same desktop power at a greatly reduced TCO (total cost of ownership). The cost is lower because the administration is centralized on a server, where it is done in bulk for many systems simultaneously.

- The NC should really be compared to the telephone, not to the PC. They are both "zero system administration at the client" information appliances.

- When NCs first appeared, the system and applications software was not ready to fully support them. In the intervening two years, Java office applications software like Lotus e-suite, Applix Anywhere, Star Office, and Digital Harbor's Wav word processor, have become readily available.

- Corresponding PC management and administration tools are promised for delivery in NT 5.0 around the year 2000.

CHAPTER 12

- Software Frameworks

- Microsoft's COM Model

- JavaBeans and Enterprise JavaBeans

- The Industry's CORBA Model

- Java and Databases

- Summary

Component Software, Enterprise Computing, and Databases

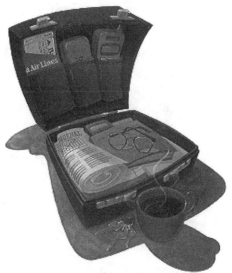

Now at last it is time to start bringing together the different strands in this narrative. The previous chapters have described the Internet, browsers, Java, intranets and client/server computing. This chapter describes some new and still-unfolding software initiatives of the past couple of years that build on these layers. We'll describe what are termed "software frameworks"—software like Microsoft's ActiveX, Sun's JavaBeans, and the industry-wide CORBA initiative. The natural counterpart of these frameworks is corporate databases. Software frameworks organize your code beyond the program level; corporate databases scale up and organize your data in the large. The second half of this chapter deals with databases in the new enterprise.

Software Frameworks

Software frameworks are fairly abstract concepts, so we'll get the explanation moving with a review of how Microsoft arrived at where it is with ActiveX. That discussion will give a good explanation of what you can do with a software framework (also called a component framework), why they are increasing in importance, and why all computer industry professionals need to be familiar with them.

In the Beginning, There Was DDE

The Windows operating system gave PCs a simpler and more accessible computing environment, but there was still the problem of lack of consistency between different programs, especially programs from different software vendors. The problem was on two levels. The different programs all used different keystrokes for identical commands like "save to a file." And they all used different file formats for their data, so spreadsheets created by Lotus123 couldn't be updated by Excel. Added to this, early PCs couldn't run (very well) more than one application at a time. If you needed a spreadsheet and a word processor and a communication program and you might want to use more than one at the same time, you needed a very big computer.

ISVs thought that integrating suites of different programs into one single massive program was the answer. So, suite applications were built that had all of the pieces in one package, but to stay within a reasonable size, they had to compromise on the quality of the components. Thus, Works had a spreadsheet that wasn't nearly as capable as Excel and a word processor that was inferior to Word and so on. But the market rejected complicated, overblown products like Claris-Works and Microsoft Works, and these integrated applications still couldn't share data with each other. Something on a more fundamental level was needed. The GUI guidelines for Windows helped to give different programs a consistent set of commands by using pull-down menus. Microsoft came out with DDE to address the second problem of incompatible file formats.

DDE (Dynamic Data Exchange) let different Windows programs share data with one another through links like the hypertext links we saw in an earlier chapter. The example that everyone always uses is a spreadsheet embedded in a word processor file (perhaps, a status report explaining the figures in the spreadsheet). It's a good example because it's easily understandable, and we'll stick with it here.

Microsoft's DDE allowed data files to be linked together, as shown in Figure 12–1. Whenever you changed the figures in the spreadsheet, those new figures would automatically appear in the word processor document when you next ran it.

DDE was a good first step, but it had its limitations. Although you could automatically import the spreadsheet data into the word processor, you couldn't update it there. To update the spreadsheet, you had to invoke the spreadsheet program. Then, you had to save the new data and invoke the word processor program again. It was only marginally better than simple cut'n'paste to switch between applications in this way. Worse, the links were fragile and would break if you moved the data files around.

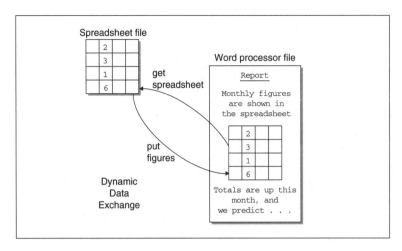

Figure 12–1
Dynamic Data Exchange Example

So, Microsoft moved on to a better arrangement that they called OLE 1, launching it in 1990. OLE meant "Object Linking and Embedding," which pretty much captured the essence of its capabilities. When you were working in your word processor and wanted to bring in the spreadsheet figures, you could instruct the program as to whether you wanted to *link* to a spreadsheet file or *embed* the spreadsheet file. Linking was the same as DDE—the word processor made a note of the path name to the spreadsheet data file (in fact, OLE 1 was built on top of DDE). The new feature of embedding meant that users could physically bring a snapshot of that data into the word processor, and save it out in the word processor data file. Figure 12–2 illustrates the difference between linking and embedding in OLE.

Linking was advantageous when the different data files were large or frequently changing and imported by several different documents. Embedding was preferred when the data files were small, didn't change much, or weren't shared by several documents. One example of embedding would be applying a little graphic icon (the company logo, say) to some headed notepaper. You might as well embed that image in the word processor file if it's small. You aren't going to be continually changing the image, and there's a convenience factor to having everything in one place.

Compound Documents

The idea with OLE 1 was to support the concept of *compound documents*. As the name suggests, these are data files in which different pieces are processed by different application programs. The idea was to give users the concept of a doc-

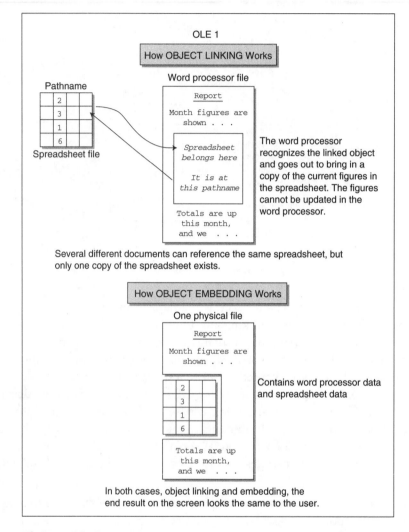

Figure 12–2
OLE 1—the Difference Between Linking and Embedding

ument-centric view of computing, in which they could focus on their data, not on the programs that created and processed it. The document-centric concept was rolled out with a big fanfare and promoted as the best thing since Neapolitan ice cream. But compound documents are simply data files that were created by either linking data files together, or completely copying the contents of one data file into another. It does not deliver the crucial benefit of making the data *independent* of the application program. If document-centric computing meant that I could in practice use any of Excel or Lotus123 or any favorite spreadsheet software to process my spreadsheet models, then it would indeed be delivering a significant benefit. However, document-centric computing does not provide this level of data independence.

OLE 1 allowed different applications programs to share data files just as DDE did, and it allowed the new feature of embedding data. However, it did not solve the problem of ponderously switching from one application into another to update the data from the other application. Nor did it have any awareness of computers other than the single desktop on which it ran. That's why OLE 2 was developed.

OLE 2 was where Microsoft started to get theoretical about what had started out as simple data sharing. The OLE 2 designers regarded compound documents as one case of a more general issue: How should different programs (like a spreadsheet program) send objects to each other (i.e., send data or ask for data or other services)? If programs could send objects to each other, couldn't the objects be code, just as well as data? The answer was to create (drumroll, please) a software framework that could be used for more than just compound documents. The framework was called the Component Object Model (COM), and OLE 2 was built on top of it and launched in 1993.

The true value of compound documents is that they enable component software. You can group objects together, store them in a file, send them over a network, invoke other objects on them, display them on a screen, and so on. There will likely be a software component to carry out each of these operations. An HTML file containing embedded links to media, data, and applet executables is one example of a non-Microsoft compound document. In the Java world, such a file can be wrapped up in one physical JAR (Java archive) file.

The most visible improvement of OLE 2 over OLE 1 was that it used the COM framework to allow in-place editing. The most visible drawback of OLE 2 was that it was hideously and quite unnecessarily complicated to program; for this reason, it has never been popular.

If you have a compound document with word processor parts and spreadsheet parts, you can fire it up with either application and switch to the other application just by clicking on the words (to switch to the word processor) or the spreadsheet table (to switch to the spreadsheet). The overall window that contains the running application stays up, and all the menus change to the menus of the other application. In-place editing makes it easy to switch between the different applications that process a given document. It still takes a few seconds of watching your screen go blank and listening to your disk spin at top speed, however. OLE 2 also introduced support for printing, automatic format conversion, and automation

Compound documents

Compound documents are simply data files that were created by either linking data files together or completely copying the contents of one data file into another. Don't be fooled by the name "document"—you can put anything in there, including text, images, or data.

The significance of compound documents is that they facilitate *software components*—pieces of independently invokable software that are smaller than an entire application. Software components are well known in the PC world but are still unfamiliar on UNIX. Inprise's Delphi software for Windows was one of the early products that legitimized and enabled a software component industry. Delphi was a variant of Pascal that was particularly well attuned to building user interfaces and connecting them to PC databases. It offered a visual toolbox of components that could easily be "snapped" together to make crude but working programs.

The reason that software components haven't caught on to the same degree in the UNIX world is that software components do much the same thing as UNIX pipes. Software components allow the reuse of software in a loosely coupled manner. However, software components often have a visual or GUI aspect that is missing from UNIX pipes. Indeed, with the right software glue, any individual scrollbar, text field, or other graphical widget can be a "control" that inputs, processes, or outputs data to other controls. Some programmers point out that third-party Motif widgets are a UNIX version of software components. An entire program can be built out of software components.

through a Visual Basic scripting language (like AppleScript). Figure 12–3 illustrates in-place editing; when you click on the graphic (A in the figure), the paint program menus replace the word processor menus allowing you to modify the graphic (B in the figure). You can switch back by clicking on the words.

Microsoft's COM Model

The Component Object Model (COM) framework allows the word processor program to talk to the spreadsheet program, telling it things like "The user just clicked on the spreadsheet, so start yourself up in my window, put your menus here, look for the data here in the file, and let me know when you're ready to change over again, OK?" The COM framework (notice how I'm slipping that "framework" term in along with these practical examples, to give you a good feel for what it means and does in practice) enables any pieces of software to talk to each other: libraries, system software, utilities, not just application programs. The trick is to define protocols that are not only abstract enough to allow the components to be created independently and to find out about their neighbors at run time, but are also concrete enough to let the components share screen space and file access.

At this point, the Microsoft marketing department stepped in with its "value added" and made the following important changes. The version number was

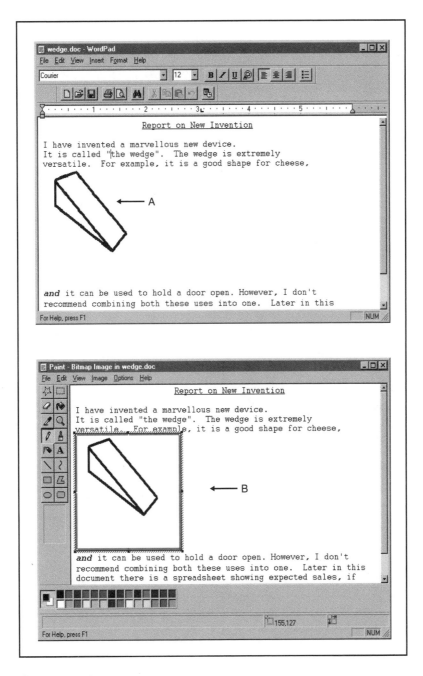

Figure 12-3
In-place Editing with OLE 2

dropped from OLE 2, and it ceased to be regarded as an acronym. Furthermore, the term "OLE" was applied to pretty much all software that was built using the COM protocols. Microsoft strong-armed ISVs into following the OLE 2 standard by withholding the "Designed for Windows 95" logo unless they did. This policy even applied to software, like games software, that had no prospect of ever doing OLE-style operations.

Although all our examples have been about spreadsheets and word processors, data from any program that uses the COM protocols can be put in a compound document. This data includes sound files, audio clips, payroll records, calendar/appointment information, and any other kind of data. The compound document stores not just the data, but also a note of the executable that can manipulate it. This information is stored in a standard form that makes it easy for other COM software to read, understand, and invoke it.

Windows 95 also introduced a new standard: OCX, meaning an *OLE Custom eXtension* component. An OCX is a piece of code, usually smaller than an entire application program but able to contain its own user interface. OCX started life in 1994 as VBX—Visual Basic eXtensions—and the idea of software components that were more than a function but less than an entire program turned out to be useful enough to be supported outside the Visual Basic environment. Three examples of OCX components might be a spell checker, a synonym provider, a technical acronym expander. The idea is that anyone with minimal programming skills should be able to bundle together OCXs to form customized applications. Figure 12–4 illustrates the use of OCX controls.

Definition: ActiveX

ActiveX is the family name for the set of Windows-specific computing technologies that
- Adds executable content to web pages (like applets)
- Allows compound documents to invoke viewing software for themselves
- Is based on Object Linking and Embedding
- has authentication, but lacks other pieces of a security framework

In a phrase, ActiveX is network-capable Object Linking and Embedding. The basic element of ActiveX technology is the ActiveX control, which is the name given to the OCX control, simplified and slightly jazzed up for the Internet.

An ActiveX control is a software *component*—a chunk of executable code larger than a function but smaller than an entire program. With the COM framework, individual pieces in a compound document can invoke methods in a component.

In the Java world, JavaBeans is the technology that corresponds to ActiveX.

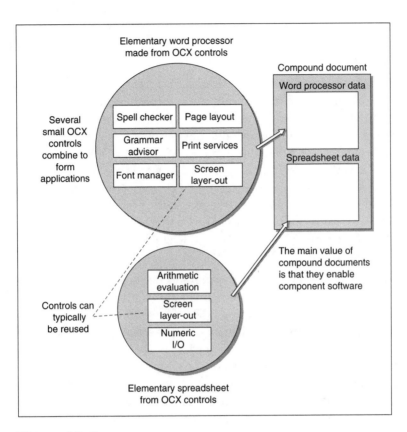

Figure 12–4
Building Applications Out of OCX Controls

In spring 1996, Microsoft retooled the terminology once again, bringing in the marketing term "ActiveX." First the term "Network OLE" was introduced, then dropped, then OLE was demoted to just referring to the technology used to create compound documents (Object Linking and Embedding, remember?). In summer 1998 the term "DNA" was launched for a bundle of technologies including ActiveX. ActiveX is now the family name for the computing technologies that

- Add executable content to web pages (like applets)

- Allow compound documents to invoke viewing software for themselves

- Provide a mechanism for downloading, caching, and running arbitrary files. The mechanism does the same thing as, but is different than, Java applets.

- Were scaled up from the desktop, and so lack a security framework.

The ActiveX relationship with COM and OLE is that COM components are the most common format to be downloaded and that almost all of these components support Windows OLE interfaces.

COM (the Component Object Model) is a set of object-based interfaces that allow Windows applications to communicate with other applications and objects on the same computer. It's comparable to something like Inter-Process Communication for Windows objects. COM was extended in partnership with Digital Equipment Corporation to create DCOM—the merger of Microsoft's OLE with Network OLE and DEC's ObjectBroker software. Part of COM was based on technology that was transferred from IBM to Microsoft under a patent cross-license agreement in the days when the two companies were cooperating on OS/2. IBM has its own version of COM, called System Object Model, that is technically superior but is irrelevant at this point. COM was extended to support more languages than C/C++, and rechristened COM+ in 1998.

Microsoft maintains that COM/OLE is portable because it has funded companies like MainSoft and Software AG to implement the Windows APIs, including COM, on non-Wintel architectures including UNIX. However, COM+ lacks binary portability, it's unlikely the results will enjoy mainstream use, and the technology remains Microsoft proprietary. Microsoft tried in late 1996 to pay The Open Group to bless some nonstrategic pieces of COM as an open standard. The attempt foundered when computer industry executives explained to the board of The Open Group that the board was being played for patsies and everyone knew it. Also, IBM pointed out that some of the technology that Microsoft was trying to give away actually belonged to IBM. It's important to Microsoft to be able to claim support for COM on non-Windows platforms, so they swallowed their pride, adjusted the proposal, and succeeded in sticking The Open Group with just enough COM to run on other platforms as a client of Windows.

Despite repeated claims to the contrary, COM was only intended to be a single desktop solution. It was never designed for distributed processing, which is why a separate new piece had to be invented. It only acquired network aspirations late in 1996 when Microsoft got Internet religion. The distributed processing version of COM is (naturally) called Distributed COM or DCOM. Distributed COM became available in Beta form in September 1996.

ActiveX Withering on the Internet

The basic element of ActiveX technology is the ActiveX control, which is the new name given to the OCX control, simplified and slightly jazzed up for the Internet. If you're beginning to suspect that there's rather a lot of marketing noise going on here, you're right. The technology started as OLE, became OLE2, was renamed to Network OLE, then launched again as OLE, before being given a fresh coat of

COM, COM, and DCOM explained

(Note to the reader: there are, of necessity, a lot of buzzwords in this section. For this I apologize in advance.)

The term "COM" has been used by Microsoft in two different ways. The modern meaning is "Component Object Model," which refers to the technology that supports OLE and compound documents on MS Windows. The Component Object Model has been described as "interprocess communication for Windows objects." Object Linking and Embedding is built on top of the Component Object Model. In other words, COM is how OLE talks to objects. The Component Object Model is the building block that allows different objects on a single PC to find and talk to each other.

Microsoft has also used COM to mean "Common Object Model," referring to the merger of the single-PC OLE framework with DEC's multiplatform CORBA-compliant ObjectBroker ORB. The resulting Common Object Model competes with the overall Object Management Architecture developed by the Object Management Group. Microsoft's Windows-only *Component* Object Model is a subset of the *Common* Object Model. It is unfortunate that two related terms have the same acronym.

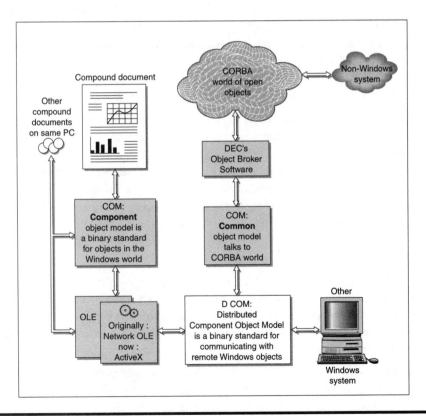

paint as ActiveX. Just one problem: ActiveX never took off on the web. Technology correspondent George Gilder said that Activex "is withering on the Net" in a Aug 1997 report in the Wall Street Journal.

After a couple of high-profile security breaches, ActiveX dropped from use on the Internet. One poll concluded that Java applets outnumbered ActiveX components by seven to one. Microsoft further downplayed ActiveX when it switched to promoting its DNA initiative. DNA—Distributed interNet Applications Architecture) is what we in Silicon Valley call "market-tecture." It is a bundling together of old technologies under a new name. DNA is just an umbrella term for repackaging COM, COM+ (the extension of COM to multiple languages, and other simplifications), ActiveX, a browser, DHTML, etc.

The downside of ActiveX in the intranet is twofold. We have already discussed at length the lack of security for ActiveX controls. This is an issue on both the Internet and intranets. The second issue is that ActiveX controls are based on OLE, which in turn is a platform-specific ABI (binary code standard). If you embed an ActiveX control in a web page, only a browser running on Windows can execute it. Browsers on the Mac or a UNIX system won't be able to execute it, no matter what languages it was originally written in. Even if your company has standardized on Windows, your partners, customers, and suppliers may not have. In the new world of extranet computing, your new software should run on all platforms. COM and ActiveX do not offer a cross-platform solution.

Microsoft is now positioning DNA as an alternative to Java by saying that it makes it easy for developers to build distributed computing solutions that are integrated with the web. Certainly, the COM+ part will help in bridging the growing interoperability gap between the different Windows APIs. But DNA has the same old Microsoft problem: it supports several languages to write for only one platform. Java provides one language to write applications for all platforms on the Internet and the intranet.

JavaBeans

JavaBeans is a component object model along the lines of Microsoft's COM, but JavaBeans is not tied to Windows and runs on all computers. The most popular feature of JavaBeans is its overriding simplicity, however. To write a Java software component or "bean," a programmer just needs to follow a few simple naming conventions. That's it! No special processing, compiling, or linking.

Software components are so clearly a "right" way to get software reuse (object inheritance is another "good" way) that they have a very bright future. The technique is in its infancy now, but some commentators think that within a few years a large part of software development will consist of connecting together components that were already written by someone else. If that happens, it's great! Programmers can spend their time solving new and bigger problems instead of repeatedly reinventing the wheel by reimplementing new versions of the same old systems. Software development will be easier and faster, and thus cheaper. JavaBeans are the best shot the industry has at making this come true.

JavaBeans, like software components in general is an abstract concept that is a little hard to describe. Think of it this way. Software components are like Lego bricks. Just one of them isn't much by itself. But if you have a box of assorted Lego bricks you can easily fit them together to make pleasing and useful structures. So it is with software components. Say I have three JavaBeans: one can read mail, one that can save text to a file, and one can encrypt text, I can connect these beans (program fragments) together, and voila, I have a mail program that saves its files securely. The JavaBean framework is a kit for doing exactly that: taking self-contained partial programs and fitting them together without recompiling or changing any of them.

There are a lot of competing Bean editors from premier software companies. Table 12-1 shows some Bean building tools that are commercially available. The tool for connecting software components is typically some kind of visual editor.

You drop an iconic representation of the bean into a window, and drag lines or click on neighboring beans to connect them. The visual editor usually displays the names of the input and output methods in each bean. You read the documentation to confirm what each does.

Table 12-1 Bean building tools

Company	Bean builder product name	URL
Inprise	JBuilder2	www.inprise.com/jbuilder
BulletProof Corp	JDesignerPro	www.bulletproof.com/JDesignerPro
Imperial Software	Visaj	www.ist.co.uk/visaj/index.html
IBM Corp	VisualAge	www.software.ibm.com/ad/vajava/
Lotus	BeanMachine	www.lotus.com/beanmachine
Penumbra Software	Super Mojo	www.PenumbraSoftware.com/
Sun Microsystems	Java Studio	www.sun.com/studio/
Supercede	Supercede Pro	www.supercede.com/
Tek Tools	Kawa	www.tek-tools.com/kawa/

The following illustration is an example of a bean-building tool in use. This is a screen dump of the VisaJ tool from Imperial Software Technology. The screen shows how a programmer would connect a button press (the object and event highlighted on the left half of the screen) with the code that should be called to deal with it (the object and method highlighted on the right half of the screen.

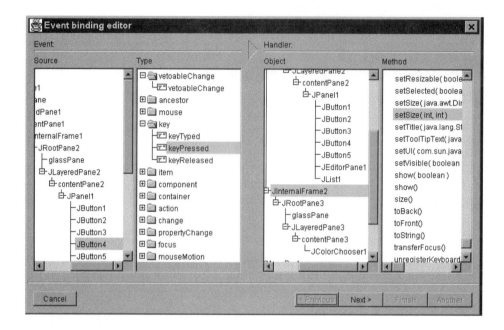

The programmer connects the beans by dragging, clicking, and/or highlighting. Any necessary (minimal) "glue" code is generated automatically behind the scenes. The beans can be fitted together without a single line of new code being written by hand, so quite sophisticated programs can be built up

You may also hear the term "Infobus." The Infobus API is a good way for Java-Beans to pass large amounts of data among themselves at run time. Neither bean has to know about the other, so Infobus maintains the "loose coupling" which is desirable in reuseable components. The term "bus" is analogous to a memory bus that is the channel for hardware data communication. Infobus can also be used to share data between several applets, replacing a variety of ad-hoc techniques here. Infobus was developed by a software architect at Lotus, and contributed back to the Java community for the good of all,

Java Bean components are not restricted to only the Java world. Beans are able to plug into other component architectures such as Microsoft's COM architecture. But unlike COM and DNA, Beans are supported on all systems that support Java, not just on Windows. Right from the start Beans had the goal of being simple and lightweight. JavaBeans allows users to do everything that COM can do, but more simply and in a portable way.

JavaBeans make it easier for developers to write applications by blending together and reusing smaller fragments of code. The traditional example is our old friend the spreadsheet embedded in a word processor document, as shown earlier in this chapter. The application of software components is potentially much wider and more significant than that.

Components are assembled visually, so less skill is needed. Some people think that if a company created a whole range of Beans corresponding to its business objects, nonprogrammers, like accountants or managers, could fit them together to model new business processes. Personally I think that history shows that pipe dream is unlikely to come true. (COBOL was originally sold under the same message 40 years ago. But regardless of the job title of those who will use them, Java Bean components bring a great new flexibility into the software world. This is truly a promising technology with a bright future.

Enterprise JavaBeans

JavaBeans were originally conceived for use on the client part of a multitier system. Users would interact with them directly. Visual controls in a GUI (scrollbars, text fields, panels, progress bars) are all beans in Java. That makes it very easy to use a bean builder to create GUI code.

Programmers quickly noticed that Java component software was equally useful outside the client tier. The use of JavaBeans on servers and front-end databases has come to be called "Enterprise JavaBeans." Unlike client-side beans, Enterprise JavaBeans don't have a GUI. They are more concerned with operations like "read a record from a database," "calculate billing information," "update customer data," "validate purchase order" and other kinds of business logic. These kinds of programs can be invoked automatically on a webserver by an http request. They are termed "servlets," just as java code on the client is an applet. The Java Web Server product provides an easy framework to get this running.

Enterprise JavaBeans operate in the same space as Microsoft's Transaction Server (MTS) product. MTS is a DCOM-based transaction processing monitor for the Microsoft NT platform. It is bundled with some other software as part of "Back Office." Applications written for MTS can be deployed only in MTS and possibly one or two other specialized TP monitors, but only on the DCOM/NT platform.

You cannot deploy an MTS component on any non-NT system. Enterprise Java-Beans allows you to write components once and reuse them in any Enterprise JavaBeans-enabled environment, on any platform, with any Beans-enabled middleware. Does that sound like a good investment in "future proofing" your software? Applications written using Enterprise JavaBeans can be deployed on all Java-enabled server systems, regardless of what hardware/OS/transactional-environment combination is used, as long as the server-side system is Enterprise JavaBeans-enabled.

Enterprise JavaBeans are already widely used in web applications, replacing a hodge-podge of Perl scripts with reuseable object software. Compaq has declared its ambition to be an Enterprise computing supplier, and is bundling the Java-based application server from vendor Novera to house and transport distributed Java applications.

Enterprise JavaBeans has extended the Java "write-once-run-anywhere" model to server-side applications. The Enterprise JavaBeans specification was developed jointly by industry leaders including Baan, BEA Systems, Inprise, Gemstone, IBM, Informix, Lotus, Netscape, Novell, Oracle, Sybase, and Tandem. These vendors are writing Enterprise JavaBean wrappers for their existing data access products. Programmers thus do not need to know the specifics of each teleprocessing monitor, which also promotes code reuse and portability.

The Industry's CORBA Model

The Microsoft DCOM protocol was launched to compete with an earlier initiative supported by essentially all the rest of the computer industry. At the last count, something like 600 companies were working together under the auspices of an umbrella organization called "The Object Management Group." The only computer company of any consequence that is not a supporter of the OMG is Microsoft (they are a member so they get the specifications and plans, but they do not actively support it).

Over the last seven years, the OMG has gradually done the impossible: created industry agreement on an industrial-strength Object Management Architecture, defining among other things what common services a distributed-object framework should provide.

The jewel in the crown of the OMA is a piece of middleware termed an Object Request Broker. The specification that describes what an Object Request Broker must do is termed CORBA—Common Object Request Broker Architecture. CORBA is a lot of things, but one thing it is not (alas), is easy to teach, describe, or learn.

Definition of CORBA

CORBA—the Common Object Request Broker Architecture—is a standard that specifies how computers can treat objects available on a server as if they were actually present in a client program, without the development overhead of worrying about sockets, protocols, packets, and so on.

Different vendors have different names for their CORBA implementations. CORBA products often have more value-added, like the ability to queue requests from clients, inspect the queues visually, and administer the load on a server. The fastest-growing CORBA vendor is Iona Technologies. Iona has the implementation closest to a pure CORBA 2.0 ORB and supports it on the largest number of systems.

The (slightly oversimplified) summary of CORBA is that it does the same thing as DCOM does in the Microsoft world, namely, lets objects locate and make method calls to other objects on the network. A big difference between DCOM and the OMG approach is that DCOM is tied to the Windows environment, whereas OMG has made interoperability with all different vendors a priority. The biggest difference, however, is that DCOM came out of COM, a single-system linking mechanism that is trying to grow up in a distributed network world; CORBA has been a networked design from the start.

CORBA is not tied to any one language and was originally laid down with C++ in mind. All the object frameworks—DCOM, JavaBeans, CORBA, SOM—let software components do similar kinds of things:

- Publish their existence and find other components

- Handle layout and presentation

- Handle events, like user mouse clicks

- Provide a way to save an object to a file (persistence)

- Support aggregation with other components to create an application

Although neither has a very large installed base, CORBA is at least two to three years ahead of DCOM in design, sophistication, and implementation. With CORBA, the objects running on a client can talk to other objects on a server, just like non-object-oriented software can communicate on a network by using Remote Procedure Calls. The server and client can be different makes of computer with different object models. As long as a CORBA-compliant ORB is the intermediary, it will all "just work."

Enabling objects on different computers to talk to each other (without worrying over issues of hardware and operating system) allows you to build much more complicated and capable systems that support true distributed processing. It's not

intended for a single programmer working on a lone PC. Distributed processing is highly useful in a large enterprise with terabytes of data distributed in databases on dozens of mainframe class systems connected to hundreds or thousands of clients.

Where an Object Request Broker fits in

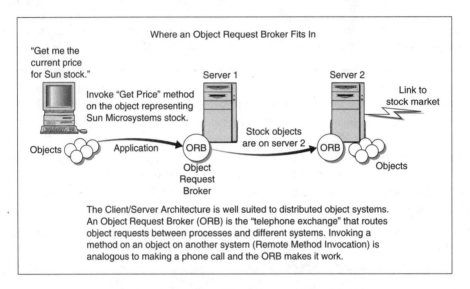

Where an Object Request Broker Fits In

The Client/Server Architecture is well suited to distributed object systems. An Object Request Broker (ORB) is the "telephone exchange" that routes object requests between processes and different systems. Invoking a method on an object on another system (Remote Method Invocation) is analogous to making a phone call and the ORB makes it work.

The CORBA-compliant ORB allows any client to talk to the objects on any server, even if they come from different vendors. In the previous chapter, we used an analogy with the phone system to explain how the hardware worked. Now put that analogy out of your mind as we will look at the corresponding diagram for CORBA software. We're saying "the phone system is like the hardware in these ways" and "the phone system is like the software in these ways"; it's not surprising they both map onto phones because ultimately the hardware and software fit together, too.

Figure 12–5 compares various object framework models.

The first CORBA specification was released in 1991, and an updated version 2.0 was released in December 1994. CORBA implementations now have the benefit of several years of practical experience. All CORBA implementations are language neutral; they achieve neutrality by having an interface language (it looks close to C)

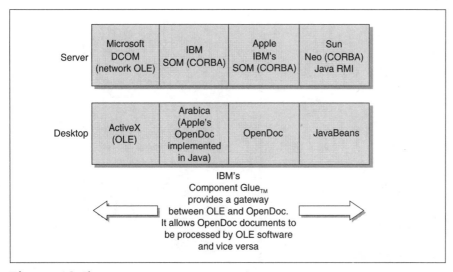

Server	Microsoft DCOM (network OLE)	IBM SOM (CORBA)	Apple IBM's SOM (CORBA)	Sun Neo (CORBA) Java RMI
Desktop	ActiveX (OLE)	Arabica (Apple's OpenDoc implemented in Java)	OpenDoc	JavaBeans

IBM's Component Glue™ provides a gateway between OLE and OpenDoc. It allows OpenDoc documents to be processed by OLE software and vice versa

Figure 12–5
Comparison of Different Object Framework Models

that other languages must map into when they call CORBA services. Making CORBA language independent was a very far-sighted decision on the part of the original designers; it means Java. There are two main reasons for using CORBA when you want objects to communicate across different systems:

- It is an object framework that is language independent. If you're using multiple languages, or you want to leave that option open for the future, or you want to access C++ legacy systems, CORBA makes it easy.

- The CORBA initiative started before Java, and the CORBA code is a little more tried and tested. The equivalent Java Remote Method Invocation (RMI) code is newly launched and doesn't have an extensive user base. Nor does CORBA, but it is further along.

CORBA is a complicated solution to complicated problems. RMI just provides a means for Java objects to communicate across systems. It does not provide the rich plethora of common middleware services that CORBA also supports. But if you're writing everything in Java, don't use CORBA—it's simpler and easier to use the Remote Method Invocation of Java. Sun and a number of CORBA vendors are working together to ensure Java RMI and CORBA can coexist well.

Sun is partnering with Inprise Corp. to transition from Sun's object request broker technology, NEO ORB, to Visigenic's VisiBroker for Java and Visiobroker for C++ ORB technology, which Inprise recently acquired.

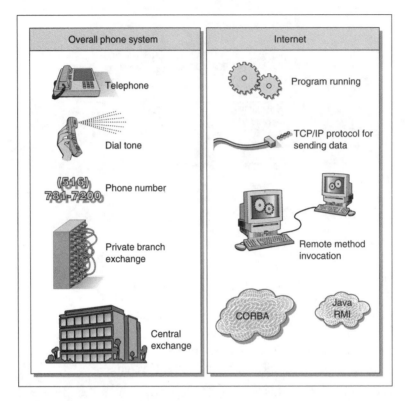

Overall phone system	Internet
Telephone	Program running
Dial tone	TCP/IP protocol for sending data
(516) 781-7200 Phone number	Remote method invocation
Private branch exchange	CORBA Java RMI
Central exchange	

This analogy breaks down if you push it too far. Whereas all the pieces of the telephone network interoperate (any telephone anywhere in the world can call any other telephone), that interoperability is currently far from being the case in the object intercommunication world.

Interface Definition Language (IDL)

IDL is the way CORBA achieves language neutrality. You describe in IDL the signature of the methods and data that CORBA will pass back and forth for you. IDL looks somewhat like C, but it is purely for describing interfaces, not for writing actual programs. IDL is only for people using CORBA. Most Java systems won't use the CORBA framework, so most Java programmers will never use IDL.

Most CORBA implementations in the market support versions 1.1 and 1.2 of the standard; others support some of the more advanced features found in version 2.0. One important component of 2.0 is the Internet Inter-ORB Protocol (IIOP). The IIOP specification allows ORBs from different vendors to send messages to remote systems via TCP/IP. Even with the common CORBA standard, ORBs are implemented and behave differently. IIOP bridges that gap and allows different ORBs to talk to each other. Companies such as Iona Technologies provide ORBs that can interface with other object models such as Microsoft's DCOM. There is no one *best* object framework. The key attribute systems designers should strive for is good intercommunication with all the models.

Java and Databases: JBDC

Java has a bright future in enterprise computing. Large enterprises stand or fall by the quality of their corporate databases. MIS departments fell in love with web browsers because the browser and CGI made it so easy to write and deploy database access programs, compared with traditional client/server techniques. Now Java makes it possible to write even more flexible and more efficient programs by using that approach. So, providing database hooks for Java was obvious, precisely because developers saw the value of web tools in database applications before they saw the light about Java.

The very first library that Sun provided after the Java Development Kit was the JDBC (Java DataBase Connectivity) library. Sun designed the JDBC to allow access to any ANSI SQL-2 standard database.

We'll describe the JDBC in full here, and to get the most out of this section, you really need to understand database terms and techniques (like SQL). We'll sketch out some of these, but the topic really requires a complete book of its own (and this isn't it).

About SQL and Relational Databases

Extracting information from a database and writing it back is done in a language called SQL. SQL—Structured Query Language—has been refined over more than two decades and is the language used to access essentially all modern databases.

Years ago, there were several fundamentally different architectures for databases: hierarchical databases (like IMS), network databases (like the CODASYL model), and relational databases. It is now almost universally accepted that the relational design is superior to the other alternatives. We're also starting to see early use of object-oriented databases, some of which are accessed in a relational fashion. The collision between "object-oriented" and "relational" databases is an area of emerging technology.

The database gurus have their own terminology of relations, tuples and "Nth normal form," but (in plain words) the idea central to a relational database is that data is kept in tables. In a way, a table in a relational database is like an enormous spreadsheet. It might have millions of rows and hundreds of columns. Each column contains only one kind of data. A row in a table corresponds to a record.

The database can contain several tables. A programmer will use SQL statements to merge tables and extract data from them. Figure 12–6 illustrates a relational database.

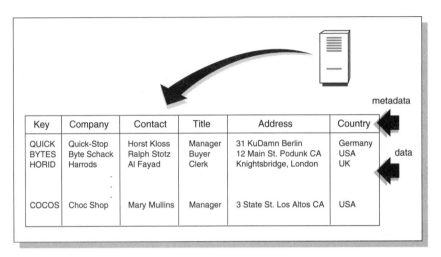

metadata

Key	Company	Contact	Title	Address	Country	
QUICK	Quick-Stop	Horst Kloss	Manager	31 KuDamn Berlin	Germany	data
BYTES	Byte Schack	Ralph Stotz	Buyer	12 Main St. Podunk CA	USA	
HORID	Harrods	Al Fayad	Clerk	Knightsbridge, London	UK	
.						
.						
COCOS	Choc Shop	Mary Mullins	Manager	3 State St. Los Altos CA	USA	

Figure 12–6
A Relational Database

The JDBC classes do their work in terms of SQL, so it takes an understanding of SQL to describe what these are. SQL is an elaborate programming language in its own right, customized to handle tables, rows and columns. Describing SQL would take more room than is available here. Suffice it to say that SQL has statements like SELECT, INSERT, DELETE, and UPDATE. SQL operates on tables, merging, matching, and extracting from them and provides its result sets in the form of tables. We don't want to make Java replace SQL; we just want Java to be able to bundle up SQL queries, direct them to the right database, and listen for the answers. The package that holds the Java code for the JDBC is called java.sql.

The JDBC API defines Java classes to represent database connections, SQL statements, result sets, database metadata (data about data), etc. It allows a Java programmer to issue SQL statements to read/write a database. The JDBC itself is written in Java, will run anywhere, and (from JDK 1.1 on) can be downloaded as part of an applet. However, more software than just the JDBC is needed to talk to a database. The JDBC package just lets your Java program ship SQL queries out. A database-specific driver is needed to listen to these queries, send them into the database, listen for the results, and send the results back into the Java world. Standard security restrictions bar an applet from connecting to any server except the one that served the applet. The implication is that any database middleware will also need to be hosted on that server so applets can open sockets to it.

The JDBC consists of an API (the specification of a library or application programmer's interface) and a package containing about 20 Java classes to implement the application program side of the API. The database side of the API is also needed, and this is the database driver mentioned above. Java programs call methods in the JDBC package to connect with databases through the database drivers, then retrieve, process, and write information, as shown in Figure 12–7.

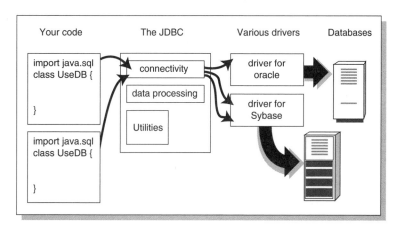

Figure 12–7
How Java Programs Talk to Databases

Note that we are not saying what kind of database is upstream of the JDBC. Your Java code knows very little about this; what your program does know is that by talking to the JDBC, it can indirectly talk to a database, just as by talking to a broker you can accomplish a transaction (sell a house, buy a diamond) with a third party you might never meet directly. This approach was pioneered by Inprise (then known as Borland) with the Borland Database Engine and its IDAPI protocol. It was also one of the virtues claimed for Microsoft's ODBC.

Vendor independence is one of the reasons that the large commercial database users are excited by the Java-DBMS integration. These companies see great value in front-end software that doesn't lock them in to one particular database supplier. The distributed-network feature of Java is an additional boost, making it almost trivial to build true distributed data processing systems.

The JDBC-ODC Bridge

At first, every database vendor had its own special database query language. Users eventually got fed up enough to create an industry standard around IBM's SQL. There was the SQL'89 standard, followed by the SQL'92 standard, both created under the ANSI umbrella. But SQL is still fragmented into many subtly different, slightly incompatible dialects.

In the early 1990s there was a further development in the SQL world. Microsoft got involved in the process and used its monopoly leverage, just as IBM used to, to impose the ODBC (Open DataBase Connectivity) standard on the industry. ODBC is an Application Programmer Interface that allows C programs to make calls into an SQL server and get back results. ODBC provided a unified way for Microsoft applications, such as Access, Excel, FoxPro, Btrieve, to talk to IBM, Oracle, Paradox and other back-end database systems. Every database vendor was then pretty much obliged to provide not only a driver for their own dialect of SQL, but also an ODBC driver that would allow ODBC to communicate with their protocols. If they didn't support ODBC, they would be locked out of the high volume PC desktop market.

Most of the ANSI SQL-2 databases out there now have ODBC drivers. So, to provide instant Java connectivity to lots of products, Sun joined with Intersolv to create the jdbc.odbc package, which implements the java.sql package for ODBC databases. This was an inspired move because it leveraged Microsoft's earlier work to claim desktop access to databases for its own. By creating a standard for its desktop applications to connect to anybody's database, Microsoft also inadvertently provided a way for Java to connect to their standard, and thence to anybody's database. The JDBC-ODBC bridge implements the JDBC by making the appropriate calls to the ODBC Standard C API. Figure 12–8 illustrates the JDBC-ODBC driver.

The JDBC-ODBC bridge is a little inefficient perhaps, using a driver to talk to a driver, but it provides instant connectivity to all popular databases. As mentioned above, ODBC is a C language interface, so the bridge needs to take Java types, unhand them into C types on the way over to ODBC, and rehand them on the way back. The JDBC-ODBC bridge is a separate C library that needs to be accessible to your code. There is a Java part that is a driver manager for the bridge and a native code part that's the driver. Since it's native code, separate versions of the bridge driver are needed for each computer architecture.

Java Blend

Java Blend is a further development on top of JDBC. It makes it easier to program database applications by representing them in terms of Java classes. Java Blend is a new library that includes both a development tool and a run time. The higher

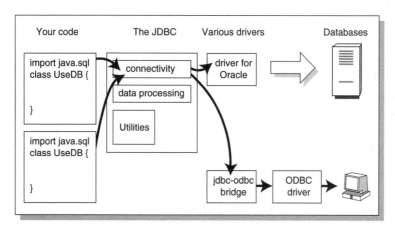

Figure 12–8
The JDBC-ODBC Driver

level abstractions presented to the developer do not involve database schemata or SQL statements (as they do with JDBC). All queries are made in terms of Java classes.

Unlike products based on conventional database access techniques, Java Blend software allows developers to write entirely with Java programming language objects. Java Blend transparently and automatically maps database records to objects and objects to databases, so that developers can avoid translating programming language data structures to database tables. Developers do not even need to know SQL or to understand database schemata. Java Blend means that "all Java programmers are now database programmers!" Java Blend was codeveloped with the Baan Company, a worldwide provider of enterprisewide business software solutions and consulting services.

The object-relational conversion in JavaBlend makes any relational database look like an object database to the programmer. You can use the new ODMG standard OQL language instead of SQL to do your queries, even if the database server you are using only understands SQL. Or you can just stick to Java if you prefer.

Java Blend provides automatic persistence for a network of objects. It keeps track of updates to persistent objects, and when a transaction commits, all updates made by that transaction to persistent objects are automatically applied to the database. The programmer no longer needs to code this task explicitly.

Java Blend will work with any database for which a JDBC or ODBC driver is available. You can map a database schema to Java classes or Java classes to a database schema. Applications written using Java Blend are portable across databases.

The major database vendors (Oracle, Sybase, Ingres, Informix) have all already launched drivers to allow their products to be accessed from Java. This also is an area of rapid opportunity for third-party tool vendors.

Summary

- Starting with OLE 2 in 1993, and bolstered by Borland's Delphi language, the Windows framework has been put in place that allows "software components" (miniprogram fragments) to exist and maybe even prosper. The components can be invoked on the different pieces in a "compound document."

- So far, software components have appeared on PCs (OCX) and Macs (Open-Doc). There is no corresponding facility in UNIX, but Java changes that with the JavaBeans model, which competes against the Windows-only ActiveX (OCX) technology.

- There are three contenders for object middleware on the server: Java's RMI, the OMG's CORBA, and Microsoft's DCOM. Interoperability is the name of the game to future-proof your systems.

- Objectware is important, but database access is the bread and butter of current enterprise computing. Java has a family of APIs called Java Database Connectivity (JDBC), that allows Java programs to extract from and update databases using SQL. Java Blend is a refinement that hides the SQL aspects of database access.

- The JavaBeans framework defines a portable, platform-neutral set of APIs for software components to talk to each other. JavaBeans is a component model for visual construction of reuseable client-side applications in Java. Enterprise JavaBeans is a component model for building mission-critical, server-side applications in Java.

CHAPTER 13

- Summary of Conclusion

- The Changing Computer Industry—
  Retooling the COBOL Programmer

Conclusions

T his endpiece brings together the key conclusions of each chapter, and finishes with a note on the changing computer industry. The key conclusions from earlier chapters are:

- The Internet is a loosely organized collection of networks using TCP/IP protocols to packet-switch data to almost anywhere in the world at a very low cost. We are still near the beginning of a global revolution to use it for business, education, and recreation.

- The World Wide Web was largely responsible for the great explosion in popularity of the Internet. It vastly simplified the use of the Internet, enabling ordinary users to access its communication power.

- Java is challenging the Windows 32 APIs as the next high-volume desktop interface. Software application companies can write their software to run in browsers instead of writing to an operating system interface. This makes it easier for users to run the software (just browse a URL), and it eliminates maintaining different versions of the product for different operating systems. Best of all, it provides type safety and productivity gains that are missing in Windows and C++.

- Java is a new programming language designed by Sun Microsystems. It has been universally adopted since its release in mid-1995. Java is popular because it is "web friendly": Java makes it simple to communicate with Internet protocols.

- An *applet* is a Java program embedded in a web page. When a browser looks at that web page, the applet is downloaded onto the system with the browser and executed on that system. This means the applet is using local (client) computing resources, and all the server need do is serve up the page (send the file contents over the network). Unlike CGI scripts Java applets can interact with the user in real time.

- The availability of application software for a system is directly proportional to the installed base of that system. The higher the installed base, the greater the amount of available software. All major OS vendors now bundle Java in their products, giving Java a huge installed base. Over time, the number of applications will follow.

- Java was designed to be "Write Once, Run Anywhere," meaning that the binaries run on all computers. By using Java, end users can retain their investment in software while upgrading or changing operating systems.

- Now that the security and privacy infrastructure is in place, the hottest growth area on the Internet is web-based commerce. Since there is a computer at both ends of an e-commerce transaction, a wide variety of automated processing becomes possible, such as comparison shopping, inventory control, and order fulfillment.

- E-commerce is a natural evolution of existing business methods like TV advertising and placing orders by phone. It combines these elements with the Internet as a communication channel. On-line retailing is a lot cheaper than other methods of displaying and selling goods.

- Special attention has been given to the security aspects of downloading and executing code automatically. This ensures that the same kind of malicious viruses that occur in the Microsoft Windows world cannot occur in Java.

- Java offers all three elements of computer security and thus can safely be deployed in an intranet or to bring in executable content from the Internet.

- The Java language supports:
  - Uniform data types—the same on all computers
  - Threads—more than one thing happening at once
  - Exceptions—better error handling and recovery

- Automatic control of memory deallocation—memory corruption and memory leak bugs can no longer happen

- Java comes with a very rich set of standard libraries that cover all important areas of computing, including windowing, networking, and enterprise database access.

- The Swing Java library bundled with JDK 1.2 (and available unbundled for JDK 1.1) provides a toolkit at least as good as any other modern toolkit, and in some respects far better. Java GUI programs can change their look and feel to suit the preferences of individual users.

- Microsoft's stated strategy for containing Java is to undermine its portability. The rest of the computer industry's best shot at containing Microsoft lies in supporting Java and Java portability.

- Client/server computing is a computing model that distributes resources among many client hosts and some fewer number of server hosts. Its strength lies in its ability to adapt to a large variety of business climates and structures, and to permit rapid structural changes to occur. It has two principal drawbacks: more difficult system administration, which leads to a somewhat higher price tag, and somewhat reduced security over a centralized model.

- An intranet is a private internal network of client/server systems implemented using tools and techniques designed for the Internet. An intranet is the TCP/IP network glue allowing clients to connect to any server. A web browser is the software. Intranets are redefining distributed processing and dramatically lowering costs compared with older forms of client/server. Because of its simplicity and immediate benefits, browser-based computing is in an explosive phase of growth.

- Java runs on the client, on the server, and in any layer connecting the two. You can now easily build information systems that otherwise need a mish-mash of different technologies and tools. The appeal of accessibility to data is so great that the most ubiquitous piece of software today is the Java-enabled web browser.

- Three-tiered systems running on an intranet and using Java in the middle layer, with network computers running Java applets in the client layer, offer cheap, robust, secure distributed computing. You can now build information systems that formerly could not be built at all.

- The single most expensive part of PC computing in an office environment is the hidden cost of system administration. It dwarfs the original purchase price.

- The promise of Network Computers is that they offer fundamentally the same desktop power at a greatly reduced TCO (total cost of ownership). The cost is lower because the administration is centralized on a server, where it is done in bulk for many systems simultaneously.

- The NC should really be compared to the telephone, not to the PC. They are both "zero system administration at the client" information appliances.

- When NCs first appeared, the system and applications software was not ready to fully support them. In the intervening two years, Java office applications software like Lotus e-suite, Applix Anywhere, Star Office, and Digital Harbor's Wav word processor, have become readily available.

- The JavaBeans framework defines a portable, platform-neutral set of APIs for software components to talk to each other. Software components is an emerging area of technology that holds great promise for encouraging software reuse.

The Changing Computer Industry— Retooling the COBOL Programmer

It seems appropriate to wrap up this book with a review of industry trends, just as we have reviewed some key industry players.

First, we should remark on the accelerated pace of change in the new Internet world. By allowing instant product distribution to anywhere in the world, the Internet has compressed the traditional schedule for software development. A Beta version can be made available while in-house testing is proceeding, and if the Beta version turns out to have bugs, you just put up a new version a week later. It's no big deal, as long as customers only use Beta releases to familiarize themselves with the technology and don't start building products around them. The software business is a volume business, as explained in Chapter 5, and by shipping early, you can capture the high ground. So, the frantic pace of development in the industry will continue.

The industry is plainly splitting into two camps: Microsoft and the ERW (Entire Rest of the World) alliance. This is a little different from the way things worked out in the 1960s and 1970s when IBM owned the computer industry and it was IBM and the seven dwarfs, or IBM and the BUNCH (Burroughs, Univac, NCR, Control Data Corp, and Honeywell). The Bunch never hit on the idea of banding together, and even if they had, they had no common elements. In contrast, by banding together now, the ERW can pool their resources to support common Java software while still competing on hardware. Write Once, Run Anywhere brings the volume of applications software that everyone needs to stay in business. Not a single tools vendor has followed Microsoft's initiative to create Window-only Java. Not a single tools vendor supports the Microsoft-only WFC or native interface.

Will we see the use of software components and rented components? It's too early to say. Most of the component infrastructure is there to support this model if people want it. As a PC user, I would certainly far prefer that my ISP had the job of buying and configuring software and that I just paid for the software I used. Rented software components is a model that many people will like, especially the software vendors. People will be a lot more willing to try new software if it requires an initial investment of $1 to rent it for a day rather than $200 to purchase it outright.

We have discussed thin clients, but there is no reason to suppose that thin clients should be smaller or less powerful than regular PCs. We finally got to the position in 1996 where the top of the line PCs are marginally capable of displaying real-time video streams and when storage products like Digital Video Disk (DVD, also called Digital Versatile Device) have the capacity for an entire movie. Wouldn't it be nice to build a really powerful thin client and get the best of both worlds: superior multimedia and zero client administration? Video streams on the desktop is a nice idea, but do current intranets and the Internet have the bandwidth? At 30 frames per second (as in the current NTSC standard) and a display area of 1024 × 768 pixels, each with three bytes of color information, that's 70 megabytes/second of bandwidth. That's 50 times the capacity of the typical network in use today. And that's one stream on behalf of one user! We can look forward to continuing high demand for more bandwidth as more companies start to run on e-mail and on-line tools instead of paper memos and policy manuals.

Fat-client operating systems will continue to grow. The NC is probably going to be as much an adjunct to the PC as a replacement. All the OS things that people are working on today—primarily scalability, performance, internationalization, and 64-bit address spaces—will continue to be important. Java is actually 64-bit capable now. All the Java run-time routines that return results about memory (amount free and so on) return a 64-bit value. So, converting to 64-bit address spaces in the years ahead can be done without changing a single line of code, though it will take a recompilation and/or change in the JVM. All those vendors that didn't future-proof their operating systems in terms of address space or adaptability to other locales will be regretting it.

Simplicity and ease of use are cornerstones for Java and help explain why take-up on the language has been so swift. The world grappled with C++ because it was the only game in town. The world is now putting C++ aside as it migrates to Java. Those MIS organizations that never detoured into C++ can leapfrog it entirely and retool their COBOL programmers for the world of network-centric computing. IBM is doing exactly that. The migration to Java isn't a journey that will be completed overnight. In the ten years that Windows has been on the market it has accumulated an estimated 400,000 programmers. At the end of 1997, the estimate for the number of serious Java developers was the same, around 400,000. But Java only took 2.5 years to reach that number. The number of Windows programmers is holding steady, while the number of Java programmers increases by tens of thousands each month. Volume is everything in the software business. Companies that don't use volume technology inevitably endure higher costs until they retrain and move into the mainstream.

What does it mean to retool COBOL programmers? Fortunately, this activity can be approached in phases. First, programmers need to learn object-oriented programming, which is based on a small number of simple techniques. Second, programmer desktops need to be connected to a server, and the server needs to be connected through a firewall to the Internet. If existing computer systems are used, this connection will cost a few hundred dollars. Finally, the programmers need to experiment with putting a low-cost, high-benefit system on line: the company phone directory, or a training manual, or shipping documents. The application doesn't matter as long as it is simple. Don't change too many things at once, and don't start with something critical.

Whenever people have invented wonderful new languages in the past (Ada, C++, Modula 3, Perl spring to mind), the languages have always done the *same* things in ways that the proponents said were better, faster, cheaper, or whatever. Java is different, as it offers the chance to do *new* things very cheaply. It's easy to open a socket connection to a remote computer. It's simple to make a Java client program that can be downloaded and run on demand from a server. And these new things happen to be exactly in line with the emerging paradigm of network computing. Java is reasonably simple for a programmer to learn. It doesn't require heroic intellectual feats, and when you have learned it, you can write windowing and network programs that run on all computers. On top of all that, Java bytecode itself runs on every computer system. What we are seeing here is the "better mousetrap" phenomenon with the world beating a path to Sun's door.

With the platform portability of object code, Java dramatically changes the model of software economics. Software vendors will still migrate to the largest executable platform, but that platform is now the Java Virtual Machine, not the Windows APIs. By implementing the JVM on their OS, all hardware vendors can share in this boon. Smaller hardware vendors can now compete on quality, performance, and cost with the volume hardware vendors, without the obvious handicap of less application software. This is good for hardware vendors, good for the industry, and good for computer consumers. The only companies that don't bene-fit from this are those that have hitherto enjoyed a position of monopoly domi-nance: Microsoft and Intel.

In the end, the IBM domination of the computer industry ended when IBM failed to anticipate new industry paradigms like the phenomenal growth of the PC undermining centralized computing. Microsoft has not been especially perceptive to notice that the Internet is big news—you'd have to be living in a cave to have missed that—and it was only in December 1995 that they tied the product strat-egy to the Internet. Many aspects of the Internet, like open protocols and mass distribution channels available to all, are actually a thorn in the side of Microsoft. Microsoft is strongly placed to prosper from its position in the computer industry, but now other winners will emerge, too.

We mentioned above simplicity and ease of use. These qualities are critical not just for application software, but for all points in the chain stretching back to sys-tems administration and the development products themselves. Java provides a solid foundation. It is a programming language with which many have reported favorable experiences. Many library classes (not all) just work the way an average programmer would expect them to.

The proletarianization of the Internet is probably the most significant paradigm shift ever in the computer industry. It is still unfolding as the impact on intranets (a term that didn't exist before 1995) and extranets (1997) becomes clearer, and Java is a key part of the trend.

When Steve Jobs came to ship the Macintosh in 1984, there was a faction that wanted to make sure it was easy enough to use, that it could ship without any manuals at all. The industry wasn't quite ready for that, but it was a bold idea.[1] The challenge for us as systems implementors is to push this kind of intuitive operation back into application software. If we can make a desktop computer as simple to operate as a TV, and as cheap as one, we'll expand the market tenfold. *That* is the promise of network-centric computing as we head into the new millen-nium.

---

1. On the other hand, Steve Jobs personally prevented the implementation of a hard disk for the first Mac, and that decision turned out to be a huge mistake.

INDEX

A

ABI standard, portability through, 107-17
Abstract Window Toolkit (AWT), 217-18
Acrobat Amber Reader, 70
ActiveX, 153-56, 292-94
    controls, and the Internet, 294-96
    in the intranet, 296
Ada, 167
Advanced Imaging API, 215
albany.net search site, 52
Algol, 169
AltaVista, 52
"Altered GOTO," COBOL, 194
Amazon.com, 103
    case study, 134-37
        affiliate marketing, 136-37
        business model, 137
        buying a book online, process of, 136
ANDF (Architecture Neutral Distribution Format), 113
Andreessen, Marc, 47
ANSI C, 169
Anti-aliasing, 221
API standard:
    defined, 107
    portability through, 107-17
Apollo Computer, 26
Apple Computer Inc., 116
AppleScript, 77
AppletMagic, 112
Applets, 71, 314
Application Binary Interface (ABI):
    defined, 108, 109
    standard, 107-17
Application Programmer Interface (API),
    defined, 109
Applix Anywhere (Applix), 277
Architecture neutral, use of term, 114, 115
ArithmeticException, 201
ARPANET, 26
ArrayIndexOutOfBoundsException, 201
.arts, 121
Authentication, and computer security, 139
autoconnect.com, 130
Automatic memory management, 194-97, 198

B

Backward compatibility, use of term, 115
Baratz, Alan, 89
Barnes & Noble, 134
BeanMachine (Lotus), 297
Berners-Lee, Tim, 44
biz.yahoo.com, 97
Bounds Checker, 230
Brochureware applications, 244
Browsers, 47, 49, 125
    applets, 71
    competition between, 55-61
    and e-commerce, 58-59
    importance of, 58-60
    plug-ins, 69-71
    programming techniques in, 65-87
    URLs (Uniform Resource Locators), 65-68
Buffer overflow vulnerability, 248
Bytecode, 111-12

C

C++, 75, 91-92, 110, 113, 167-72
  and backward compatibility, 170, 182-83
  complexity of, 170
.ca, 121
CAMRA (Campaign for Real Ale) case study, 61-62
Cascading Style Sheets (CSS), 83
CCITT X.25 packet switching standard, 32
CDF (Channel Definition Format) (Microsoft), 86
Cedar, 182
CEPIS (Council of European Professional Informatics Societies), 159, 161-62
CERN, 44-47
Certification:
  Sun Certified Java Developer, 100, 224
  Sun Certified Java Programmer, 100, 224
CGI, 270
  defined, 75
CGI scripts, 59, 71, 75, 77, 87, 314
  how they work, 76
  invoking directly by a browser, 77
Charles Schwab, online trading market, 131
Chorus Systems, 275
CIA (Central Intelligence Agency), web site break-in, 142-45
Cisco Systems, 264
C language, 107
Clarke, Jim, 104, 124
ClassNotFoundException, 201
Client/server, 315
  advantages/disadvantages of, 239-41
  case study, 253-54
  defined, 235
  and the intranet, 235-57
  need for, 236-39
  tiers, 249-54
    middleware, 252
  timesharing compared to, 236
Client/server model, 94
cnnfn.com/markets/9806/02/marimba/in-dex-txt.htm, 97
COBOL, 107, 169, 207
  "altered GOTO," 194
CodeCenter, 230
.com, 121
Comcast Cable, 131
Common Gateway Interface (CGI), 270
Common Hardware Reference Platform (CHRP), 109
Compaq Corporation, 8-9, 128, 273
  Java strategies, 9
  opportunities/threats, 9
  profit margin, 4

  strengths, 8
  weaknesses, 8-9
Compatibility, 111
comp.lang.java.programmer, FAQ list for, 38-39
Component frameworks, *See* Software rameworks
Component Object Model (COM), 289, 290-96
Compound documents, 287-90
Compuserve, 96
Computer Incident Advisory Capability (CI-AC)(U.S. Dept. of Energy), 248
Computer industry:
  changes in, 316-19
  industry trends, 3-22
  players, 5-22
    Compaq Corporation, 8-9
    Hewlett-Packard Corporation, 10-11
    IBM/Lotus, 12-14
    Intel Corporation, 15-16
    Microsoft Corporation, 17-22
    Sun Microsystems, 5-7
Computer security:
  comparison, 152-53
  decompiling, 157-58
  defined, 139-40
  denial-of-service attacks, 158
  DNA (Microsoft), 152-56
    ActiveX, 155-56
    as a "blame assignment" architecture, 154
    lack of security with, 153-56
  encryption, 158-60
  finer-grained security, 156-57
  IP spoofing, 142
  Java security measures, 145-52
  NIS attacks, 142
  openness vs., 160-65
  packet capture (snarfing), 142
  plug-ins, 152-53
  Secure Socket Layer (SSL), 128, 160
  security attacks, early history of, 151-52
  security cost/need trade-offs, 140
  security spectrum, 140-41
  single-user do's/don'ts of, 145
  subversion, 142
  web site security measures, 141-45
Conditional variable, 192
Confidentiality, and computer security, 139
Connected networks, layers of, 123
Cookies, 75
CoolTalk, 69, 101
CORBA, 252, 300-305
  defined, 301
  first specification, 302-3

Interface Definition Language (IDL), 304-5
Object Request Broker, 300, 302
Core libraries, 209-10
Counting semaphor, 191
CSS (Cascading Style Sheets), 83

D
Database-specific middleware, 252
Data packets, 30
Data race conditions, how to prevent, 191-94
DDE (Dynamic Data Exchange), 286-87
Debugging, 194
Decompilation, 157
Decompiling, 157-58
Deja News, 52, 164
Dell Computer, 128-29, 273
profit margin, 4
Denial-of-service attacks, 158
DHTML (Dynamic HTML), 71, 82, 83
XML compared to, 86
Diba Company, 280
Distributed processing security issues, 139- 65
DLLs, 102
DNA (Microsoft):
ActiveX, 155-56, 165, 296
as a "blame assignment" architecture, 154
defined, 296
lack of security with, 153-56
and security, 152, 153-56
Document Object Model, 83-84
Domain names, 121
DOSMGR callout API, 104
DVD standard, 91
Dynamic memory management, 195

E
e-commerce, 58-59, 119-37, 314
advantages of, 132
and banking services, 129, 130
and browsers, 58-59
and catalog goods, 130, 131
and classified advertising, 130, 131-32
current state of, 128-29
and electronic delivery of products,129
and entertainment products, 130
evolution of, 125-28
and financial products, 130
future changes for, 133-34
and payment of bills, 129, 130
products suited for, 129-33
shopping online, 133
stages of, 126-28
business to business, 127-28
informational web site, 127
non-Internet-based e-commerce, 127
retail operations, 127
and ticket purchases, 130, 131

.edu, 121
Eiffel, 182
Electronic mail (e-mail), 36
Embedded Java API, 213
Employees, defined, 4
Encapsulation, 175-77, 205
Encryption, 158-60
Enterprise JavaBeans, 211, 299-300
Error-prone memory management, problem
of, 196
e-suite (Lotus), 277
Excel-compatible Java spreadsheet (Visual
Components, Inc.), 277
Exception handling API, 103
Exceptions, 197-203, 314
defined, 197
Exite, 52
Extranets, defined, 242

F
FAQ:
defined, 39
Java, 38-39
FARC (Revolutionary Armed Forces of Co-
lombia), 163
Farmer, Dan, 141-42
FBI's web site, 69
FDDI (Fibre Distributed Data Interface), 122
Federal Express case study, 253-56
FileNotFoundException, 201
File Transfer Protocol (ftp), 32, 66
Filo, David, 52
Filter, firewalls, 246
finger, 32
Firewalls, 146, 246
.firm, 121
Flight Simulator, 111
Floating point, 186
Forms, 71, 87
how they work, 76
Fortran 77, 107
Fortran 90, 107
FORTRAN, 169
Forward compatibility, use of term, 116
Frames, 60
free() system call, 194
Frost, Jim, 230-32
fruitfly.berkeley.edu, 97
ftp:, 32, 66
Funnel sites, 133

G
Gates, Bill, 17, 273
Gerstner, Lou, 13
Gigabit Ethernet, 122
Gilmore, John, 164
.gov, 121

Groupware-specific middleware, 252

H
Hardware/application APIs, 212-14
    Embedded Java API, 213
    Java Card API, 213
    Java Electronic Commerce Framework, 213
    Jini, 213-14
    miscellaneous Java products/APIs, 214
    Personal Java API, 212
Hewlett-Packard Corporation, 10-11, 116, 273
    Java strategies, 11
    and Merced chip, 10
    opportunities/threats, 11
    profit margin, 4
    strengths, 10
    thin-client products, 11
    weaknesses, 10-11
Hitachi, Ltd., 116
Home page, defined, 51
HotJava, 71
HTML (HyperText Markup Language), 47-49,
    242
    CSS (Cascading Style Sheets), 83
    DHTML, 82, 83
    drawback of, 82
    feature enhancement, 71-72
    forms, 71-75
    ordering form, example of, 73-74
    tags, 47
    XML (eXtensible Markup Language), 84-87
http:, defined, 66
100% Pure Java, 224-25
100baseT ethernet, 122
Hypermedia, 46
Hypertext, 44-49
    defined, 44, 46
    HTML (HyperText Markup Language),
        47-49
Hypertext browsing, how it works, 45
HyperText Transfer Protocol (HTTP), 32, 66

I
IBM/Lotus, 12-14, 116, 128, 275
    computers/operating systems, 110-11
    e-suite, 13
    and JavaOS, 14
    Java strategies, 14
    opportunities/threats, 13
    profit margin, 4
    strengths, 12
    System Network Architecture (SNA), 32
    weaknesses, 12
Iceberg model, 260-64
Identification, and computer security, 139
IEEE 1394 high-speed I/O bus, 91
IEEE Standard 754, 185

IllegalAccessException, 201
industry trends, 3-22
.info, 121
InfoBus API, 210, 298
Inheritance, 177-79, 205
Integrity, and computer security, 139
Intel Corporation, 15-16, 164
    Java strategies, 16
    opportunities/threats, 16
    profit margin, 4
    strengths, 15
    weaknesses, 15
Intel x86 processor, and dynamic memory
    management, 195
Interface Definition Language (IDL), 304-5
Internet:
    ARPANET, 26
    backbone tariffs, regulation of, 28-29
    browser-based desktop office applica-
        tions, 60
    browsers, 47, 49, 125
        applets, 71
        competition between, 55-61
        features of, 59
        importance of, 58-60
        programming techniques in, 65-87
        software "lock-in" through unique
            features, 60-61
    connecting to, 122-24
    defined, 26, 39
    distributed administration, 120-21
    early applications, 29
    and e-commerce, 119-37
    electronic mail (e-mail), 36
    how it runs, 120
    Internet Engineering Task Force(IETF),
        120-21, 128
    map of early Usenet sites, 27-28
    modem communications, 28
    NSFNET, 26
    number of computers on, 126
    origins of, 26-29
    TCP/IP protocol, 30-36
    using for learning, 36-39
    web browsing, 124-25
Internet casinos, 53-55
Internet Engineering Task Force (IETF), 120-
    21, 128, 160
Internet Explorer, 248
Internet Explorer (Microsoft), 55, 57-58, 128
    API, 104
    bundling of, 57
    plug-ins, 70
Internet Inter-ORB Protocol (IIOP), 304

Internet Movie Database, 136
Internet Protocol (IP), 30-31
    defined, 35
    standard IP services on UNIX, 37
Internet Registry, 121
Internet Service Providers (ISPs), 28-29
    changing role of, 281
InterNIC, 121
Intranets, 241-47, 315
    defined, 242
    firewalls, 246
    growth of, 245-46
    Java security, 247-48
    protocols, 247
    security, 246-47
IPSec, 128
IP spoofing, 142
ir.chem.cmu.edu/applets, 97
ISDN, 122
ISO/IEC JTC 1, 107

J

Java 2D Graphics API, 211, 214
Java 3D API, 214-15
Java, 75, 313
    application software, 277
    C/C++ features omitted from, 182
    defined, 78
    DHTML compared to, 86-87
    exceptions, 197-203
        predefined, 201
        run-time, 201
    features added to C to create, 183
    garbage collection, 194-97
    initiatives, 224-26
        100% Pure Java, 224-25
        Java Lobby, 225-26
        programmer certification, 224
    Java Runtime Environment (JRE), 116-17
    license agreements, 116
    and network computers, 281
    object-orient programming (OOP), 174-83
        child, 178
        class/data type, 175-76
        constructors, 176-77
        defined, 174
        encapsulation, 175-77, 205
        inheritance, 177-79, 205
        methods, 176
        parent class, 178
        polymorphism, 179-83, 205
        subclass, 178
    in operating systems, 226-28

overflow, 185-87
performance, 172-73
philosophy, 167-73
platform-independence of, 100, 101-4
and programmer productivity, 228-32
threads, 187-91
uniform data types, 183-85
UPSP use of, 203-5
use of, C++ use vs., 173
XML compared to, 86-87
Java applets, 70, 89-118, 314
    adoption of look/feel of system, 96
    commercial applets for Internet/extra-net/intranet, 97
    complex content-rich applets on educa-tion/research sites, 97-98
    defined, 92-93
    Internet Service Provider/Content Pro-vider utilities, 96-97
    Java Plug-In, 101
    security restrictions, 96
    and system administration, 95
    uses of, 95-98
    and viruses, 150
    WORA (Write Once, Run Anywhere), 98-100
Java Archive (JAR file), 149
JavaBeans API, 216, 296-99, 316
Java Blend, 308-10
Java Card API, 213
JavaChips, 281-82
Java Communications API, 211
Java computing, 270
Java Database Connectivity library, 252
Java Electronic Commerce Framework, 213
Java Enterprise APIs, 211
Java FAQ, 38-39
Java Foundation Classes (JFC), 209
JavaHelp, 211
Java libraries, 207-34
    core libraries, 209-10
    hardware/application APIs, 212-14
    internationalization, 222-24
    JavaBeans API, 216
    Java Media Framework APIs, 214-16
    Java Swing API, 217-20
    process/purpose, 207-14
    standard extension libraries, 210-12
Java Lobby, 225-26
    URL, 226
Java Mail API, 210
Java Media API, 210, 214-16
Java Media Framework library, 16
Java Messaging, 211
Java newsgroups, 38

FAQ list, 38-39
JavaOne, 89
JavaOS, 275
Java phenomenon, 89-92
Java Plug-in, 70, 101
Java Runtime Environment (JRE), 116-17
JavaScript, 59, 70, 71, 75, 77-82, 87
    capabilities of, 82
    features, 78
    role of, 78
Java security, 145-52
    applets, 146-51
        code signing, 149-51
        language, 146-47
        sandbox, 147-49
    intranets, 247-48
    Java applets, 145-46
JavaSoft, 113
Java Sound API, 215
Java Speech API, 215
JavaStation, 6, 275, 278
Java strategies:
    Compaq Corporation, 9
    Hewlett-Packard Corporation, 11
    IBM/Lotus, 14
    Intel Corporation, 16
    Microsoft Corporation, 22
    Sun Microsystems, 7
Java Studio (Sun Microsystems), 297
Java Swing API, 217-20, 315
Java technology, licensing of, 89
Java Telephony (JTAPI), 216
Java Transaction Service, 211
Java Virtual Machine (JVM), 112, 273
    design, 112
    running other languages on, 113-14
Java Virtual Machine Specification, 109
JBridge (Corel), 277
JBuilder2 (Inprise), 297
JDBC (Java DataBase Connectivity), 305-10
    JDBC-ODC bridge, 308
    relational databases, 305-7
    SQL (Structured Query Language), 305-7
JDesignerPro (BulletProofCorp), 297
Jini, 213-14
Jobs, Steven, 319
.jp, 121
Junk e-mail, 36

K

Kawa (Tek Tools), 297
Kiosk-style applications, 278-79

L

Language generations, 169
Lawton, Stephen, 241

Linux software, 264
LISP, 169, 182
Live3D, 69
LiveAudio, 69
LiveConnect, 82
LiveVideo, 69
Locks, 191-94
    conditional variable, 192
    counting semaphor, 191
    monitor, 191, 192
    mutex lock, 191
    reader/writer lock, 191
Lycos, 52
Lynx, 55

M

McLain, Fred, 153-55
malloc(), 194
Marimba Castanet software, 271-72
mars.graham.com/wits/, 97
Martin, James, 169
Media Framework API, 215
Memory management, 194-97, 198
mendobrew.com, 69
Methods, 176
    and exceptions, 202-3
microJava, 282
Microsoft Corporation, 17-22, 55, 116
    browser presence, 57-58
    CarPoint site, 131
    Component Object Model (COM), 290-96
    "Content Bar," 133
    disadvantages of, 134
    Expedia, 131
    Java strategies, 22
    and Linus operating system, 21
    and Netscape Communications, compe-
        tition between, 55-61
    opportunities/threats, 20-21
    OS versions, 102
    partnering strategy, 19-20
    and software development, 18
    strengths, 17-18
    and system software security, 18-19
    undocumented APIs, 103
    U.S. government antitrust action against, 21
    weaknesses, 18-20
    web-based retailing case study, 134-37
    Zero Administration for Windows
        (ZAW), 265-68
Microsoft Foundation Classes, 100
Microsoft Windows NT, versions of, 276
Middleware, 252
.mil, 121
MMX technology, 91
Modems, 28, 122

Monitor, 191, 192
Mosaic browser, 47, 49
Motorola, 116
MSNBC (Microsoft-NBC), 96
MS Quick C/Windows 1.0 API, 103
MT-hot, 193
MT-safe, 192-93
MT-unsafe, 192
Multithreading, 187-91, 194
    timesharing vs., 188
Mutex lock, 191

N
Naming and Directory Interface API, 211
Nasdaq, 131
National Center for Supercomputing Applica-
    tions (NCSA), 47
.net, 121
Net income, defined, 4
Netscape Communications, 47, 55-56, 124
    Communicator, 55
    frames, 60
    and Microsoft Corporation, competition
        between, 55-61
    Secure Socket Layer (SSL), 128, 160
Netscape Communicator, 69
    plug-ins, 70
Netscape Navigator 2.0, 82
Netscape Navigator 3.0, 279
Network computers, 259-83, 316
    appeal of, 275
    application software, 277
    cost of running, 274
    hidden costs of PCs, 259-60
    fat client PC costs, 264-69
    iceberg model, 260-64
    and Microsoft, 264-69
    security/reliability, 262-64
    and Internet Service Providers (ISPs), 281
    and Java, 281
    niches for, 277-80
        appliances, 280
        kiosks, 278-79
        set-tops, 279-80
        single-function applications, 277-78
        webtops, 277
    thin client, 269-72
        defined, 269-70
        and Marimba Castanet software,
            271-72
Network File System (NFS), 235
Network news, *See* Usenet
Newsgroups, 38-39
Nicely, Tom, 164-65
NIS attacks, 142

.nom, 121
Non-Internet-based e-commerce, 127
Nortel, purchase of Bay Networks, Inc., 91
notify() method, 192
Novell, 116
NSFNET, 26

O
Object class, 181
Objective C, 182
Object-orient programming (OOP), 174-83
    child, 178
    class/data type, 175-76
    constructors, 176-77
    defined, 174
    encapsulation, 175-77, 205
    inheritance, 177-79, 205
    methods, 176
    parent class, 178
    polymorphism, 179-83, 205
    subclass, 178
Object Request Broker, 300, 302
OCX (OLE Custom eXtension), 292-93
OLE (Object Linking and Embedding), 44, 287,
    289-93
OMG (Object Management Group), 300
One-tier system, 249
On-line Web-based business, 51
Onyx, 26
Open Software Foundation (OSF), 113
Open system, defined, 108
Open Systems Interconnection (OSI) Network
    Model, 35
Opera Software, 55
.org, 121
OS Communications middleware, 252
OSF ANDF initiative, 113

P
Packages, 211
Packet capture (snarfing), 142
Packets, 30
Palm Pilot PDA, 273
Pascal, 107, 195
Password handling under NT 3.1 and 3.5 API,
    103
Perl, 75
Personal computers (PCs), hidden costs of,
    259-60
Personal Java API, 212
picoJava, 282
Ping, 31, 35-36
Ping of Death, 31, 36
Platform independent, use of term, 114, 115
Plug-ins, 69-71, 87
Polymorphism, 179-83, 205
Port, 36

Portability, 315
    through API and ABI standards, 107-17
Portal sites, 133
Porting software, costs of, 106
POSIX, 108
    threads, 194
print() method, 181
Profit margin, defined, 4
psych.psy.uq.oz.au/~ftp/Crypto, 160
Pure Software, 196
Purify, 230

Q

QuickTime, 69

R

Reader/writer lock, 191
RealAudio, 70, 101
.rec, 121
Regulation of the Web, 53
Remote Object Communication middleware,
    252
Resource control, and computer security, 139
Revenues, defined, 4
Routing tables, 30

S

SABRE reservation system, 130
Sandbox, 147-49
San Francisco (IBM), 277
Santa Cruz Operation, Inc., 116
Scripting language, 77
Script standardization, 80
Seagate, 128
Searching the Internet, 51-55
Search sites, 51-52
Secure Socket Layer (SSL), 128, 160
Security, defined, 139-40
Security attacks, early history of, 151-52
SecurityManager class, 147, 202
Server, defined, 235
Servlets, 75
SGML (Standard Generalized Markup Lan-
    guage), 48, 84
Shockwave, 70
Signed applets, 156-57
Signed class scheme, 149-51
Smalltalk, 182
Smith, Dave, 167
Snarfing, 142
SNA (Systems Network Architecture), 111
Software frameworks, 285-90
    compound documents, 287-90
    DDE (Dynamic Data Exchange), 286-87
SOHO ("small office, home office) users, 94
Spam, 36
SPARC Compliance Definition, 109

Spyglass, 59
SSLRef, 160
Standard extension libraries, 210-12
    InfoBus API, 210
    Java Communications API, 211
    Java Enterprise APIs, 211
    JavaHelp, 211
    Java Mail API, 210
    Java Media API, 210
Standardized programming languages, 107
Stateless protocols, 31
Stock trading, 131
.store, 121
Stroustrup, Bjarne, 168, 171
Subversion, 142
Sun Certified Java Developer, 100, 224
Sun Certified Java Programmer examination,
    100
Sun Microsystems, 5-7, 26, 71, 275
    Java releases from, 208
    JavaStation, 6, 275, 278
    Java strategy, 7
    opportunities/threats, 6-7
    profit margin, 4
    Solaris operating system, 5
    strengths, 5
    weaknesses, 6
Supercede Pro (Supercede), 297
Super Mojo (Penumbra Software), 297
System Network Architecture (SNA) (IBM), 32

T

T1 trunk line, 122
T3 trunk line, 122
Tcl, 75
Tcl/Tk plug-in, 70
TCP/IP protocol, 30-36, 243
    and UDP, 31-32
telerobot.mech.uwa.edu.au/java/ap-
    plets/usher, 98
TeleScript, 77
telnet, 32
10baseT ethernet, 122
Thread programming, 193-94
Threads, 187-91, 314
    race conditions, how to prevent, 191-94
Three-tier system, 249-51
Tier concept, 249-54, 315
    case study, 253-56
    middleware, 252
Timesharing:
    client/server compared to, 236
    multithreading vs., 188
toString(), 181
Transaction Processing middleware, 252
Transmission Control Protocol (TCP), 30, 34

defined, 32, 35
Two-tier system, 249

U

Ubiquitous computing, 278
.uk, 121
Unabomber, 124
Underflow, 185
Uniform data types, 183-85, 314
Uniform Resource Identifiers, 68
    URLs (Uniform Resource Locators), 65-
      68
    URNs (Uniform Resource Names), 67-68
Upward compatibility, use of term, 116
URLs (Uniform Resource Locators), 65-68, 87
    colon in, 66
    newsgroup kind of, 67
    pathname, 67
    www. prefix, 66
URNs (Uniform Resource Names), 67-68
U.S. Army recruiting home page, 69
Usenet, 36-39
User Datagram Protocol (UDP), 31-32, 33
US Pacific Stock Exchange, trading system,
    131
U.S. Postal Service, use of Java, 203-5

V

Value-Added Network (VAN), 127
Vatican's web site, 69
Video streams, playing, 69
Viruses, and Java applets, 150
Visaj (Imperial Software), 297
VisualAge (IBM), 297
Visual Basic Script (VBS), 77, 83
Visual C++ 4.0 API, 103
Volume, and software industry, 104-7

W

wait() method, 192
Wav (Digital Harbor), 277
.web, 121
Web browsers, *See* Browsers
Web browsing, 124-25
Web-browsing applets, 94
Web crawling, 52
Web page, running a program from, 93-95
Web server API, 103
Web site, cost of, 51
Web site security measures, 141-45
WebTV, 90-91, 279
Western Digital, 128
Win95 socket library API, 104
Windows 3.11 API, 104
Windows32 APIs, and browsers, 87
Windows CE, 273

WORA (Write Once, Run Anywhere), 98-100,
    113-14, 115, 314
World Wide Web (WWW), 43-63, 313
    basic commercial Web site, 61-62
    browsers, 47, 49
    home page, 51
    hypertext, 44-49
    Internet casinos, 53-55
    on-line Web-based business, 51
    regulation of, 53
    search sites, 51-52
    web site, cost of, 51
    See also Hypertext
www.ai.mit.edu/projects/anatomy_brow-
    ser/index.html, 97
www.albany.net/allinone, 52
www.barnesandnoble.com, 134
www.cadviewer.com/dwf/asesmp.shtml, 97
    www.co-operativebank.co.uk/
      internet_baning.html, 97, 129
www.fbi.gov/wanted.htm, 69
www.firstdirect.co.uk, 97
www.gamelan.com, 98
www.georgiatech-metz.fr, 164
www.goarmy.com, 69
www.imdb.com, 136
www.InfoWar.com, 142
www.internic.net/ds/about.html, 121
www.plumbdesign.com/thesaurus, 98
www. prefix, use of, 66
www.quote.com, 97
www.rmi.de/~gollog/tableuk.htm, 98
www.sba.gov.sg, 144
www.traderonline.com, 130
www.travelocity.com, 130
www.usps.gov/formmgmt/webforms/, 97
www.vatican.com, 69
www.xs4all.nl/opennet, 160

X

XLL (eXtensible Link Language), 86
XML (eXtensible Markup Language), 71, 84-87
    DHTML compared to, 86
    example of, 85-87
    matching start and end tags, 84
XMS (eXtended Memory Standard), 104
XSL (eXtensible Stylesheet Language), 86

Y

Yahoo!, 52, 96
Yang, Jerry, 52

Z

Zero Administration for Windows (ZAW),
    265-68, 278
ZippoMfg.com, 69

defined, 32, 35
Two-tier system, 249

U

Ubiquitous computing, 278
.uk, 121
Unabomber, 124
Underflow, 185
Uniform data types, 183-85, 314
Uniform Resource Identifiers, 68
    URLs (Uniform Resource Locators), 65-68
    URNs (Uniform Resource Names), 67-68
Upward compatibility, use of term, 116
URLs (Uniform Resource Locators), 65-68, 87
    colon in, 66
    newsgroup kind of, 67
    pathname, 67
    www. prefix, 66
URNs (Uniform Resource Names), 67-68
U.S. Army recruiting home page, 69
Usenet, 36-39
User Datagram Protocol (UDP), 31-32, 33
US Pacific Stock Exchange, trading system, 131
U.S. Postal Service, use of Java, 203-5

V

Value-Added Network (VAN), 127
Vatican's web site, 69
Video streams, playing, 69
Viruses, and Java applets, 150
Visaj (Imperial Software), 297
VisualAge (IBM), 297
Visual Basic Script (VBS), 77, 83
Visual C++ 4.0 API, 103
Volume, and software industry, 104-7

W

wait() method, 192
Wav (Digital Harbor), 277
.web, 121
Web browsers, *See* Browsers
Web browsing, 124-25
Web-browsing applets, 94
Web crawling, 52
Web page, running a program from, 93-95
Web server API, 103
Web site, cost of, 51
Web site security measures, 141-45
WebTV, 90-91, 279
Western Digital, 128
Win95 socket library API, 104
Windows 3.11 API, 104
Windows32 APIs, and browsers, 87
Windows CE, 273

WORA (Write Once, Run Anywhere), 98-100, 113-14, 115, 314
World Wide Web (WWW), 43-63, 313
    basic commercial Web site, 61-62
    browsers, 47, 49
    home page, 51
    hypertext, 44-49
    Internet casinos, 53-55
    on-line Web-based business, 51
    regulation of, 53
    search sites, 51-52
    web site, cost of, 51
    See also Hypertext
www.ai.mit.edu/projects/anatomy_browser/index.html, 97
www.albany.net/allinone, 52
www.barnesandnoble.com, 134
www.cadviewer.com/dwf/asesmp.shtml, 97
    www.co-operativebank.co.uk/internet_baning.html, 97, 129
www.fbi.gov/wanted.htm, 69
www.firstdirect.co.uk, 97
www.gamelan.com, 98
www.georgiatech-metz.fr, 164
www.goarmy.com, 69
www.imdb.com, 136
www.InfoWar.com, 142
www.internic.net/ds/about.html, 121
www.plumbdesign.com/thesaurus, 98
www. prefix, use of, 66
www.quote.com, 97
www.rmi.de/~gollog/tableuk.htm, 98
www.sba.gov.sg, 144
www.traderonline.com, 130
www.travelocity.com, 130
www.usps.gov/formmgmt/webforms/, 97
www.vatican.com, 69
www.xs4all.nl/opennet, 160

X

XLL (eXtensible Link Language), 86
XML (eXtensible Markup Language), 71, 84-87
    DHTML compared to, 86
    example of, 85-87
    matching start and end tags, 84
XMS (eXtended Memory Standard), 104
XSL (eXtensible Stylesheet Language), 86

Y

Yahoo!, 52, 96
Yang, Jerry, 52

Z

Zero Administration for Windows (ZAW), 265-68, 278
ZippoMfg.com, 69

NOT JUST JAVA™
A Technology Briefing, Second Edition
PETER van der LINDEN

313 pages
ISBN 0-13-079660-3

NOT JUST JAVA™: A Technology Briefing is the book for everybody who needs to understand why Java and other Internet technologies are taking the industry by storm. Peter van der Linden, in this updated new edition, carefully explains each of the key technologies driving the Internet revolution.

INSTANT JAVA™
Second Edition
JOHN A. PEW

423 pages; (includes CD-ROM)
ISBN 0-13-272287-9

Instant Java applets—no programming necessary! INSTANT JAVA™ is your guide to using more than 75 easy-to-customize Java applets that are included on the cross-platform CD-ROM. This is an invaluable tool for adding Java special effects to your HTML documents!

JUST JAVA 1.1
AND BEYOND
Third Edition
PETER van der LINDEN

652 pages; (includes CD-ROM)
ISBN 0-13-784174-4

In this completely updated third edition, Peter van der Linden, the author of the classic EXPERT C PROGRAMMING, brings his well-known enthusiasm, expertise, and wit to the challenge of explaining Java and object-oriented programming as painlessly as possible.

JAVA BY EXAMPLE
Second Edition
**JERRY R. JACKSON and
ALAN L. McCLELLAN**

386 pages; (includes CD-ROM)
ISBN 0-13-272295-X

Step-by-step, working from examples, you'll learn valuable techniques for working with the Java language. By reviewing example code written by experts, you'll learn the right way to develop Java applets and applications that are elegant, readable, and easy to maintain.

HTML FOR FUN AND PROFIT
3rd Edition

MARY E. S. MORRIS and JOHN E. SIMPSON

400 pages; (includes CD-ROM)
ISBN 0-13-079672-7

The international best-seller has been updated and expanded to give you in-depth coverage of the fundamentals as well as all the hottest new HTML innovations including Dynamic HTML, XML, cascading style sheets, and frames.

WEB PAGE DESIGN
A Different Multimedia

MARY E. S. MORRIS and RANDY J. HINRICHS

306 pages
ISBN 0-13-239880-X

Anyone can design a Web page, but it takes more than basic HTML skill to build a world-class Web site. Written for Web page authors, this hands-on guide covers the key aspects of designing a successful Web site, including how to integrate traditional design techniques.

CYBERCAREERS

MARY E. S. MORRIS and PAUL MASSIE

352 pages
ISBN 0-13-748872-6

Cyberspace is now the land of opportunity. With Cybercareers™ you'll discover the skills you need to really compete for the most sought-after jobs in cyberspace. You'll also learn how to plan for maximum success and how to plot a challenging and rewarding career path.

STEP-BY-STEP ISDN
The Internet Connection Handbook

BEN CATANZARO

308 pages
ISBN 0-13-890211-9

Save time and money with no-hassle strategies for setting up your ISDN Internet connection. STEP-BY-STEP ISDN tells you exactly what to do—and what to buy—to get reliable, fast ISDN Internet connection for your business or home.

DESIGNING VISUAL INTERFACES
Communication Oriented Techniques

KEVIN MULLET and DARRELL SANO

262 pages
ISBN 0-13-303389-9

You will learn to enhance the visual quality of graphical user interfaces, data displays, and multimedia productions with this book. It will be useful to anyone responsible for the appearance of computer-based information displays.

DEVELOPING VISUAL APPLICATIONS
XIL™: An Imaging Foundation Library

WILLIAM K. PRATT

351 pages; (includes CD-ROM)
ISBN 0-13-461948-X

A practical introduction to using imaging in new innovative applications, it covers the basics of image processing, compression, and algorithm implementation and gives clear, real-world examples for using XIL™ a cross-platform imaging foundation library from Sun.

INTRANETS:
What's the Bottom Line?

RANDY J. HINRICHS

421 pages
ISBN 0-13-841198-0

This book is a decision maker's guide to intranets. You will learn all you need to know to evaluate how to incorporate intranets into your organization for effective business communications and transactions.

HANDS-ON INTRANETS

VASANTHAN S. DASAN and LUIS R. ORDORICA

326 pages
ISBN 0-13-857608-4

This hands-on guide tells you everything you really need to know to deploy an intranet quickly, securely, and cost-effectively—and how to manage it for maximum payoff.

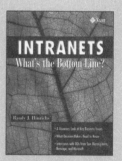

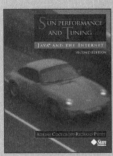

AUTOMATING SOLARIS™ INSTALLATIONS
A Custom Jumpstart Guide
PAUL ANTHONY KASPER and
ALAN L. McCLELLAN

282 pages; (includes diskette)
ISBN 0-13-312505-X

AUTOMATING SOLARIS INSTALLATIONS describes how to set up "hands-off" Solaris installations for hundreds of SPARC™ and x86 systems. Learn how to configure your site that when you install Solaris, you simply boot a system and walk away—the software installs automatically!

SOLARIS IMPLEMENTATION
A Guide for System Administrators
GEORGE BECKER,
MARY E. S. MORRIS, and
KATHY SLATTERY

345 pages
ISBN 0-13-353350-6

This book discusses real world, day-to-day Solaris 2 system administration for both new installations and for migration from an installed Solaris 1 base. It presents tested procedures to help system administrators improve and customize their networks.

SUN PERFORMANCE AND TUNING:
Java and the Internet, Second Edition
ADRIAN COCKCROFT and
RICHARD PETTIT

500 pages
ISBN 0-13-095249-4

Hailed in its first edition as an indispensable reference for system administrators, SUN PERFORMANCE AND TUNING has been revised and expanded to cover Solaris 2.6, the newest generation of SPARC hardware, and the latest Internet and Java server technologies.

CONFIGURATION AND CAPACITY PLANNING FOR SOLARIS SERVERS
BRIAN L. WONG

428 pages
ISBN 0-13-349952-9

No matter what application of SPARC architecture you're working with, this book can help you maximize the performance of your Solaris-based server. This is the most comprehensive guide to configuring and sizing Solaris servers for virtually any task.

PANIC! UNIX SYSTEM CRASH DUMP ANALYSIS

CHRIS DRAKE and KIMBERLEY BROWN

481 pages; (includes CD-ROM)
ISBN 0-13-149386-8

UNIX® systems crash—it's a fact of life. Until now, little information has been available regarding system crashes. PANIC! is the first book to concentrate solely on system crashes and hangs, explaining what triggers them and what to do when they occur.

CREATING WORLDWIDE SOFTWARE
Solaris International Developer's Guide, Second Edition

BILL TUTHILL and DAVID SMALLBERG

382 pages
ISBN 0-13-494493-3

If you're a UNIX or Motif software developer, learn how to globalize software at remarkably low cost while building a worldwide customer base. CREATING WORLDWIDE SOFTWARE will walk through every issue involved in internationalizing your software.

SOLARIS PORTING GUIDE
Second Edition

SUNSOFT DEVELOPER ENGINEERING

696 pages
ISBN 0-13-443672-5

Ideal for application programmers and software developers, this book provides a comprehensive technical overview of the Solaris 2 operating environment and its related migration strategy. It covers both SPARC and x86 platforms.

PC HARDWARE CONFIGURATION GUIDE FOR DOS AND SOLARIS

RON LEDESMA

331 pages
ISBN 0-13-124678-X

Eliminate the frustration of trial-and-error installations by following a simple, structured approach to hardware configuration for your PC. The book presents a time-tested method for installing and configuring x86 hardware for both stand-alone and networked machines.

ALL ABOUT ADMINISTERING NIS+
Second Edition

RICK RAMSEY

451 pages
ISBN 0-13-309576-2

Updated and revised for Solaris 2.3, this book is ideal for network administrators who want to know more about NIS+: its capabilities, requirements, how it works, and how to get the most out of it.

WABI™ 2:
Opening Windows

SCOTT FORDIN and
SUSAN NOLIN

383 pages
ISBN 0-13-461617-0

WABI™ 2: OPENING WINDOWS explains the ins and outs of using Wabi software from Sun Microsystems to install, run, and manage Microsoft Windows applications on UNIX systems. Step-by-step instructions, illustrations, and charts guide you through each phase of using Wabi.

INTERACTIVE UNIX OPERATING SYSTEM
A Guide for System Administrators

MARTY C. STEWART

275 pages
ISBN 0-13-161613-7

Written for first-time system administrators and end users, this provides detailed examples of the most common INTERACTIVE™ UNIX® issues facing system administrators and is based upon actual customer questions and issues handled by Sun's service support lines.

PROGRAMMING WITH THREADS

STEVE KLEIMAN, DEVANG SHAH,
and BART SMAALDERS

534 pages
ISBN 0-13-172389-8

PROGRAMMING WITH THREADS is the definitive guide to multithreaded programming for both novice and experienced threads programmers. The book provides structured techniques for mastering the complexity of threads programming with an emphasis on performance issues.

THREADS PRIMER
A Guide to Multithreaded Programming

BIL LEWIS and DANIEL J. BERG

319 pages
ISBN 0-13-443698-9

Written for developers and technical managers, this book provides a solid understanding of threads—what they are, how they work, and why they are useful. It covers the design and implementation of multithreading as well as the business and technical benefits of threads.

MULTITHREADED PROGRAMMING WITH PTHREADS

BILL LEWIS and DANIEL J. BERG

350 pages
ISBN 0-13-680729-1

Based on the bestselling THREADS PRIMER, this new book gives you a solid understanding of Posix threads—what they are, how they work, when to use them, and how to optimize them. Special emphasis is placed on cancellation, error conditions, performance, hardware, and languages.

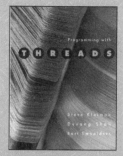

SUN MICROSYSTEMS PRESS

THE ENTERPRISE

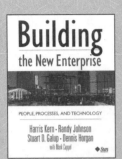

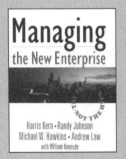

BUILDING THE NEW ENTERPRISE
People, Processes, and Technology

HARRIS KERN, RANDY JOHNSON, STUART GALUP, and DENNIS HORGAN, with MARK CAPPEL

416 pages; (hardcover)
ISBN 0-13-079671-9

People, processes and technology — in that order — are the key drivers of success with client/server and Internet technology. BUILDING THE NEW ENTERPRISE delivers practical ways to maximize all three. It's filled with how-tos, metrics, forms, checklists, sample organization charts, job descriptions, schedules, methodologies, policies — everything you need to get results. It's the first practical guide to the day-to-day "blocking and tackling" that makes the difference between success and failure in distributed systems.

RIGHTSIZING THE NEW ENTERPRISE
The Proof, Not the Hype

HARRIS KERN and RANDY JOHNSON

326 pages; (hardcover)
ISBN 0-13-490384-6

The "how-to's" of rightsizing are defined in this detailed account based on the actual experiences of Sun Microsystems as it re-engineered its business to run on client/server systems. This book presents you with proof that rightsizing can be done—and has been done.

MANAGING THE NEW ENTERPRISE
The Proof, Not the Hype

HARRIS KERN, RANDY JOHNSON, MICHAEL HAWKINS, and ANDREW LAW, with WILLIAM KENNEDY

212 pages; (hardcover)
ISBN 0-13-231184-4

This book is about revolution and change in corporate computing. It provides a solid technology foundation for the advanced networking and systems you need to build your New Enterprise and it tells you how to re-engineer your traditional IT practices, all the while reducing costs!

NETWORKING THE NEW ENTERPRISE
The Proof, Not the Hype

HARRIS KERN, RANDY JOHNSON, MICHAEL HAWKINS, and HOWIE LYKE, with WILLIAM KENNEDY and MARK CAPPEL

264 pages; (hardcover)
ISBN 0-13-263427-9

NETWORKING THE NEW ENTERPRISE tackles the key information technology questions facing business professionals today—and provides real solutions. It's the first end-to-end, business person's guide to planning, implementing and managing networks that truly support the goals of your enterprise.

COMPUTER SECURITY POLICIES AND SUNSCREEN™ FIREWALLS

KATHLYN M. WALKER and LINDA CROSWHITE CAVANAUGH

121 pages
ISBN: 0-13-096015-2

How to get the most out of the SunScreen products (SunScreen EFS 2.0 and SunScreen SPF-200 1.0), how to design a security policy and then how to translate that policy for the SunScreen products. You will also learn fundamental security concepts relevant to firewall technology and about SKIP, the security technology used by the SunScreen products to provide encryption capability.

INTRANET SECURITY
Stories From the Trenches

LINDA McCARTHY

260 pages
ISBN 0-13-894759-7

This is a collection of real-life security nightmares that could happen at any company. Security consultant Linda McCarthy shows how breaches occurred; what steps were taken to deal with them—and how well they worked; and what could have been done to prevent the crises.

READ ME FIRST!
A Style Guide for the Computer Industry
SUN TECHNICAL PUBLICATIONS

256 pages; (includes CD-ROM)
ISBN 0-13-455347-0

User documentation should be an asset, not an afterthought. This style guide can help technical publications groups outline, organize, and prepare high quality documentation for any type of computer product. Based on the award-winning Sun documentation style guide.

THE UNIX BOOK OF GAMES
JANICE WINSOR

223 pages; (includes CD-ROM)
ISBN 0-13-490079-0

We've brought together ten of the world's favorite games to keep you entertained. Every game comes with comprehensive rules, hints, lore, history, and complete installation instructions—or just play from the CD-ROM. The games come ready-to-play on Solaris and Linux.

VERILOG HDL
A Guide to Digital Design and Synthesis
SAMIR PALNITKAR

396 pages; (hardcover); (includes CD-ROM)
ISBN 0-13-451675-3

Everything you need to know about Verilog HDL, from fundamentals such as gate, RTL and behavioral modeling to advanced concepts such as timing simulation, switch level modeling, PLI, and logic synthesis. The book stresses the practical design aspects of using Verilog.

EXPERT C PROGRAMMING
Deep C Secrets
PETER van der LINDEN

353 pages
ISBN 0-13-177429-8

This is a very different book on the C language! In a conversational and often humorous style, the author reveals coding techniques used by the best C programmers. This book is a must read for anyone who wants to learn more about the implementation, practical use, and folklore of C.